Social Media

Strategies for Engaging in Facebook, Twitter & Other Social Media

Marketing

Liana "Li" Evans

800 East 96th Street,
Indianapolis, Indiana 46240 USA

Social Media Marketing

ISBN-13: 978-0-7897-4284-1
ISBN-10: 0-7897-4284-5

Library of Congress Cataloging-in-Publication Data:

Evans, Liana.
  Social media marketing : Strategies for engaging in facebook, twitter & other social media / Liana Evans.
     p. cm.
  Includes index.
  ISBN 978-0-7897-4284-1
  1. Internet marketing. 2. Social media. 3. Online social networks.
I. Title.
  HF5415.1265.E93 2010
  658.8'72—dc22

                                          2010018994

Printed in the United States of America

Fourth Printing: May 2011

Trademarks

All terms mentioned in this book that are known to be trademarks or service marks have been appropriately capitalized. Que Publishing cannot attest to the accuracy of this information. Use of a term in this book should not be regarded as affecting the validity of any trademark or service mark.

Warning and Disclaimer

Bulk Sales

Que Publishing offers excellent discounts on this book when ordered in quantity for bulk purchases or special sales. For more information, please contact

U.S. Corporate and Government Sales
1-800-382-3419
corpsales@pearsontechgroup.com

For sales outside of the U.S., please contact

International Sales
international@pearson.com

Associate Publisher
Greg Wiegand

Acquisitions Editor
Rick Kughen

Development Editor
Rick Kughen

Managing Editor
Kristy Hart

Project Editor
Lori Lyons

Copy Editor
Krista Hansing

Indexer
Erika Millen

Proofreader
Water Crest Publishing

Technical Editor
Amanda Watlington

Publishing Coordinator
Cindy Teeters

Book Designer
Anne Jones

Compositor
Gloria Schurick

Reviewers
Mack Collier
Beth Harte
Kim Krause-Berg

CONTENTS AT A GLANCE

About the Author

Liana "Li" Evans has been active full-time in the search marketing arena since 1999, becoming well versed in all avenues of social media and search marketing. Li runs the Search Marketing Gurus blog and is the Director of Social Media for Serengeti Communications, a Washington, DC-based Online Marketing Consulting firm. Li has led the SEO strategy for an Internet Retailer 500 company, and was the SEO and Social Media architect for a Fortune 500's multi-million page entertainment Web site. As a database designer and programmer since 1992, Liana has developed technical expertise in dealing with large-scale retail sites and their dynamic natures. She holds degrees in both Public Relations and Information Technology, which lend well to working with client strategies in Social Media and Search Marketing. She speaks and trains Social Media and SEO at Search Engine Strategies and other industry conferences.

You can reach Li at www.lianaevans.com and on Twitter at@storyspinner.

Dedication

This book is dedicated to my father David G. Evans who, although gone from this world, has still had significant impact on my life every day; and to my mother Dolores E. Evans, who amazes me every day by her willingness to accept and try anything new (even Facebook and Twitter). Without my dad's encouragement, his willingness to share what he learned, his silent prodding, and without my mother's love of sharing, networking, and relating stories and both their love and support, I would not be where I am today. Thank you Dad, you're always in my heart, and thank you Mom, without you I wouldn't be who I am.

Acknowledgments

First, I need to thank my editor Rick Kughen and my tech editor Amanda Watlington for all their help, encouragement, refinement of my thoughts, and generally for just putting up with me getting the knowledge I wanted to relate to all of you, on paper. It has been a long journey, and I've learned so much from the two of them—they are a godsend to any author.

I would also like to extend my sincerest thank you for all the encouragement, cheering on, advice, pointing to examples, and loving support from so many people who have helped me in my career. It's so hard to name all the people who've gotten me here along the way, but there are some I need to thank specifically because without them, this book would not have been possible.

My boss, mentor, and friend, Nan Dawkins—for your constant belief and support of me, the guidance you provide, and your ever source of wisdom that never ceased to amaze me. Thank you.

My friend, mentor, and general overall marketing guru, Mike Grehan—without your constant sharing of knowledge and brain trust, I really would be lost. You are a treasure to this industry, a fountain of wisdom that everyone in social media and search marketing should seek out. Thank you for being my friend and guiding me along the way.

My friend and colleague, Beth Harte—from Plurk to working together, wow what a journey! Thank you, Beth, for always being my sounding board and my voice of reason—you are one of the best friends a person could ask for!

To Debra Mastaler, Becky Ryan, and Simon Heseltine—my constant cheerleaders, source of encouragement, and go-to people for advice on search and social media. Without you three, I'd be so lost. Thank you for helping me find the right paths.

To Rebecca Lieb—thank you, my wonderful friend, for believing enough in me to recommend me writing this book. Your constant encouragement has helped me tremendously!

The team at Search Engine Strategies: Marilyn Crafts, Jackie Ortez, Stewart Quealy, Matthew McGowan, Dan Hoskins, and Fred Rumsey—thank you for always including me in SES and always encouraging me to be the best that I can be. If there ever was a family I wanted to have by just picking my friends, you all would be in it (yes Fred, even you).

To the team at Serengeti Communications: Stacy Moren, John Lynch, Nathan Linnell, and Kevin Olsen—Thank you for putting up with the craziness that is me. It's a privilege and an honor to get to work with each of you, I learn from all of you every day.

To Danny Sullivan—Thank you for giving me the opportunity so many years ago to step out from being just another SEO and letting me be able to share my knowledge on the stage at SES. To this day I thank you for that opportunity, and I am forever grateful and appreciative of the opportunity you granted me.

To my friends Lauren, Jason, and Karen—Thank you guys for putting up with my crazy schedules, my ranting about this industry when you have no idea what it's about, and for just being there to support me. You all have kept me sane!

Last, but not least, to my sister, Dani Scozzari, my brother-in-law Chris, my nephew Anthony, and my niece Sara for always being there. It's been a rough ride these last few years, but your constant love and unquestioning and unwavering support mean the world to me.

Oh yes—I can't forget Captain Jack and Luke...who kept me company throughout most of the chapters of this book. I couldn't have done it without my silent co-authors.

We Want to Hear from You!

As the reader of this book, *you* are our most important critic and commentator. We value your opinion and want to know what we're doing right, what we could do better, what areas you'd like to see us publish in, and any other words of wisdom you're willing to pass our way.

As an associate publisher for Que Publishing, I welcome your comments. You can email or write me directly to let me know what you did or didn't like about this book—as well as what we can do to make our books better.

Please note that I cannot help you with technical problems related to the topic of this book. We do have a User Services group, however, where I will forward specific technical questions related to the book.

When you write, please be sure to include this book's title and author as well as your name, email address, and phone number. I will carefully review your comments and share them with the author and editors who worked on the book.

Email: feedback@quepublishing.com

Mail: Greg Wiegand
        Associate Publisher
        Que Publishing
        800 East 96th Street
        Indianapolis, IN 46240 USA

Reader Services

Visit our website and register this book at quepublishing.com/register for convenient access to any updates, downloads, or errata that might be available for this book.

Introduction

I believe that social media is changing the way that companies need to interact with both their audiences and customers by listening and directly engaging with them. I'm Liana "Li" Evans, and I am the author of Social Media Marketing: Strategies for Engaging in Facebook, Twitter, & Other Social Media.

I've written this book to give any marketer, novice, or expert a deeper look into the realm of social media marketing. So much has been touted, preached, and hoisted up on a pedestal as things marketers or companies should be doing, it's hard to believe what's true and what isn't. This book can be your guide from beginning to end in understanding what's hype and what's not. From making the case of whether or not you should be actively engaging in social media, to putting the pieces together to plan a successful social media marketing strategy, I hope you will put this book to good use.

There's a lot to digest when it comes to learning the different facets that comprise the world of social media. It isn't simply just Facebook or Twitter—there's a much bigger world out there than most marketers or company CEOs or CMOs are even aware of. Understanding that your audience and customers might not be where the media thinks they are (Twitter and Facebook, for example) is an important concept to grasp if you want to be successful.

Social media is also constantly changing. The Facebooks of today will be the Friendsters and MySpaces of tomorrow. Communities ebb and flow. They depend highly on engagement and members giving their time. When members cease to find reasons to share and leave the communities, those communities can go through low periods. Some recover, some don't. For this reason, you have to be flexible with your social media strategies and constantly be monitoring and researching the conversations and where they're happening.

Throughout the book, you'll find several themes:

- **Research**—You need to research your audience and customers thoroughly. Without the research, you are only guessing at where to start. Without the research, you will be wasting a lot of valuable time and resources in areas that most likely won't help you attain the goals you want to reach with your social media marketing plan.

- **Strategy**—Social media marketing is a lot more than just a laundry list of items that a company prints out on a marketing slick. Social media marketing, just like any other form of traditional or online marketing, needs a strategy. You need a well-thought-out plan with goals set in place so that you know where you want to be and how to get there.

- **Involvement**—It's not just your social media marketing team that's involved in engaging and participating in social media communities. Just about everyone in your company has some sort of stake—whether it's the stories your customer service reps hear on the phone, or it's people totally removed from marketing (your accounts payable department, for example) who have Facebook pages stating they work for you. Everyone in your company has some sort of involvement in your social media marketing strategy. Understanding that different levels of involvement all have differing affects is key to making sure you plan the right strategy for everyone in your company.

- **Measurement**—One of the biggest questions I hear when it comes to implementing a social media marketing strategy is, "How will I know if it's successful?" I also like to put the questions out there of "How do you know if what you are doing is not successful and when do you know when to stop doing it?" Your social media marketing strategy needs to be measured. Measurement comes in many different forms, from website traffic to the number of retweets your content is getting. No two companies will measure the same things the same way. Success or failure is different for everyone.

Social media is my passion. I have found companies that understand how to harness the power that social media communities offer and have become extremely successful and usually have a loyal band of brand evangelists ready to promote them at a moments' notice. Helping companies and marketers understand how to reach and engage their audiences through the power of social media is something I love to do, and I cringe when I see or hear so-called consultants selling social media services as if it were the next gimmick they need to get into.

Social media marketing isn't a gimmick—it's hard work that can be extremely engaging when implemented in the right way. Now more than ever, it's crucial for companies to be where the questions and conversations are going on that affect their bottom line. Social media is the perfect way to do that.

My hope is that you find this book to be your guide to help you become successful in your social media marketing efforts and that it gives you both the foundation and roadmap to help you along the way to that goal. Thanks for reading!

The Basics of Social Media

It's Not Easy, Quick, or Cheap

One of the biggest misnomers of social media marketing is that marketing in this online medium is easy, quick, and cheap. The truth couldn't be farther away than Sydney is from New York City. This perception of social media marketing comes from those overnight sensations that go viral within minutes of hitting a social media network such as Digg, YouTube, or MySpace. People see reports in the mainstream media about how "fast" something went popular on a social media site and assume that because it was fast, it was easy and, therefore, cheap to implement.

Although adding your content to these social media sites is easy and free, a lot more work is involved in making that content valuable to an audience. The difficult part of finding success in social media is dedicating the resources and time to your social media strategy. This hard work behind the scenes makes the "overnight" successes seem so easy.

*Social media marketing requires research, strategy, imple-
mentation, buy-in from your team, networking, conversing, and measuring, along with a whole list of other
things that I discuss later in this book. The fact is, the
overnight sensations that you see reported on the major
news networks are few and far between.*

What Is Social Media Optimization?

Optimizing your social media marketing efforts involves everything from making
sure your profiles have the right keywords (which includes your brand, product or
service names), to ensuring the content that you are placing out into the social
media communities you become involved in is not only "findable" but relates to
what those community members are talking about.

A lot of companies miss perfect opportunities on making the link between social
media and search marketing in their online marketing plans because they don't
realize the link between social media and search is *being found*. People in these
social media communities still need to find you and your content that you are providing, so understanding how to optimize what you are doing with your social
media strategy is imperative.

Throughout this book I'll be covering different types of optimization, but the concepts of understanding how to build a social media strategy and how to relate with
the social media communities are at the heart of any social media optimization
efforts.

Overnight Successes Tend to Be Accidental, Not Planned

Frequently, big successes with social media are stumbled into—not planned. Take
for example, the Eepie Bird guys. You know them more from their viral videos in
which they drop Mentos candy into plastic bottles of Diet Coke, causing beautiful,
synchronized explosions, which are set to music. This overnight success was totally
accidental and sparked purchases and discussion of Mentos and Diet Coke. The
Eepie Bird guys didn't plan this, they didn't contact Coke or Mentos, and none of
these three entities were ready for the popularity of their experiments. How they
reacted afterwards was telling and we'll discuss this later on.

This accidental "Success", means those successes really didn't benefit the company in the way they would have if there had been a strategic effort in place. Because these companies didn't use any strategic planning when they became "overnight social media success stories," they don't know how to truly measure their successes—or even know how to repeat them.

With all the recent media hype about social media, companies are seeing and hearing more about how easy it is to come by this type of success in the online environment. Unfortunately, companies that believe success in social media comes easy often also believe that all they have to do is launch a Facebook page and they'll be a hit with their audience.

Many companies give up on Facebook when they see no activity occurring on their page. Unfortunately, the real conversation often is happening in a forum that the company doesn't even know about. Focusing efforts for a limited time and in a place where your audience isn't conversing about your company (such as Facebook) is a common mistake, which is why it pays to first create a social media strategy.

Participating in social media isn't just about creating a page, making a blog post, posing a question, or tweeting. You can't just leave "your mark" and expect success. Unlike all the media hype surrounding how great social media is, it certainly isn't that quick or easy. Social media is about holding conversations and sharing experiences with others who are connected through like-minded activities. Social media communities also involve trust—and trust is not gained overnight.

The Conversation Happens Even When You Aren't Involved

The most important point to remember about the conversations and shared experiences of social media sites is that they go on with or without your involvement, approval, or input. Conversations such as these take a lot of time and resources to become involved in legitimately. You can't control what's being said, how it's being said, or who's saying it. With social media, a community is discussing you and your products, services, or brands in a way that its members feel benefits them, not the way the company has decided it should benefit the audience.

Senior executives sometimes have a problem with this concept. Many executives believe that they are in total control of the conversation about their company, brands, products, or services. They hire armies of PR people to spin everything, including trumpeting their newest hires and launching new product. They've been brought up to believe that marketing is about delivering that very carefully crafted message and that it doesn't matter what the audience says about that message.

Social media has changed all of that. A company no longer has complete control over what is truly valuable to the people who buy their wares. Now the audience dictates the value of your company's products and services. That can be a bitter pill for top management to swallow after years of marketing the old way.

Conversing with your audience isn't always easy, either. In this day and age, consumers have become increasingly suspicious of companies entering the online marketing space—even more so as they enter social media circles. Consumers don't want to be marketed to. Unfortunately, most companies look at social media sites (such as Facebook, MySpace, and Twitter) as another place to push their marketing message. Those messages fall on deaf ears in social media communities because the audience members chalk up their actions to just another "TV commercial"—one that they choose to now ignore. Members of social media communities are no longer swayed by a coupon for 10% off or an invitation to try a new product. Instead, they want to connect. This is why social media marketing is not a quick process—it takes time to nurture relationships into conversations and create those solid, trusted connections.

Understanding that listening is required when you are entering into a conversation in a social media site can also be a tough concept for companies and marketers to grasp. That fact that it is not about "you," even though you see consumers talking about you, can be a little confusing. Social media marketing works only when the audience members find true value in your products and services, and shares their experiences with others. As discussed earlier in this chapter, years of dealing with traditional media such as TV, radio, and newspapers has conditioned marketers not to listen and to focus solely on a finely tuned marketing message.

When the Internet really started to take off, consumers started to tune out those carefully crafted messages and take more control over how they voiced their experiences with products or services. From websites to blogs, to forums and message boards, conversations started to spring up around products, brands, and companies. These conversations have had more influence on what others buy, subscribe to, and believe is valuable than any marketing message could manage.

Long before the term *social media* was coined, these conversations were happening with very few companies knowing that they were even going on, and even fewer understanding that they needed to participate in those conversations. Now that *social media* is on the tip of everyone's tongue when talking about online marketing, companies are starting to grasp the power this medium holds. It holds just as much power for the consumer advocate as it does for the "trolls" who never find good in anything and just want attention.

It's also not easy to sort through the trolls and the constant complainers to find consumers who truly want you to listen to them as they share their experience with your product. Although it's not easy to sort through, companies are still investing serious resources into their social media efforts because, at the end of the day, these real conversations lead to real relationships, and those trusted relationships lead to referrals and sales. These real conversations also produce some of your most loyal fans and greatest evangelists.

You must first begin to understand that a customer who seems to be complaining is really a customer who was very disappointed in your service or produce after putting a lot of trust into what you were selling. Then you can distinguish them from the trolls and constant complainers. However, this takes time and understanding. It doesn't just happen because you decided to participate in social media or announce that you've "arrived." It happens because you take the time to become part of the community and share on an equal level with your audience.

For all the successes in social media touted in the mainstream media, thousands more efforts launched and failed because they regurgitated offline messages to social media communities. The companies didn't plan a strategy because they figured it was as simple as transplanting their carefully crafted message within this new medium.

The reporters who feature these successes neglect to mention the companies' hours of research, man-hours of networking, and effort put into listening to audiences. Companies such as Zappos, Whole Foods, and Southwest Airlines are all putting extraordinary efforts into holding the right conversations, in the right environments, and at the right times with their audiences. Unfortunately, the mainstream media rarely highlights their efforts.

Who Owns Your Social Media Strategy Internally?

Beyond conversing with your audience in social media, understanding who owns your conversation within your own company isn't always simple, either. In big corporations, a lot of different hands are claiming that they can do social media better than the others. If you outsource some of your marketing, your vendor is thrown into the mix, too.

- Your PR department personnel think they can do it better because they know how to get the press interested.

- Your marketing department personnel think they are the people to do the job because they have the experience to craft your message.

- Your online marketing team members believe they can do the best job because this is their world, and they can get you found by combining search engine optimization (SEO) and pay-per-click (PPC) efforts with social media.

- The ad agency to which you outsource your media buying thinks its members can do it because they think the most creatively.

- Your IT department personnel might even have a hand in here, too, because they control access to servers, computers, and the Internet.

But who really is the best qualified?

Somewhere among all those clamoring voices is the answer. The tough part is deciding who it is. It's never the same answer for every company because there's no cookie-cutter solution when it comes to social media. Figuring out who is truly the best at handling social media efforts within your company can be difficult.

Is the best answer to use a mix of people from all departments, to form a new department? Or do you hand over the job to one department? The answer is as different for you as it is for your competition. It's as much about understanding your audience as it is about understanding the internal workings of your own company. No matter who ends up owning the conversation within your company, the most important piece is to make sure that all departments communicate and buy into your social media strategy.

Anyone in Your Company Can Affect Your Social Media Strategy

Getting your employees to buy into your social media strategy might seem easy, but it can be one of the toughest tasks to implement. Not only does it involve departments communicating with each other, but it also involves setting in place policies for employees who are not directly involved with your social media strategy but are active in social media platforms.

Your employees have a life after their work hours and, more than likely, are involved in some social media site in some way. Getting them to understand the impact of their actions on these social media platforms in their off-hours is just as important to communicate. Even the janitor of your building should be made aware that what he says about his job on Facebook or MySpace affects your company; he also should buy into your social media strategy.

Even if it seems inconsequential to your efforts, everyone on your team should be aware that you have some kind of social media strategy in the works. While your employees couldn't help or harm marketing efforts targeted to more traditional marketing outlets such as newspapers, radio and TV, your employees can affect your social media marketing efforts. Your employees have just as much of an affect on your social media marketing strategy as do your customers. You never know how your employees' lives can either hurt or even assist your strategy, the only way you can even begin to understand those possibilities is to ask and share what it is you are planning to do.

Don't Take the Bait

The biggest lure that brings companies into social media is the thought that this will be a quick, easy, and cheap solution to all their marketing problems. Although it seems a no-brainer to set up a Facebook page or a Twitter account and take it live in just a few minutes, that's the only easy, cheap, and quick part.

A lot of hard work goes into creating and implementing a successful social media strategy using these platforms. Don't be fooled by all the hype—there's really nothing fast, simple, or cheap about a successful social media strategy. So with all that out of the way, let's get down to understanding the hard work that goes into succeeding in social media and marketing effectively in this medium.

2

Understanding Social Media Strategies

Diving into social media without a strategy in place is the best way to set your company's efforts up for failure. Without a strategy, you are basically trying to navigate a huge sea without a compass, a map, or a spyglass to know where you are going or where you want to end up. Without a strategy you might as well place different social media sites on a dart board and fire away. Marketing in social media is no different than any other form of marketing, such as marketing by email, online, with billboards, through direct mail, or via TV. All those avenues have carefully planned strategies and measurements for success. Why shouldn't you use the same approach for social media?

Social media marketing can seem intimidating to a lot of companies when they first set out to create a strategy for it. Social media is a huge medium that includes many different types of social media sites; finding out where your audience or customers hang out and hold conversations can be a giant task in itself. Understanding how your target audience functions in these different sites is essential in succeeding in this medium. You also need to understand that people on social media sites don't just stick to one site, or even a single type of social media site. Instead, they cross-pollinate—creating user-generated content not just for one site, but for many. Taking all of this into account, you can now see that this isn't a quick, simple, and easy task.

Understanding the Types of Social Media

Social media appeals across generations because so many different types of social media sites allow users to generate their own content, commonly referred to as user-generated content (UCG). Social media also allows community members to share their experiences in many different ways. The idea that social media is only for the younger generations just coming out of high school or college is increasingly incorrect. Some of the fastest-growing demographics in social media are those above the age of 40.

So what are the various types of social media? We take a closer look in the next sections.

Social News Sites

Social news sites are sites that allow members to submit news stories, articles, blog posts, videos, and photos to the community. The community can then vote up or down for the submitted piece and can also add comments. The more votes a submitted piece gets, the more chance it has of appearing on the front page of the site.

Sites such as Digg, Reddit, NewsVine, Kirtsy, and BallHype all work in this matter. Digg is especially popular and can drive a lot of traffic to a website in a short period of time, especially if the piece appears on the front page of Digg or the top page of a category on Digg. Other social news sites are niche sites. Although they don't offer the instant slam-dunk boost in traffic that Digg does, they offer more qualified traffic that will more likely find your content or media valuable to them.

Social Networking

MySpace started all the rage with social networking, but Facebook has surpassed it in popularity (see Figure 2.1). In the last year, Facebook has climbed to more 120 million unique visitors a month by the end of 2009, according to a comparison done on Compete.com.

Figure 2.1   *Facebook has surpassed MySpace in terms of unique visitors and is the current social media champ.*

Definitely take these two behemoths into consideration when you are planning your strategy for social media, but understand that these sites have extremely different audiences. Social networking sites allow community members to upload photos and videos, tag their friends, post comments on each other's "walls," create groups, add fans, invite friends to events, post bulletins, and integrate applications. Undoubtedly, more features will be added as the need arises in these types of communities.

Note

Niche sites offer very targeted traffic and should not be overlooked when you are planning your social media strategy. For example, LinkedIn caters to professionals who want to build their network of colleagues and associates. This site allows community members to post their resumes, answer and ask questions, and form and join groups. Eons is an example of a social networking site that caters more to an age demographic—in this case, people 55 and over. Other social networking sites focus on ethnicity, such as MiGentre, BlackPlanet, and AsianAvenue.

Social Bookmarking

Social bookmarking sites allow you to bookmark and share your favorite websites with an entire community. Although it seems a bit silly at first—and you might be thinking, "Who's really going to like my bookmark about hair styles for Bichon Frises?"—likely more than a few individuals will be interested.

Sites such as Delicious, Magnolia, and Diigo are communities that have a host of fanatical collectors who want to find great sites to share with their friends as well as the community. As with social news sites, when another community member bookmarks the same page or site, the site's popularity increases, giving it the potential to hit the front page of the social bookmarking community. When this happens, as with social news sites, a website can see a surge in traffic.

Social Sharing

The common denominator across all social media sites is the ability to share. Some sites specialize in sharing particular forms of media. The social sharing sites tend to focus on two types of media: photos and videos. The two sites that you cannot leave out of your strategy are Google's YouTube and Yahoo!'s Flickr.

Social sharing has become a huge piece of the online marketing puzzle. In fact, ComScore reports that more searches were conducted on YouTube than on Yahoo! in April 2008. That's pretty amazing when you stop to think about it: People are searching for results more on a social media site than on the second-largest search engine on the Web.

With social sharing sites, community members can upload their own media, such as videos on YouTube and both photos and short videos on Flickr. Users can tag photos, add meaningful titles and descriptions, and embed the videos or photo slide shows into other sites. Both YouTube and Flickr enable users to see statistics for their media (although Flickr stats are available only to paid users at this time).

Social Events

If you've got a public event you want to get the word out about, sites such as Eventful, Meetup, and Yahoo!'s Upcoming are the places to do it. Meetup charges a fee, but Eventful and Upcoming are both free. The neat thing about Upcoming is that you can integrate photos from Flickr into the event's information, which adds another layer of sharing on this social media site that its competitors don't have.

Events can be in a physical location or virtual. Community users who plan events have several options to promote them and contact members who sign up for events to start creating relationships in these types of social communities.

With the rise of open APIs, many of these sites limit event sharing to promotions. Also, many of these event sharing sites allow outside access from other applications. For example, Yahoo's Upcoming allows community members to share photos and videos from Flickr and Yahoo Video as well as bookmarks and tags from Delicious.

Blogs

Next to forums and message boards, blogs are one of the oldest forms of user generated content out there. Blogs allow the creators to express themselves to the entire internet in a way that hasn't been very easy before. That ease of publishing thoughts, interests, opinions, ideas, photos, videos and anything else they'd like to share with an interested audience is exciting and is the lure for most bloggers. When they later find out that they can possibly earn not just a living, but the respect of their peers, this is the driving force that keeps the bloggers going.

Blogs are possibly one of the best ways to "get the word out" to a very tailored audience and allow companies to reach those people who are truly interested in their content. With that said, blogs can be one of those double edge swords. Since bloggers are not journalists, as I'll discuss in Chapter 11, "Bloggers Have No Boundaries," approaching them should be done only after a lot of research and in a very personal manner. Sending out a BCC'd press release to a blogger is a sure way to get off on the wrong foot with the blogging community.

Microblogging

So what is microblogging? Think of microblogging as a very abbreviated blog consisting of short messages (usually 140 characters or less) often sent from smart phones and laptops. Your messages are sent to people interested in seeing your posts. These people are known as "followers" and if you are using Twitter, your posts are known as "tweets." It goes without saying that the main microblogging platform used today is Twitter. There are some smaller microblogging communities, such as Plurk, but Twitter is by far the most popular platform.

Since Twitter uses an open API, Twitter has grown by leaps and bounds in both active users as well as available applications. There are now mobile apps, analytic applications, as well as URL shorteners to help Twitter users to share their messages. These messages can contain random observations or status updates (think status updates on Facebook) to URLs, blog comments, videos and photos. The power of microblogging for a business can be huge, if you add personality into your Twitter stream (your messages) and not just allow it to be automated.

Wikis

Wikis are a great way for people to share their own knowledge and expertise regarding nearly anything imaginable. While controversial in the sense of verifiable facts (most colleges, universities, and schools don't accept Wikipedia as a source for papers & reports), Wikipedia cannot be ignored for its power for quick information exchange. Wikis, though, aren't just limited to Wikipedia. There are very specific subject oriented Wikis such as ones based on the Star Trek and Star Wars franchises. Companies even launch wikis around industry related terms or popular product lines or brands with their audiences helping to contribute the content that fills these wikis.

Wikis can be powerful way to set your company up as an expert and drive traffic and interest to your brands, products or services. However, maintaining a wiki is a lot of work—from verifying information, to controlling spam and keeping members active.

Forums and Message Boards

Forums and message boards are the "granddaddies" of social media. They've been around since the beginning of the internet when programmers would post information about bugs or fixes they've encountered in the applications they were programming. When the internet started to become more common, people started to utilize forums and message boards to discuss everything from comic books to scrapbooking. These were the first places in which like minded people visited seeking information from people who have experience with the subjects they were interested in.

Even as the internet has expanded, broadband access has become readily available to most and many social media sites have sprung up, message boards are still in wide use today. In fact, message boards can hold a wealth of consumer generated content and information, and according to Charlene Li and Josh Bernoff's book, Groundswell, message boards book are the second most commonly used social media tool. Forums and message boards aren't a place to just jump in and say "I'm here!" There are rules and norms that need to be researched and prepared for before you implement your social media strategy. Later in this book, I'll address just how to do that.

3

Goals Need to Be Defined

When you set out on your family trip, you have an ending point on the map that is your goal, your destination. When you reach the particular spot you've marked on the map, you consider the course you've taken to reach your goal and can pretty much surmise that it was a success. How you got there and what happened along the way will influence whether you ever take that same path again if you need to get from point A to point B. If the road was rough and you encountered hazards along the way, the next time you need to get from point A to point B, you might not take the same route—you might opt for one with fewer hazards.

Marketing in social media is no different, except that your strategy could include many different types of goals that you are aiming to attain. Without those goals predefined, how do you know whether your strategy was a success? How do you know how hazardous the route was and whether you could have taken alternative routes? If you do not clearly define where you want to be at the end of *your efforts, how do you know whether you should continue on, adjust your course, or just stop where you are? Without these goals, you don't.*

This is why it's so tough to really know whether these so-called overnight successes were truly successful. Most of the time, a video hits YouTube without any planning and goes viral without a company knowing what has happened. They haven't set in place any kind of measurements for success, nor have they documented what they were doing. When success is largely accidental, it's very difficult to reproduce or to know whether it really helped your bottom line.

Senior management relies on clear, concise measurability when it comes to deeming something a true success. Social media marketing tends to be less concrete than other online marketing efforts, such as search engine optimization (SEO) and pay per click (PPC). With SEO and PPC, it's very clear what happens: A person searches on a site such as Google, Yahoo!, or MSN. The site returns results. The person then clicks on a result; lands on a particular website; and either performs an action, goes back to the search results, or gives up. These actions are measurable results that can show just how effective the marketing efforts were to get the person to perform the desired action or goal.

With Social Media, There's No Direct Click to Purchase

Social media doesn't encourage users to perform an action, such as purchase a product or subscribe to an email list. Instead, social media encourages users to share. Sharing in social media is a pretty tough thing for companies to measure because this action generally does not take place on the company's site. When it comes to online marketing, companies have gotten so used to driving the traffic to their own sites to measure their success that it's tough to wrap their arms around the concept of measuring the "offsite" successes that social media offers.

In a lot of ways, marketing in social media is like traditional forms of marketing when it comes to measurement. With public relations, you measure mentions and brand lift. With TV and radio spots, audience reach is important. However, it's a difficult task to measure and connect success to your marketing efforts. With the advent of the online marketing and analytics packages that measure website traffic and actions performed by visitors, online marketers have become a lot more accountable for their efforts. The mindset that everything on the Web should be measured is a logical one and is vital in measuring the success of marketing strategies.

With the rise of sites that allow users to generate their own content related to hobbies, passions, concerns, and complaints, companies have to think beyond their own websites when measuring their marketing strategy's successes and failures. This rise in areas where companies have less control over how their carefully crafted messages are delivered can be a little intimidating to even the savviest marketer. How do you measure success on a website that isn't your own or that you don't have the ability to control or see behind the scenes?

To a large extent, consumers have the ability to control who and what is marketed in their direction on social media sites and the interaction that happens there. Because consumers can comment on your products and services, ask questions, post reviews, and shut you out altogether if they so choose, companies attempting to market in social media circles need to learn how to best measure successes and failures—as well as manage their resources and strategies—that happen on sites they don't own or control.

Most of the creation of user-generated content happens on social media sites that is owned by a completely different entity, so a lot of the measuring of success or failure with social media strategies tends to be more manual in process. Because these sites are owned by someone else, companies are not privy to the behind-the-scenes measurements of community member actions as they are on their own sites. Therefore, every action that can be measured by a company planning a strategy in a social media community is public, meaning that just as the community sees what happens, so do the companies. What this means is, that if your measurement includes how many fans/friends you've acquired on MySpace or how many posts on your wall occurred in Facebook, the public can see these actions as well as the companies measuring performance—not to mention your competition.

Different Types of Social Media Require Different Types of Goals

With SEO and PPC, the click–to–purchase actions drive the measurement of goals. When it comes to social media, companies can measure a lot when it comes to actions. This is why the goals need to be worked into the strategy from the beginning. As discussed in the previous chapter, more than a few different types of social media exist, and each type has a different measure of success. In the coming sections, we take a closer look at these types.

Social News Sites

Setting goals in social news is pretty straightforward. Social news sites are one of the few types of social media sites that can drive traffic directly to your site. Obviously, you should work these sites into your strategy because you can measure more user actions when planning strategies for these types of sites:

- Number of both positive and negative votes for media submitted

- Number of comments on media submitted

- Positive and negative sentiment

- How quickly media was voted to the popular page of the social news site(s)

- Traffic brought in from the media being submitted to the social news site

- Time visitors stay on your site

- Number of pages visited from initial referral from social news site

- Number of links acquired since submitting the media to targeted social news sites

- How many social news sites the media has been submitted to beyond the original targets

Social Networking Sites

A wide array of social networking sites exists on the Internet, and each site offers community members different ways to network with one another. Social networking sites tend not to be traffic drivers to other websites. Instead, they offer a place for friends to discuss, tag, comment on, and connect with their friends. Consider these metrics that apply to social networking sites:

- Number of friends or fans acquired

- Number of comments made on updates

- Number of photos or videos added by fans or group members

- Number of photos or videos you've been tagged in

- Number of discussions started on your fan or group page

- Number of responses to questions or topics posed

- Traffic from social networking site(s)

- Time visitors stay on your site

- Number of pages visited from initial referral from social networking site

- Number of downloads or installs of your social networking application

Social Bookmarking Sites

As with social news sites, social bookmarking sites can potentially drive traffic directly to a website. Although the potential is not great enough to cause a flood of traffic that can take down a server, social bookmarking sites can bring a more qualified audience to your site that might stick around a little longer and visit more pages of your website. Consider these metrics:

- Number of bookmarks for media submitted

- Number of tags on media submitted

- Number of unique tags

- Number of times a particular tag has been used

- How quickly media was voted to the popular page of the social bookmarking site(s)

- Traffic brought in from the media being submitted to the social bookmarking site

- Time visitors stay on your site

- Number of pages visited from initial referral from social bookmarking site

- Number of links acquired since submitting the media to targeted social bookmarking sites

- How many social bookmarking sites the media has been submitted to beyond the original targets

Social Sharing Sites

Since their rise in popularity, social sharing sites offer a great potential for brand exposure. As I explained earlier, YouTube is the second-most-searched site on the Internet, just behind its parent company, Google, and before rival search engine Yahoo!. Flickr is the largest photo-sharing site on the Internet and has a very avid and loyal community. Although these types of sites are not huge traffic drivers to other sites, the opportunity to expose its community members to brands, products, and services is huge. Consider these metrics:

- Number of times a photo or video is viewed
- Number of times a photo or video is commented on
- Positive and negative sentiment
- How highly a photo or video is rated
- Number of links or embeds of a video or photo
- Number of times a photo or video is a favorite
- Number of friends or subscribers acquired
- Number of times a photo or video is added to groups
- Number of times a photo or video is submitted to other social media sites (social news, social bookmarking, social networking)

Social Event Sites

Using social event sites for marketing purposes is pretty straightforward. If your strategy includes populating the information about the event with a special link to a page on your website with even more photos, videos, or information about the event, this can be a form of measurement, too. Generally, gauging success with your marketing in social event sites is pretty easy. Consider these metrics:

- Number of views of the event
- Number of RSVPs
- Number of people who can come, tentatively can come, and cannot come
- Number who actually showed up to the event
- Number of RSVPs who showed
- Number of additional guests (if allowed)
- Number of attendees who showed who saw the event on an event-sharing site but didn't RSVP
- Traffic to a special landing page or website

- Number of photos or videos that community members added to the event

- Number of comments on the event

- Positive and negative sentiment

- Number of tags the for event that community members added

- Number of links to the event listing on an event-sharing site

- Number of times the event is listed on other event-sharing sites beyond the targeted site(s)

Blogs

Whether it's your own blog or a set of bloggers you plan to interact with, you still need to define goals and measure whether your efforts are successful. Of course, with your own blog, you can see behind-the-scenes measurements. However, you should still be developing some offsite goals and measuring them manually. When dealing with blogs, the focus is the conversation that is happening, so comments are just as important in setting goals as the number of subscribers. Table 3.1 offers some metrics to consider for each.

Table 3.1   Metrics for Measuring Blog Success

Category	Metrics for Success
Your own blog	• Number of subscribers to blog • Ratio of comments to posts (how many comments are you getting for each post) • Positive and negative sentiment • Number of times posts are submitted to social news, social bookmarking, social networking, microblogging sites, and so on • Number of links to posts
Other blogs	• Number of comments that a post about you receives • Positive and negative sentiment • Number of times the post is submitted to social news, social bookmarking, social networking, microblogging sites, and so on • Number of links to a post • Number of links to your own targeted page

Table 3.1   Metrics for Measuring Blog Success (continued)

Category	Metrics for Success
The authority of the blogger(s) who mention you	• Technorati rank • Google page rank • Ranking for keyword phrases you are targeting

Microblogging

Twitter is all the rage, but how can a company go about defining and measuring goals with microblogging sites such as Twitter and Plurk? You can set goals in place to help you understand just how successful your efforts to hold meaningful conversations are with these platforms. These metrics include the following:

- Number of followers acquired

- Real followers who hold conversations (don't count the spammers)

- Number of replies you get to your tweets or plurks

- Number of retweets your tweets receive

- If you start a conversation around a hashtag, how much conversation happens (number of tweets)

- Positive and negative conversation

- Whether people take the initiative to log or put into PDF format the conversation that happens. For example, groups on Twitter talk about certain subjects and use the hashtag to follow a conversation, such as #pr20chat or #blogchat. At the end of these conversations, contributors of the conversation take the imitative to put these conversations into PDF format for later reading and reference.

- Traffic to the website, web pages, blog, or blog posts from tweets

Wikis

Wikis are tough to measure directly unless you've started your own (and if you are in an industry full of confusing jargon and acronyms, this might not be a bad idea!). Wikis do not have many forms of measurement that a person can see. They don't offer ratings, comments, or voting as the other social media sites do. You can consider these metrics for wikis:

- Mentions in wiki pages

- Links to the website from wiki pages (photos and direct links)

- Traffic from wiki pages

- Number of bookmarks to wiki pages mentioning your company

- Conversations about you in the "talk" section of wiki pages

- Positive and negative sentiment

Forums and Message Boards

The oldest forms of social media can offer you a lot to measure, whether it's a forum or message board you start yourself, or one in which you become intimately involved. These types of sites can drive targeted and qualified traffic to specific information, products, or media, as well as initiate poignant conversations around your brand and its products or services. Consider these metrics:

- Your own forum

 Note

With your own forum, you will be able to measure a wider array of metrics such as unique visitors to the site, number of members joining during a certain time frame as well as keywords that drive people to the forum. While being able to measure a lot more is a very enticing reason to start your own forum or message board, companies must take into consideration whether or not the community is already established on another forum or message board and if there is a need for a new community. Just because you build it, doesn't mean the community will come to it.

- Number of community members

- Number of new threads started

- Number of replies to threads

- Links to forum posts

- Participation in forums (including your own)

- Number of friends acquired

- Number of replies to new threads posted

- Positive and negative sentiment

- Replies to private messages sent to community members or friends

- Traffic to your websites from forums where you're active

- Number of profile views

Final Thoughts

Of course, these are merely suggestions. As a marketer, you should realize that this is only a starting point for defining your goals and success measurements. Just as every company is different, every social media site is different. After you've done your research and decided which sites best suit your marketing efforts, take steps to understand those sites fully and in depth so that you can map out what goals you can measure and define as you interact with the community members of the specific sites.

Don't be afraid to refine, revamp, and re-evaluate your goals and your barometer for success. You might find that you've set the bar too low or too high, so don't hesitate to change it, especially if you are just starting out. You never know how community members will react when you start interacting, so don't dig in your heels and hold on tight to some measurement point. Be a little flexible in defining—and redefining—your goals as you learn the ropes of each different social media community.

4

It's ROC (Return on Conversation), Not ROI (Return on Investment)

When it comes to understanding how to develop successful strategies in social media marketing, you need to alter your thinking from the traditional ways of measuring success (to learn more, see Chapter 3, "Goals Need to Be Defined"). When it comes to social media, the primary issue is the investment that companies make in the conversations that are happening instead of the ads they are sending out to those social media communities.

Measuring the Conversation

The different types of measurable goals explained in Chapter 3 are just the beginning. You can measure many more metrics, although doing so can get quite resource intensive. Doing this type of in-depth analysis of conversations happening within active communities can lead to wildly successful projects. These successful projects can create healthy returns on marketing efforts for the companies, as well as result in fans and evangelists who willingly market for you without expecting anything in return. But this kind of success takes time, resources, and investment in real conversations to produce real relationships that garner hardcore evangelists.

Developing conversations within social media sites that have active participants who are interested in your industry, products, services, or brands is essential in developing the trust that goes into building solid, reliable relationships. By building these types of relationships and sharing the experiences the community members are having, you gain a trustworthy foothold within the community. This is essential when both good and bad things happen.

Community members want to connect, and connecting requires human beings, not marketing messages, coupons, or physical items. People might love their iPods, but the experience and the sharing—being part of that Apple group—brings them together. The iPod itself isn't the link to the audience. People want to know that real humans stand behind the products and services. They want to know that someone within the company will listen to them, answer questions, and share experiences. Utilizing social media is a great way to start the conversation and let the community members know, "We're here" and "We're real."

Word-of-mouth marketing relies heavily on the conversation. Social media and word-of-mouth marketing are inextricably intertwined. People talk, people recommend, people suggest. They recommend products and services to their business associates, families, friends, neighbors, and others in social media circles. They talk to complete strangers. They share their experiences with products, brands, services, events, and so on. And if they are well connected, they can touch hundreds—and sometimes thousands—of people just by having a conversation that shares their own experience.

You Need to Monitor the Conversations about Your Company

So where do you start? How do you start developing conversations that will actually garner your company some type of return on your efforts? You start by monitoring your brand, product, and service's keywords.

You can use buzz-monitoring tools for this, some that come free and others that are included in a paid service. Consider these two examples:

- **Google Alerts**—With the free service Google Alerts, you manually determine which keywords to monitor. The service is limited in scope and returns basic information—just a URL of the site the mentions the keyword you are monitoring.

- **Radian6**—Radian6 is an enterprise-level buzz-tracking software service that you pay a fee to use. Radian6 and other similar tools give you a lot more information about what's being monitored. Currently Radian6 only allows you to see the previous 90 days of activity.

- **Techrigy**—Techrigy is an enterprise-level buzz-tracking software service that you pay a fee for as well. Like Radian6, it gives you a lot more data than Google Alerts, such as basic sentiment analysis. Currently Techrigy can draw information as far back as October 2007 and return it in a report format.

If you're on a budget, Google Alerts is a great place to start. If you have the budget, you can invest in one of these tools to help you monitor the conversations you are interested in:

- Radian6 (www.radian6.com)

- Techrigy (www.techrigy.com)

- BuzzMetrics/Neilson Online (www.nielsen-online.com)

- TrackUR (www.trackur.com)

Think of Social Media as "Social Conversations"

Start thinking of social media as social conversations. Conversations can take many forms, especially in the realm of online communities. From videos, podcasts, and photos, to messages on forums, to tagging and friending on social networks, all these forms of social media offer some way to converse with one or many people. Social media allows people to engage and share, and it all boils down to conversation.

Being active in conversations and responding to what you are monitoring in a respectful fashion, you will gain your company respect, trust, and a certain amount of authority. For example, consider a conversation on Twitter between a restaurant patron who was disappointed by his visit and a representative from the establishment (see Figure 4.1).

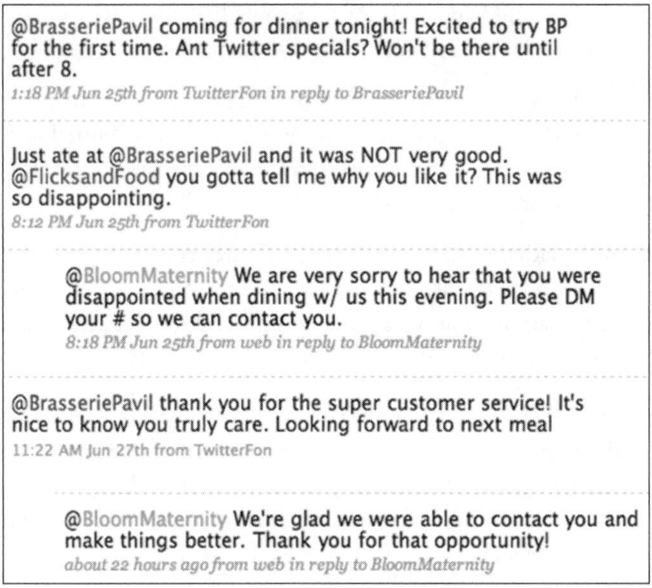

@BrasseriePavil coming for dinner tonight! Excited to try BP for the first time. Ant Twitter specials? Won't be there until after 8.
1:18 PM Jun 25th from TwitterFon in reply to BrasseriePavil

Just ate at @BrasseriePavil and it was NOT very good. @FlicksandFood you gotta tell me why you like it? This was so disappointing.
8:12 PM Jun 25th from TwitterFon

@BloomMaternity We are very sorry to hear that you were disappointed when dining w/ us this evening. Please DM your # so we can contact you.
8:18 PM Jun 25th from web in reply to BloomMaternity

@BrasseriePavil thank you for the super customer service! It's nice to know you truly care. Looking forward to next meal
11:22 AM Jun 27th from TwitterFon

@BloomMaternity We're glad we were able to contact you and make things better. Thank you for that opportunity!
about 22 hours ago from web in reply to BloomMaternity

Figure 4.1   *An example of a conversation in which the company had a prime opportunity to turn negative feedback into positive buzz. (Image courtesy of Trustworthy Blog—"The Undo Button" http://blog.gettrustworthy.com/2009/06/29/the-undo-button.)*

Figure 4.1 demonstrates a few points about conversations in social media.

- **Realizing the benefit of monitoring**—As Figure 4.1 shows, Brasserie Pavil was clearly monitoring its name in the social media space—in this case, on Twitter. If the company had not been monitoring its Twitter account and staying actively engaged, it would have missed out on BloomMaternity sharing her experiences about her visit to the Brasserie Pavil restaurant in Austin, Texas.

- **Engaging in conversations**—A more in-depth look at the Brasserie Pavil Twitter account reveals that the company is clearly engaged in conversations with its audience by tweeting, retweeting, and replying to followers, not just tweeting out the daily specials (see Figures 4.2 and 4.3). Also note the ratio of followers to those being followed, which clearly shows the company is actively seeking out people to follow.

- **Understanding the power community members hold**—Brasserie Pavil personnel recognized the power that BloomMaternity's shared experience would have on her followers. Instead of allowing the tweet to make a negative impression on BloomMaternity's followers, they tried to amend the situation and turn negative to positive by authentically caring and interacting with BloomMaternity.

Loved by beer lovers and others! Our soup today is Double
Chocolate Stout and cheddar cheese with fried spinach.
1:36 PM Jan 9th from CoTweet

Come watch the Cowboys today at Pavil's Bar. We have a selected
Beer Bucket Special: $16 for 6 beers. Go Cowboys!!!
12:03 PM Jan 9th from CoTweet

Our former exec sous chef, Isaac Cantu-now chef de cuisine
@watermarkgrill-walks 6900 steps each 8-hour shift!
http://budurl.com/stepsaddup
11:57 AM Jan 9th from CoTweet

@sahomesales Thank you! We appreciate all of the Twitter support
from loyal followers like you.
11:17 PM Jan 8th from Tweetie in reply to sahomesales

:(RT @spurs: Final from the @attcenter, Spurs 103 - Mavericks
112.
10:56 PM Jan 8th from Tweetie

Glad you liked it! RT @satscribe: @TanjiPatton I finally enjoyed
some absinthe at Pavil. Nice!
10:54 PM Jan 8th from Tweetie

@TanjiPatton Thank you for the tweet today, Tanji. We always
enjoy seeing you.
10:53 PM Jan 8th from Tweetie in reply to TanjiPatton

RT @WineTwits: What have you been drinking tonight? Please
share @WineTwits...
10:49 PM Jan 8th from Tweetie

@TanjiPatton: Wow..the French do it so well. Pavil's Gruyere &
Ham sandwich with a glass of Sancerre-comment dites -vous THE
BEST!
10:48 PM Jan 8th from Tweetie

Thank you, @SABizJournal for the mention today in your article
about using social media. It's been a fun ride for us.
10:43 PM Jan 8th from Tweetie

@Lizzieloushoes Thank you for retweeting.
5:14 PM Jan 8th from Tweetie in reply to Lizzieloushoes

@LBaehrUSAA Perfect timing. We look forward to seeing you.
5:14 PM Jan 8th from Tweetie in reply to LBaehrUSAA

Figure 4.2   *Brasserie Pavil is clearly engaged in conversations with its audience by tweeting, retweeting, and replying to followers, not just tweeting out the daily specials*

This company actively seeks out people to follow

Figure 4.3   *Note the ratio of followers to those being followed.*

- **Being humble**—Brasserie Pavil personnel did not argue or take offense to BloomMaternity's tweet; they simply embraced it as an opportunity to make a bad situation better. They were open to the possibility that the establishment did not do everything right, said they were sorry for the bad experience she encountered while there, and essentially acted humble. In doing so, they gained more respect from not just BloomMaternity and her audience, but from their own followers as well.

- **Creating fans and evangelists**—By being honest and forthright, genuinely caring about BloomMaternity's experience, and demonstrating that care with engaging conversation, Brasserie Pavil personnel likely created at least one avid fan in BloomMaternity, who will relate this experience to her audience in a positive manner.

Participate Without Expecting

Working in social media can be a lot like networking in face-to-face instances. Consider the following example of a local pizza shop. The owner knows that his customers are the local community. He establishes relationships with his customers by talking to them when they come in—not about pizza, but about themselves. He remembers that every Friday at 5:30 you call and order a large pizza with extra cheese, and you need to give only your first name, even though 10 other Bobs likely call that same day. You remember the extra effort he takes in having your pizza ready right as you walk into his shop.

The local pizza shop owner also realizes that his community isn't limited to just the people who come in and buy pizzas and sandwiches. He gives back to the community through local organizations and charities. He knows his community consists of the local boys-and-girls club that needs a sponsor for their trophies, the veterans group that needs a special meal to honor one of their members, and the church that needs someone to donate drinks and paper goods for its music festival.

These situations might not be directly related to people buying something from his pizza shop, but the owner gives to the community without expecting anything in return. By being a good community member, starting conversations and contributing to the greater good, he sees a return in conversation by new customers that are referred to him because he has become a trusted and well-respected community member.

The same situation applies online when participating in social media communities. However, instead of the local boys-and-girls club, a company might become involved with the *national* boys-and-girls club and engage its active adult advisors. Instead of providing a meal to the local veterans club, a company might serve as a resource of information that family members of veterans can access to help pre-serve a veteran's cherished memories. All these peripheral conversations eventually return to companies that genuinely engage in them.

Join a Random but Relevant Conversation

Conversations are constantly going on. They happen on Twitter, on YouTube, in forums, and on Digg and StumbleUpon, just to name a few. People love to connect and discuss topics that appeal to them. They love to share commonalities and debate differences. But the question is, should you just jump in?

When it comes to representing a larger entity (such as a company) instead of a sin-gular person, it's always wise to first watch the conversation and get a feel for who's participating and how open they are. Joining a somewhat random conversation on Twitter based around a hashtag (#) can actually be a boon for finding like-minded individuals. Social media community members use hashtags to make it easier to follow a particular conversation not just in text and not just in Twitter, but across other social media platforms such as Flickr and YouTube. In finding these individ-uals, you open the door for creating more trusted relationships built around com-mon subjects. The opportunities are limited only by the time and resources you can dedicate to developing.

Joining these random but relevant conversations, such as #blogchat on Twitter (Sundays starting at 9 p.m. EST, spearheaded by community-building expert Mack Collier of the Viral Garden Blog), can open you to conversations and thought lead-ership opportunities that you might not have been thought of before. These types of random but relevant conversations have begun to spring up on microblogging plat-forms, but they've essentially been alive and thriving in forums for ages. However, the quickness and immediateness of platforms such as Twitter and blogs appeal to community users who want to know the most relevant issues and information now.

During a Sunday night session of #blogchat, Mack Collier was discussing his atten-dance at South by South West Interactive in March of 2009. If you represented a company that created dashboard tools, being part of this conversation and interact-ing with someone like Mack or the other followers, could help position your com-pany as a thought leader.

> One of the themes I heard last week during SXSWi was that people didn't necessarily want more social tools, they wanted better ways to organize the available information.
>
> —Mack Collier, *The Viral Garden* (March 23, 2009)
> (http://moblogsmoproblems.blogspot.com/2009/03/
> what-i-learned-from-last-nights.html)

Join the Conversation on Several Platforms

Very rarely does one conversation have an immediate return on investment (ROI). Most people do not have a conversation with one person and then go to Sears and buy their new washer and dryer set. With so many avenues of information available, the average person listens to a neighbor and then goes to Amazon, Epinions, or Yahoo! Answers in search of more relevant information to back up or debunk the neighbor's raving review. This is why monitoring more than just one source is vital and why recognizing that humans don't stick to just one site is vitally important to understanding how conversations migrate and propagate throughout social media.

Plan for resources to engage community members, but also plan for those resources to be active in conversations across many platforms in social media.

5

Know Who Your Audience Is and What They Are Doing

To succeed in social media, you not only need to hold real conversations, but you need to hold those conversations with the right people. That means you need to know who your audience is and what that audience is doing in the social media space. You have to go where your audience is engaged and holding a conversation if you want to see some real progress from your efforts.

Just holding conversations about your product or services in some random social media site likely won't get you far down the road of success. Knowing who your audience consists of and what your audience is doing are two of the major keys to success in the social media sphere.

Most companies have a pretty good handle on who their target audience is. A lot of research goes into understanding who is buying a product or service and why. This research helps a company develop its marketing strategies and finely tuned messages for the right people so that they are more likely to respond in the manner the company envisions. The carefully crafted messages speak to a highly refined demographic that the company believes is the most receptive.

Most traditional marketers would like to believe that this demographic information transfers directly to the online world from the offline world, but sometimes the audience changes, especially when moving to an online environment. So before you assume that your audience is the 45- to 65-year-old woman who has raised her kids and still lives in the family's three-bedroom, two-bathroom house, take some time to investigate whether your audience has changed when you move to the new medium (the Internet).

Taking the time to understand who your audience members are makes it easier to figure out what they are doing. Knowing what your audience is doing can save your company time, resources, and money when implementing social media strategies. By taking the time to listen to the entire buzz around not only you and your branded terms, but the industry you are in, you'll be able to get a better handle on where you should be holding your conversations and how you should be holding them.

Hearing a social media site hyped in the media—Twitter, for example—might get you thinking that your company needs a Twitter account. But without doing research on your demographic and what your audience members are doing in the social media space, how do you know whether your customers are actively holding conversations in Twitter? You might be surprised to learn that the core of your audience doesn't use Twitter, but instead uses a niche forum dedicated to discussing your industry.

Finding where your audience is and what its members are doing in social media isn't exactly easy; it takes some time and research to understand where the conversations are being held. Sometimes the conversations are happening in multiple places; most people don't settle for just one social media platform. People move from video sharing, to MySpace, to a community forum with such ease and without much thought. That means your social media strategy needs to be as flexible as your audience.

Undertaking all this research on where your audience is and who they are might seem like a daunting task, but some resources can help. In *Groundswell*, by Charlene Li and Josh Bernoff, the authors identified six distinct groups in social media based on their actions on different social media platforms:

- Creators
- Critics
- Collectors
- Joiners
- Spectators
- Inactives

By segmenting social media users, marketers can get a better grasp on where their audience might be hanging out and where the conversations are happening. Let's take a quick look into those six groups:

Creators

Creators are socially active people who create blogs, videos, wikis, forums, and so on. These people are enthusiastic about their hobbies, passions, dislikes, or love of a product, brand, or service—and they've taken it to the next level by creating something dedicated to conversing about it and sharing their experiences with others.

Even a website owner who has a fan site dedicated to *Buffy the Vampire Slayer* can be considered a creator. Creators tend to hold a lot of influence over their audiences and are seen as an "authority" on their content because they care so passionately about something that they research and vet information for others.

Critics

Critics are active in social media by commenting on blogs, writing reviews about products or services, and responding to threads in forums. Critics also like to rate products, services, and so on. Critics are quite vocal on Twitter about their opinions and want those opinions to be heard.

Although the term *critic* can carry a negative connotation, doesn't mean that this type of person is a bad thing to deal with. Critics can be some of your better allies, especially if you have a great customer service department, are a beloved brand, or have products or services that your customers find valuable. Even if the expression is negative, you have the opportunity to turn vocal critics into your greatest evangelists.

Collectors

Collectors love to find and share things on the Internet. They collect bookmarks and submit them to social news sites. This group of social media users tends to be dedicated to bookmarking sites such as Delicious, or submitting stories to sites such as Digg or Stumbleupon.

Collectors sometimes are known as power users. They wield a lot of influence on how fast a submission can become popular and be pushed to a position of prominence on the community site. Depending on the site, collectors can potentially generate a lot of traffic in a short amount of time, especially if the collector has decided to bookmark or submit your content and share it with friends or the entire community on a popular site.

Joiners

Joiners interact in places such as Facebook, MySpace, and LinkedIn, or within a forum or message board. This is where real communities and groups develop and where they hold conversations and share their experiences about certain topics. Forums and message boards are the "granddaddies of social media" and have been doing just this since the inception of the Internet.

Joiners want to feel like they belong to something. Joining networks and community forums makes them feel connected to people who are a thousand miles away or more and who love to share their experiences about a shared topic. These networks—whether they are niche networks created on the popular Ning platform or a Facebook group—allow people to connect with one another in ways they cannot in their lives away from the Internet. This ability to connect with many people over great distances is a huge draw for joiners.

Spectators

Spectators love to sit back and watch. They are avid blog readers and most likely have a feed reader. They will make a friend of CNN or ESPN in Twitter so they can follow their news updates while they follow their other friends in Twitter.

Spectators also read ratings and reviews and can come to a conclusion based on those reviews, whether or not you as a company are actively involved in those conversations. Basically, a spectator is someone you will always have in your audience in some form.

Inactives

This classification is as simple as it sounds. Basically, these people are on the Internet but are not yet participating in social media. This generally tends to skew to an older crowd; however, as in all things, that demographic is changing, too.

The Groundswell Profile Tool

Now that we've discussed the classifications that Li and Bernoff have laid out to help marketers navigate the world of social media, we can take a look at the tool that goes along with the book. The Groundswell Profile Tool uses the most recent data from Forrester's surveys to help users understand where their target demographic lies within these six groups. It's a helpful tool for marketers to find starting place when doing their research on where their audience is, and it can save companies time and wasted effort.

 TIP

Download the Groundswell Profile Tool at
www.forrester.com/Groundswell/profile_tool.html.

The Groundswell Profile Tool enables users to search for an age group, a gender, and a country, and provides information about that demographic's typical social media classification (based on the most recent Forrester survey statistics).

This tool doesn't tell you what specific social media sites each demographic uses most, but it does identify the type of people within each demographic. Marketers then can apply the information to their social media marketing efforts.

Using the Groundswell Profile Tool

Let's take a look at a hypothetical company that manufactures pots and pans. The company is targeting an audience of women, in the United States, ages 45–54. Using the Forrester profile builder, we see that the majority of our audience leans toward being spectators (see Figure 5.1). So what does this tell you?

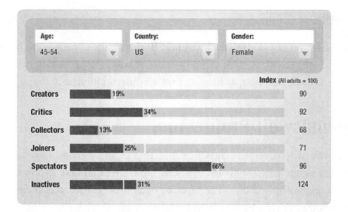

Figure 5.1   *The Groundswell Profile Tool can tell you a lot about your audience's social media tendencies. (Image courtesy of Forrester Research.)*

Developing a MySpace profile would be a wasted effort in both time and resources for this target demographic. Instead, this fictional company could benefit from building a cooking blog focusing about all things cooking related—recipes, healthy eating, equipment, and more. As you can see, this demographic also includes critics, so the blog would allow audience members to voice their opinions and experiences not only with their products, but also on the other subjects the blog would cover. If the fictional company actually sold these items online, it would behoove them to add ratings and reviews for the products, too.

However, relying on just this tool can be a little misleading. Social media sites are in constant flux and demographics are constantly changing, sometimes faster than what a tool like Groundswell can keep up with. That's why it's always good to do your research. Supplementing the tool with research for this demographic would show that Facebook's fastest growing segment is women over 45. With this knowledge, creating a Facebook fanpage might be the exception to the Groundswell data.

Companies looking for conversations with their demographics on different social media sites might at first be a little disappointed because no real conversations are going on about "them." This could mean that the people in the communities are not using the company name, brand name, or name of a particular product or service. This is more common with smaller companies that don't get a lot of press or mentions in the media, or with small, more locally focused businesses such as contractors, lawyers, photographers, or DJs. Although this can be a little deflating to the ego, it also presents a great opportunity to position a company as a thought leader locally, regionally, or nationally on a particular subject or even regional location.

If your company falls into this category, you still need to do your research and understand where your audience is. However, your marketing efforts should focus on industry conversations and ways you can provide valuable content to community members. Instead of basing the conversation on a specific product or company name, you need to build the conversations around information related to the industry. This is a great way to build inroads with communities and position a company as a thought leader. Eventually, the content provided becomes valuable to the community, and the small company's name and products then become connected with that value. Word-of-mouth throughout the social realm spreads, and the company becomes known as the "go-to" people.

The key to doing this and turning a little-known company into a thought leader— whether it's locally, regionally, nationally, or globally—is doing due diligence into your target audience and where they are holding the conversation. It's no different than a multimillion-dollar company trying to reach its target audience.

When you know not only who your audience is, but what your audience members tend to do in social media, you make your strategy easier to implement and at a smaller cost. You also tremendously raise your chances for a successful venue into social media.

Not Knowing Your Audience...Can Lead to Egg On Your Face

Many larger companies think they can bypass the research part of knowing where their audience is and what they are doing. This can lead to failures in social media as well as pretty public and embarrassing mistakes.

The following example demonstrates common missteps companies take in social media. As you'll see, this company's biggest misstep was not really knowing what their audience is doing or where they hang out.

In April of 2009, Pizza Hut announced they were looking for a "Twittern" to reach out to the college age demographic. Unfortunately beyond getting some of the lingo wrong in their press release and publicly announcing they were intending on leaving their social media marketing on a global platform to an intern, they didn't understand their demographic of choice wasn't active on Twitter.

A simple look at the Groundswell Profile tool shows us the demographic of college age students are overwhelmingly Joiners not Creators. That means this group is very active on places such as Facebook, Foursquare and MySpace, but they aren't as active creating content on Twitter (see Figure 5.2).

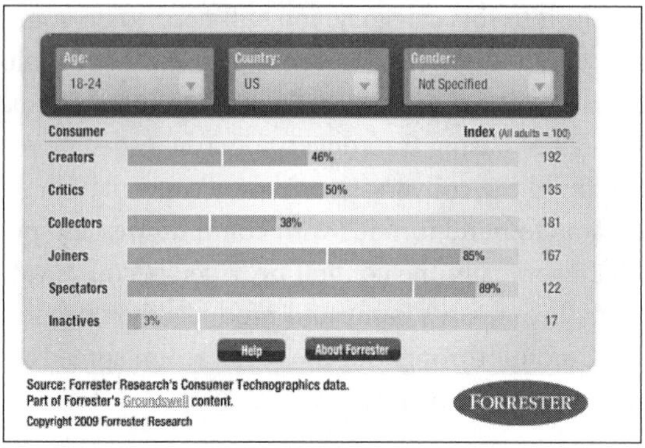

Figure 5.2 *Using the Groundswell Profile tool, you can get a better handle on what the audience you hope to reach is doing with social media.*

What was even more surprising was that there was a lot of conversation happening on Pizza Hut's Fan Page on Facebook but Pizza Hut wasn't even participating in the conversation. Opportunities to create evangelists, such as the person who posted "I feel at home" at Pizza Hut (see Figure 5.3) were slipping by. Pizza Hut also missed opportunities to control some embarrassing and vulgar wall posts because they weren't actively participating.

Figure 5.3 *Pizza Hut missed some opportunities to engage with people visiting its fan page on Facebook. Photos and names intentionally blurred to protect the posters' privacy.*

Final Thoughts

Understanding where your audience is and what they are doing in social media circles is at the foundation of whether the social media strategy you implement is successful or not. Instead of being lured in by the newest, coolest and hippest tools, such as Pizza Hut was with Twitter, take the time to know whether your audience that you are targeting is actually participating in that social media community.

Not only will taking the time to research and understand what your audience is doing in social media help you succeed, it will also help you with your bottom line. Your resources will be better utilized and not wasted in areas that will only end up draining your team's time and effort on tactics that won't bear success in the end.

II

It's About Conversation

6

The Conversation Happens With or Without You

A funny thing happened when the Internet went main-stream. Ordinary people could talk to more people than just their neighbors, co-workers, and social club friends about what they were passionate about. Believe it or not, this started happening long before the term social media was even a forethought in anyone's mind.

Conversations about brands, products, and services started happening online with the advent of message boards, forums, and web-based chat rooms. From 1992 on, comic book collectors could talk all about which series they loved, advertise any extras for sale, speculate on what might happen in the next issue of their favorite comic, and announce whether they were planning to attend local or national comic cons (conferences dedi-cated to comic collectors) through message boards and forums dedicated to the topic.

These conversations weren't just on a national level, either. People from around the world could now speak about their passion for comics to fellow enthusiasts in countries thousands of miles away. Have a rare comic you'd like to trade? Wondering what really happened to Gambit in the last issue of the XMen comics? Wondering if Stan Lee would make an appearance at the latest comic con? These are just a small sampling of the types of conversations that still go on in these forums.

Even When You Aren't Listening, People Are Talking About You

All this was going on without DC or Marvel really understanding the hidden treasure trove that had sprung up without spending even a dime of their own marketing money. As the years progressed and online marketing moved toward banners and flashy graphic ads, ads for comics or movies based on comics or conventions began to appear in these forums. Eventually, forum members became banner blind; most just ignored the ads they had seen hundreds, if not thousands, of times.

Unfortunately, these comic book companies really missed out on an opportunity to connect with a very passionate audience early on. Instead of using banner ads and flashy graphics announcing a new issue, or a special event at a comic conference, they could have had a representative in the forums talking with the community members about upcoming issues, conferences, or maybe even gripes about current plot lines. This would have garnered a lot more engagement and interest than a banner advertisement ever could have.

The conversations in these forums went on without "official" input from any major comic book publishers. And this still happens today. Many companies miss prime opportunities to engage with customers or their audience on social media platforms because they believe that because they aren't involved, nothing is being said. They don't realize this point:

The conversation goes on with or without you!

The people in these social media communities who are actively engaged in conversations about you, your brands, or your products and services do not adhere to your carefully crafted marketing messages, or your public relations timelines for releasing news, or when your CEO thinks you should be on the front page of the papers for your latest release. They talk about you whenever they want, however they want, and to whomever they want. It doesn't matter if it's a journalist from the *New York Times* or a fellow scrapbooker—community members will share their experiences. And they don't share just the good or the bad experiences, either—they share any experience. To community members, the simple act of sharing with one another drives these conversations.

Forums and message boards are some of the oldest and most powerful places on the Web where these conversations happen, but they are far from the only places where people are discussing your company. Conversations can also seem one-sided until you look deeper into comments, ratings, and reviews of the user-generated content on these social media sites.

Blog posts, for example, can seem like they are written by someone just spouting off their thoughts, opinions, or experience with your brand or products. But take a closer look. Do you see comments or trackbacks? Who else is mentioning this blog post about your company or its products or services? If a blog has comments and trackbacks, a conversation certainly is going on, and you might want to become active in it if you aren't already.

With videos, perhaps you find one of your TV commercials on YouTube, but you haven't released it on your website. This could be a huge signal that your offline media is affecting the online world. Finding that people have pulled your commercials and put them online tells you that the audience either really likes them or finds them incredibly annoying. The only way to tell is by the descriptions, title, and comments.

Missing Out on Opportunities to Converse

AT&T has a great line of commercials that show people in precarious situations that they could've avoided if they'd subscribed to AT&T's service and gotten an important call. My favorite of these is the "Techno Twins" commercial—and based on the 1,000-plus comments and more than 3,000 saves to Favorites on YouTube in less than a year, I'm apparently not alone (see Figure 6.1).

Although the positive takeaway from this is that AT&T finally put the videos online (these commercials were not on AT&T's account when the commercials first started appearing on video-sharing sites), the company is missing out on a conversation. AT&T also is missing out on a prime opportunity to promote these clever commercials on their website, or even lead people to view them via their YouTube accounts on their website. As you can see in Figure 6.2, there's no obvious way to find the commercials by going directly through the AT&T home page.

Figure 6.1   *AT&T Techno Twins Video on YouTube.*

Figure 6.2   *The AT&T home page doesn't link directly to the commercials that are creating buzz about AT&T.*

These commercials and subsequent videos on YouTube get people talking. The comments might not be directly related to AT&T's products or its wireless service, but they're still a vehicle to start a conversation with the more serious commenters.

Now imagine if AT&T had these commercials on their website and allowed their actual customers and audience members who are more directly interested in their products and services to comment on these videos. Can you imagine the kind of feedback they could get and what they could learn? Talk about missing out on insightful conversations! People are also embedding this video in blog posts and linking to it. This particular video also has seven video responses, plus homemade spoofs of the video. All the videos in the series, which are now viewable videos on YouTube, are conversation starters.

I don't say that AT&T needs to start the conversation, because that's what these clever videos do. Although they make you laugh, because you wouldn't want to be caught in this situation, they also make you think. AT&T could be asking, "Have you ever been stuck like this with your own version of the Techno Twins? Tell us your story!"

So much opportunity exists here for active engagement, from conversing with the company's own "built-in audience"—customers that come to the AT&T website to pay their bills or learn about services—to capitalizing on the spoof videos and video responses posted on the commercial housed on YouTube. Unfortunately, this also shows AT&T that the conversation about these commercials and AT&T is going on without the company's active involvement.

User-Generated Content and Media Give More Control to the Consumer

With the advent of user-generated content and media—and the ability to share any of it via social media sites on the Internet—companies have to be aware that these conversations exist and that they really have no control over them. Trying to control the conversations can only result in revolt by said communities and more bad press than any company could ask for. Listening and actively participating is a company's best course of action when discovering any kind of conversation in the social media environment.

Being humble when you first discover the conversations and trying to enter and participate in them is key. Just because you own the company, product, or service doesn't always mean you know everything about how your customers find value in it. Sit back and listen first; ask questions and then offer advice or information in a way that doesn't offend the community. The last thing you want to be marked as in these communities is a "marketer" or a "know-it-all."

Understanding that these conversations are going on is the first step in social media planning. The second step is finding your audience and understanding how and where members are having these conversations. From there, you can plan a strategy that involves getting engaged in the conversations in a positive manner.

No longer can companies afford to ignore social media or play the "we did not know" card. Consumer-generated content is having wide-ranging effects on both the perception of a company and whether a purchase is eventually made. These effects are not immediate, but somewhere along that decision cycle, a conversation in social media will most likely have had an impact on the purchase decision.

The question now becomes, can your company afford not to participate in the conversation?

7

Bring in Legal Early

Nothing can stop a great social media strategy faster than a lawyer with a stack of documents telling you why you can't talk about this or upload that. Of course, the legal department isn't out to thwart all creative and fun marketing strategies; it's really there to protect the company—and you.

Interacting with your customers or audience in a more one-on-one situation can result in employees stepping into murky legal waters. The immediacy of the medium involves less of a filter than traditional marketing channels such as ad campaigns or press releases. Whereas your legal team probably reviews your traditional marketing pieces before they're released to the public, social media interaction generally happens without the benefit of prior legal counsel.

When employees comment in forums or in groups on Facebook, Twitter, YouTube, or any other social media site, their words stay on the site and in the minds of customers or audiences. Even if an employee says something on a social media site and the comment is removed, there's still a chance that someone in that community has a record of what the employee has said via screen captures or printouts.

Legal Isn't There to Ruin the Fun

Contrary to the old stereotype of stodgy old men who smoke cigars and say "no" all the time, the legal department isn't out to ruin the fun of a creative social media strategy. If you take early steps to invite the members of the legal department to join your conversation about your social media strategy, you might find yourself very thankful you did so. If you ask the right questions and tell legal personnel what you are attempting to do, they can help guide you in how to put together your strategy without getting the company into a heap of legal trouble.

These troubles can take many forms, from employees mistakenly saying something they shouldn't resulting in libel or slander claims, to having to issue apologies for things that were done or said that can damage business relationships. The last thing you want is to have the legal department find out about your social media strategy when they have to clean up a mess that an employee created while attempting to act in the best interests of the company. After you've been burned in the social media arena, it can be very difficult to persuade your legal department to sanction further interactions in social communities.

Having your lawyers involved in the process from the beginning isn't just a wise move—it also can be a tremendous cost saver. Think about it this way: Would you rather spend resources to have your legal team advise on the right social media strategy in the beginning, to help ward off potential (and costly) missteps by your social media team? Or would you rather pay a ton of money to fight it out in court because an employee who thought he was being helpful promised a group of community members something he shouldn't have, and now those community members are suing you?

Teach Legal about Social Media

Social media is a vast new area of the Internet that a lot of legal teams know little or nothing about. Before you have team members dive headfirst into some possibly treacherous waters, teach them about the different kinds of social media. Create a social media presentation that navigates them through the different types of sites discussed in Chapter 2, "Understanding Social Media Strategies." Show them Digg,

Facebook, Twitter, and YouTube, and explain to them how people interact on these sites. Make sure you also give them information to take with them so they can refer back to it.

Taking the time to educate your legal team helps them get a better handle on what exactly they are dealing with when it comes to your social media strategy. If you explain the benefits the company will reap from participating in social media, your legal team will be more willing to assist you and will be less likely to just say "no." Better yet, if your initial social media strategy might've place the company into legal jeopardy, the newfound understanding of social media will help your legal team steer the company around legal trouble.

No one wants to stop a strategy that can help the company improve profits and its presence in the marketplace—and that includes the legal department, which tends to always be seen as the "bad guys." However, if the harm outweighs the benefits, legal needs to step up and steer the company away from the potentially harmful situation. That's not only their job, but ethically, it's their duty.

Make Legal a Part of Your Team

Work with the legal team to develop and streamline the process of getting things approved before you start actively engaging in social media. It's best to include legal as part of your social media team from the beginning. This will give your legal team a vested interest in helping your strategy succeed and steer clear of legal issues.

When you include legal as an essential part of your team, personnel will be a lot more willing to propose alternatives to strategies that could get you into trouble. Your lawyers will be able to spot proposed strategies that could be legally problematic and set you on the right path before you expend time, energy, and money on a strategy that could land you in legal hot water.

Understand Your Industry's Legal Ramifications

Certain industries have to be more cautious about their marketing and should be aware of their actions in social media. In particular, companies that deal with anything medical, such as pharmaceuticals and medical equipment, should have the legal department (sometimes referred to as "regulatory") vet everything that is presented to the public. The same issues can be encountered by any industry that is heavily regulated such as insurance, financial or banks. The entertainment industry also has copyright issues and concerns to address whenever they are planning to implement any type of marketing campaign. Anything to do with social media will likely have to go through the same scrutiny.

If you know that you need legal's approval before you launch or participate in anything that is remotely marketing related, you can better plan your social media strategy accordingly. If legal needs to approve your blog posts first, work with the department to develop a smooth and easy way for both of you to approve those posts, especially if you expect to post every day.

Work with your legal team on a comment policy that defines what can be approved and what can be addressed in comments, as well as what needs to be held for legal review. This will keep your conversations fresh and active and make your content relevant to what's going on in the world and your industry. Because social media is more about what's going on now, it's important that you create a smooth channel of review and approval to keep those active conversations going in the safest way possible.

Have Legal Help Create Your Social Media Policies

Whether it's the trackback and comment policy for your blog, how your employees speak to consumers in social media forums, or what happens when employees are active in social media sites outside their normal work hours, you need to have legal involved. This team of people will work tirelessly to make sure the company's social media marketing efforts don't place the company in legal peril. Figure 7.1 shows an example of how you might integrate legal in your social media strategy planning.

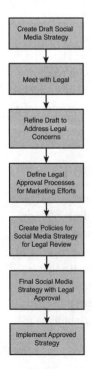

Figure 7.1   *A sample flowchart showing how to involve legal in your social media strategy planning.*

- Guiding your **trackback and comment policies**— While its crucial to create trackback and comment policies as discussed in an earlier chapter, its even more important to have your legal team help guide you in creating these policies. The legal department can help you better define what kinds of comments and trackbacks are acceptable and unacceptable. This includes racist or vulgar comments, profanity, and even terrorist threats. Your legal department can help you word these policies so that others can clearly understand what you won't accept and why.

- **Defined approval processes**—Having your legal team assist you in defining a clear path for approval of all marketing efforts in social media saves a lot of headaches. The legal team knows the ins and outs of the legal world and how much time it takes to understand the impact of your actions on the company's legal position. If the legal team is involved in this process from the beginning, expectations can be better set for what needs to be vetted and appropriate turnaround time.

- **Employee conduct on social media sites while working**—The legal team can be a great resource to you in setting up policies governing how employees should conduct themselves on social media sites when they are working and representing the company. Your legal department will help you establish ground rules for employee participation in work-related social media efforts and will help enforce sanctions against employees who disregard those rules.

- **Off-hours and employees in social media sites**—Just as important as the hours an employee spends at work is the time that employee is away from your office and how she represents you in the social media realm. Policies for both on-hours and off-hours activities and conduct within social media communities need to be clearly defined, and repercussions of policy violations should be spelled out.

The tricky part in all of this is what your employees do in their off-hours. That's their time and you aren't paying them for it, so the general thought is that the employees can do whatever they want. You want to ensure that your company's image and reputation is safeguarded. Remember, the actions of your employees—even in their own time—can affect your company's reputation.

If employees act in a way that is unbecoming or harmful to the company in social media platforms, your legal team can help advise you how to proceed. They can advise you on how to walk this tricky tightrope and develop policies that keep your company safe, legally.

Your legal department also can help you address other policies when it comes to dealing with social media. The ones I've just listed are the most pertinent for the companies I deal with when planning social media strategies.

You pay your legal team to keep you on the straight and narrow, so use it for this very purpose in social media. The key is teaching legal personnel about these technologies and how they affect the company, and to integrate legal in a smooth and painless manner. You can save a lot of time, effort, and resources by including them from the very beginning.

Set Up a Plan of Action in Case Something Goes Wrong

Always have a contingency plan, in case something goes wrong, especially in social media. This is important because, in social media, great potential exists for something bad to spread across the globe in seconds. One mistweet on Twitter by your employee in Kansas can cause a boatload of trouble for you in your China office. Legal can help you with these types of contingency plans.

Legal understands the workings of the legal system. If you are a global company, you likely also have people on your team who understand the legal systems of different countries. Consult with them to develop a plan to address issues when things go wrong with your social media marketing strategies.

Your legal team is skilled enough to know what kind of actions the company must take in different types of scenarios. For example, if you discover that an individual in a social media community is violating a company trademark, your legal staff will know what actions to take. It's an entirely different scenario, however, if an employee leaks vital and private company information through a social media site.

As stressed before, your legal team is acutely aware of and extremely skilled in knowing what actions to take for different situations that arise, so make sure legal personnel are involved in any contingency plans you are developing. Having these types of plans in place when something goes wrong saves a lot of headaches and heartaches when all the dust settles. It also keeps your company from reacting with a trigger finger and possibly doing something that will result in more trouble than you originally were in.

What If I Don't Have a Legal Team?

Smaller companies might not have the luxury of an entire legal team—or even any legal staff. If your company has just a small legal staff (possibly just one person), it might not be feasible to make legal part of your social media strategy. In that case, the best course of action is to line up everything you need and then have your legal counsel review the documents, policies, and plans to ensure that you are following a path that will keep your company out of legal trouble. Sometimes general legal counsel is not as skilled in dealing with social media, so don't be surprised if your legal counsel refers you to a more specialized attorney to review your documents.

If your company does not have any in-house legal representation whatsoever, it might be worth the expense to have outside counsel review your plans and help deal with legal issues as they come up.

Whenever you are dealing with policies—especially those that deal with employee conduct—make sure your legal counsel reviews exactly what those policies mean. Doing so in advance helps ensure that you are well versed in the potential repercussions of those policies and your ability to legally act upon them if the policies are violated.

Dealing with legal might sound scary, and might even seem a bit of a deterrent to entering the social media space, don't think of it that way. Think of legal as your partner to help steer you on the right path. Your legal team ultimately wants you to be as successful as possible in your marketing efforts, while staying on the right side of the law.

8

Don't Be Afraid of the Negative

Every day I deal with potential clients who are reluctant about getting into social media marketing because of the "bad things" people can say about them. This is the biggest stumbling block for a lot of CEOs or corporate-level managers to get over because they aren't in control of what people are saying about them in the online environment of social media.

Thinking that you can prevent negative things from being posted about you on social media sites just by staying out of social media marketing is a huge mistake for any company to make. In today's world of online reviews, blog posts, and picture sharing, is that the conversation about your company is still going on, whether or not you are actively involved. Companies cannot control these conversations or their tone, either—regardless of whether they participate in social media. So if people are going to talk about your company with or without you, doesn't it make sense to get involved and turn some of those negatives into positives?

Anyone Can Be Involved in Social Media, Even Your Grandma

As the popularity of sites such as Flickr, YouTube, TripAdvisor, and Yelp grow, companies can no longer ignore social media sites. Twitter—which is hugely popular with the over-30 crowd—has grown exponentially in the past year. Furthermore, one of the fastest-growing demographics on Facebook is users over the age of 45, which drives home the fact that growth in social media sites is not limited to a young demographic.

 Tip

> See mashable.com's statistics on the Twitter phenomenon here:
> http://mashable.com/2009/07/16/twitter-june-2009-growth/. To learn more
> about the Facebook boom, see istrategylab's July 2009 article here:
> www.istrategylabs.com/2009-facebook-demographics-and-statistics-
> report-513-growth-in-55-year-old-users-college-high-school-drop-20/.

Although anyone can be active in social media, some types of social media tend to be more popular with a certain demographic. Your customers or potential customers are increasingly becoming involved in social media in some way, even in ways you might not have considered:

- They're reading blogs and reviews.
- They're sharing their opinions and uploading photos to Yelp and TripAdvisor.
- They're creating their own blogs and vlogs to offer insights, tips, and reviews of companies, products, and services.

And they can do all this without your permission.

You can't let the fact that customers are increasing their power, gaining control, and expressing their opinions scare your company away from becoming involved in social media. Negative opinions will always exist. How you embrace and react to the negative opinions is what matters in social media.

When dealing with social media, companies need to fully understand they are no longer totally in control of what is being said. The public relations team can no longer be in sole control over what people are saying about you to the press. Journalists have become more savvy and are completely tapped into the online world of blogs and social networking sites when they are digging around for information about you beyond the fluff of a press release.

Journalists no longer rely on the spin of a press release designed as a glowing report of your newest venture. They want more: They want a balanced story. In search of that balance, they do searches on Google, Yahoo!, and Bing, and even look to immediate searches on social sites such as Twitter, Technorati, or even Digg. Journalists visit all different kinds of social media sites to find the "other side" of the conversation. Do you even know what is being talked about in those other conversations?

Don't Be Tempted to Let Outside Sources Handle Your Social Media Efforts

Although the job of your public relations team is to help get your company the attention you duly feel it deserves for its accomplishments, this team also tries to control what is being said about you, both good and bad. Trying to bring that control to social media can backfire in many ways. The problem with just leaving your public relations company or ad agency to "handle" your social media "issues" is that the public relations agency isn't you.

A lot of companies let an outside PR company, ad agency, or search engine optimization (SEO) resource handle their social media. Those entities assert that they have the skills to navigate this world and better represent you in these types of environments. They might have better social media skills initially, but that won't be the case for long. In fact, you and your staff will need to hone your social media skills and then look to your ad agency or SEO professional to help you with the finer points, such as dealing with the negative side of social media.

As an example, imagine that you have a micro-brewery. Your public relations firm, ad agency, or even SEO/PPC (pay per click) firm tells you that they can handle your social media for you. Your initial reaction might be, "Great! One more thing I don't have to worry about." However, take a step back and re-examine the situation. As personnel from your outsourced company are tweeting, responding in forums, or even writing your blog posts, they aren't you—and they do not know what is intricately involved in the beer-making process.

If your strategy includes being active in Twitter and one of your audience members asks about something directly related to the beer-making process, how will PR personnel answer the question? Will they know that one of your beers has such a beautiful amber glow, or that the taste of the beer you make has a subtle but delightful hint of apricots in it? They won't, and you probably wouldn't want them trying to answer anyway. So they have to come back to you for the answer. Unless your outsourced company has one of its own team members onsite and integrated into your own marketing team when the question is being asked, the elapsed time between when the question is asked and then answered will not be as fast as people in

Twitter expect it to be answered. You'll lose out on the opportunity to engage that audience member when his interest was at its highest.

Let's take this micro-brewery example a step further. If your outsourced agency is monitoring Twitter for you, that company is likely either using a tool such as Tweetbeep to monitor your company name or using chosen keywords (such as the names of your beers). If the outsourced agency is tweeting for you, they also have access to your replies and direct messages through your account. Now say, for instance, that someone from your audience visits your establishment and is tweeting about a horrible experience.

The team handling your Twitter account will report this negative situation back to you and seek direction on how to handle it, because just saying "I'm sorry" won't be enough to soothe this audience member. Let's say you're on a flight to a beer-tasting contest and you don't get that email until you land. By now, six or eight hours have passed, and this person in your audience has told everyone following her not just that she had a bad experience, but every detail of that bad experience.

If someone from your team who had been trained to handle customer experience had managed the situation internally, that team member could have responded to the concern or complaint in a much more timely fashion. Your team member could have turned that bad experience into a positive one and stopped the negative information from spreading for those six or eight hours. This could have been an opportunity to turn a negative into a positive, a chance to turn an disgruntled critic into a raving fan, and a chance to bring positive attention to your establishment. An outsourced company can't do that in a quick and efficient manner unless they have someone truly integrated and part of your team.

Knowing the Difference Between the Constant Complainer and an Upset Customer

Even in the offline world, companies have to deal with both legitimate complaints about their business and constant complainers who are out to get as many free services as they can from the company. In the offline world, your staff comes to know the difference between the "trolls" and customers who have been duly wronged by your company. When online, you don't have that face-to-face interaction with your customers, so the job of deciphering the difference is a little tougher.

You don't want your staff chasing their tails and wasting their time with the trolls and complainers. These types of people aren't really and truly the social media community types because they're focused only on themselves. After a while, they get pretty easy to spot.

How to Spot the Troll or Constant Complainer

A few signs can help you sort the trolls from legitimately upset customers:

- They complain about everybody and everything, not just your company.

- The world has wronged them.

- They don't complain on just one site, such as Yelp; they complain on a lot of sites, all the time.

- They use the same username and/or avatar across social media sites so that they can be found easily.

- Other companies have tried to appease them, to no avail.

- They have a new gripe every day or every week.

- They tend to not have a lot of fans or friends.

- They engage in arguments with community members quite often.

If you do realize that you are dealing with a troll, the best course of action is to just acknowledge their displeasure in a professional manner and apologize for any inconveniences they encountered. It's best not to engage this type of person any further. What's most important about this is that most of the other community members are smart enough to know the trolls will never be made happy. They will also notice your polite and businesslike manner of acknowledgement and will respect you for your approach.

How to Spot the Upset Customer

You can spot the legitimately upset customer with these signs:

- Until the incident that has them upset, they talk positively about you.

- They communicate in a friendly manner with the entire community.

- They actively create new content for the community.

- Unlike the constant complainer, they rarely badmouth anyone.

- They have a lot of friends and fans.

- They're generally helpful with other community members and attempt to resolve issues or disagreements.

The Power of the Community to Spot Constant Complainers

Paying more attention to the upset customer than trying to "feed a troll" will improve your bottom line and your reputation in the community. Members of social media communities are pretty quick to identify and know full well which members are the constant complainers and will never be made happy. If they see that you are catering to the constant complainer, you can lose respect in the community. This is why it's important to understand who you are dealing with.

Consider the example of Royal Caribbean Cruise Lines. In May 2008, the company opted to take the unusual measure of banning a couple whom they considered constant complainers. The couple from Cleveland wrote reviews of their cruises on social media forums geared toward travel on cruise lines. Each time they complained, the cruise lines responded by giving them some type of discount, which the couple duly reported in the forums.

The members of these communities took notice and also felt rather strongly about this couple's actions. The community as a whole took action, and community members wrote to the president of Royal Caribbean.

> Some board members felt the <name withheld> had complained their way to an unfair discount and posted their displeasure. They felt that the <name withheld> were teaching others how to "scam" Royal Caribbean. Some went so far as to contact Royal Caribbean's president and chief executive, Adam Goldstein to complain about the <name withheld> getting any compensation at all.

 Note

You can learn more about how Royal Caribbean handled this sticky situation at MSNBC, www.msnbc.msn.com/id/24711659/.

Handling the Negative with Style

Being present in social media can go a long way toward giving you authority and respect when dealing with negative situations. On social media sites that allow community members to review companies, their products, or their services, it's becoming more important for companies to be directly involved in these sites.

To understand the world of social media more intimately, I use social sites for just about everything I do. Recently, I took a trip to Key West, Florida, and used TripAdvisor to find a hotel. I wanted a smaller hotel, closer to the downtown but far enough away from the hustle and bustle of Duval Street. I searched the listings that TripAdvisor returned and found one that stood out above them all.

The Palms Hotel on White Street in Key West is active in Trip Advisor. Hotel staff monitor their comments and actually respond to both negative and positive reviews. When there are negative reviews, they don't discredit the reviewer. Instead, they explain the situation to the complainant, as in the example shown in Figure 8.1. The Palms is a pet-friendly hotel, but it does have weight limits on the pets you can bring. Unfortunately, that rule was just recently put in place, which is a big disappointment for guests who visited before with dogs above the new weight limit.

Figure 8.1   *The right way to handle a negative review.*

As you can see, management responded. They acknowledged the complaint and didn't discredit the complainant, but they also explained why the rule had changed. This wasn't the only response The Palms had within TripAdvisor, either. How The Palms responded in each situation—whether it was negative or positive—had a big influence on my decision to stay there. As more people use sites such as TripAdvisor to make their decisions about where to stay on vacation, it becomes increasingly important for property owners to become involved with these communities and the reviewers.

We Deal with the Negative All the Time

When you are involved in a business, you have to deal with negative aspects sometimes. Although we have been conditioned to handle problems by traditional means, such as utilizing a PR company, today's online world and social media sites are requiring businesses to become more intimately involved with their customers and both their praises and complaints. The difference in the online world is the speed at which customers can share their experiences.

Social media sites can propel a person's experience with your company across the globe within seconds. Not being active in these social media sites can be detrimental to your company and its marketing efforts, whether that customer's experience was good or bad. Of course, negative experiences can cause significant damage, especially if you are not involved in the conversation. This is why you cannot be afraid of what people are saying in social media sites. You need to be aware, understand the situation, and then address it.

If you respond in the right way to the negative reviews, comments, or other type of media placed in social media sites, you can actually turn negative situations into positive outcomes. It's all a matter of how you as a company respond.

9

Understanding
Each Community

Social communities, whether they are online or offline, have interesting dynamics. To make any kind of headway with the community, you need to understand how each individual community functions before charging in and saying, "Hey! Can I join the party, too?" A lot of different factors can affect whether you are accepted into the community. It's imperative that you understand what makes the communities in which your business is discussed tick. If you don't, you could find yourself on the outside looking in.

In Chapter 1, "It's Not Easy, Quick, or Cheap," I explained how important it is for companies to research where their audience and customers are in the realm of social media. That's only the first step in dealing with communities. A lot more goes into developing the type of respect, authority, and relationships in communities that generate successful strategies and attain goals for companies.

When you've done your in-depth research into where your audience is communicating in the world of social media about you or the broader industry that your company is part of, you have a little more work to do. It doesn't just end at saying, "Hey! I found my audience," and charging in waving your marketing message like the paper boys used to do on the street corners. Doing that will only garner you more than a few cold shoulders.

Working with communities of any kind—whether it's a forum, a group on Facebook, or a bunch of people on Twitter—discussing a particular subject every week takes both care and time. The care comes in developing true relationships with your audience by helping community members gain information they need or by solving their problems. By taking this approach, you can slowly establish their trust in you and build a solid foundation of a great consumer relationship. However, this doesn't happen overnight, no matter what brand or company you are.

Read the Rules

One of the simplest things marketers can do to understand where a community draws its lines and defines its norms is to read the rules. Generally, these rules are posted in plain sight or are part of your service agreement when you create an account. Most rules are prominently displayed where all members can access them. Often community members will point other members directly to them for reference purposes. For example, consider the rules and regulations of a forum called Cre8asite Forum (www.cre8asiteforums.com), shown in Figure 9.1.

See the callouts in Figure 9.1. You will notice that this particular set of rules informs page rank seekers (people who just try to post replies in forums that contain links to their pages in the hopes of improving their website's Google page rank) that they won't get any value from posting them into the forum. The second point to note in this figure is that the rules state what "You may not" do. After years of dealing with spammers, this forum has defined what types of actions will and will not be tolerated.

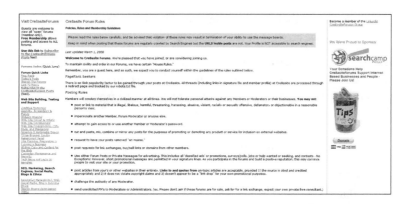

Figure 9.1   *An example of the community rules at a social media site.*

The owners of the forums and social media communities have been dealing with spammers since search engines became the golden cash cows the spammers perceive them to be. Forum owners know the power their communities have within certain topic areas. Furthermore, forum owners have learned that they must combat the spammers and unscrupulous marketers, to keep honest conversations going in their communities. This is why it is so important for marketers to read the rules for any online community in which they want to participate. These rules can serve as a guide or map for learning how each of these communities operates.

Often the administrators or owners of the community will add information about the number of links you can post in your signature or in a post or reply. Admins also can add stipulations regarding your avatar or how marketers may contact people within the community. If you violate one of these rules, you can find yourself out of the community without even a second thought—and your chance to engage with the captive audience you found will be blown.

Observe, Look, Listen, and Learn

The old adage "God gave you two ears, two eyes, and only one mouth" is a wonderful way to think about how you should get started with social media. You just cannot come waltzing into a community with guns blazing claiming to be the ultimate authority on your industry, your product, your service or your brand. Even though you do own it, if you come in with the attitude that no one knows your products better than you, that will only manage to get you more enemies than friends.

Having a bit of humility is important, especially when dealing with online communities. If you take the time to observe what's going on around you, you can learn a lot from people in social media communities. If you enter this space with an open mind, you can gain so much more than if you come into the community thinking you know everything about your products and industry. You may learn a lot from people who use your product or service every day.

Sometimes the truth is hard to take, however. When you sit back and listen in social media communities, you get the unabated truth. Many times tuning in to these communities is more informative—and less costly—than paying thousands of dollars for focus groups. When you just observe, you can get a full view of what actual customers think about your product or services, how they are using them, and why they recommend them or "diss" them to the community.

A great example of listening to the audience via a social media channel is the case of Canadian grocery store chain, Loblaws. Loblaws knew they had a winner with their store brand BBQ sauce. Loblaws won first prize at a BBQ festival in the Ozarks. They heard from their customers how great the sauce tasted, but still couldn't understand why it wasn't selling better. Once Loblaws put product reviews on their website they discovered —the bottle design. Apparently it was too tall to fit in most fridge doors and always had to be on the top shelf. Once they listened and knew what the customers really wanted, they addressed it and now sales of their BBQ sauce are great!

Often focus groups can be very contrived, in that the attendees feel they need to "please" whoever is administering the focus group. Worse still, attendees might feel as though they're present just to give quick answers, get their money for participating, possibly saying anything that will help them finish sooner. Neither of these reasons tell you what the audience truly feels. When observing social media communities, there's no predisposed situations. It's just the community sharing honest opinions and experiences with your brand, products, or services. Stopping to look, listen, and observe these communities can mean the difference between a successful social media strategy and a strategy that produces mediocre results or fails.

Understand the Norms

Along with observing how the community is talking about you and your product or services comes learning to understand the norms, or unwritten rules, of the community. These unwritten rules can sink a ship or help it sail successfully to its destination. For example, in communities that speak about medical conditions, it's perfectly normal to post pictures of dirty baby diapers so that the mom who's concerned can determine whether her child has a food allergy. Posting these types of photos on your Facebook page isn't the norm and could likely have a lot of your friends scratching their heads wondering why you are posting such things.

These norms can be as simple as jargon—that special language a particular company or industry uses to describe everyday things. They can also be as complicated as how you link to sites (for example, when you are allowed to add links and whether the community has a preferred or mandated method for doing so). Communities can be fickle; if you break one of their unwritten rules, you may have to deal with an incredibly cold shoulder.

Many marketers fail to realize that rejection isn't the only consequence for their unwanted approaches in social media communities. What they don't realize is that these community members talk behind the scenes, where you can't see or participate in the conversations. They talk through instant messengers, private intercommunity messages, emails, and direct messages on Twitter. Often they share things in private that they're not comfortable sharing in public.

These behind-the-scenes conversations can have a huge influence on other community members. If you break one of their norms, you can pretty much count on the night's discussion revolving around your marketing blunder—and that all goes on without your knowledge.

The key to understanding all these norms is to first observe the community in action and learn how members interact with one another. After a few weeks of watching and observing the interactions within a community, you can pick up on those small idiosyncrasies that you'd missed if you had just jumped right in claiming to be the expert or used a buzz-monitoring tool pull out the posts about you. Buzz-monitoring tools help you find audiences, but they don't give you a guide to interacting with them. You can get that only by taking the time to stop, listen, and observe how the community interacts and what norms they follow.

Learn the Pecking Order—Who's the Boss?

Along with uncovering a community's unwritten rules, companies need to determine the "pecking order" in a community. When you learn who the true influencers in the community are, it can make your efforts a lot easier. Knowing the pecking order, from administrators, to influencers, to those who are just learning, can help you build a much more stable strategy for integrating you and your company into the community.

That's not to say that you need to target the influencers as soon as you sign up. Being aware of who has the influence to affect how other community members view or perceive your brand, product, or service is more important than even striking up a conversation with them. Understanding that you need to engage the whole community is a huge factor of success within the social media sphere. However, you need to approach each type of community member differently.

With influencers, you must recognize their power without announcing it publicly. Silently and subtly acknowledging the power they wield is key to working with this group. This can be done by simply replying to a poster in the forum and adding that the poster has quite a lot of experience in this area and might have insights to offer you. To some degree, you must come bearing gifts, whether those are compliments, offers to demonstrate your new products, or even coupons or free trials. Sit back and observe the influencers first, and understand what drives them to share their experiences and give recommendations.

With community administrators, you must be forthright and honest about who you are and why you are there. Don't try to just "slip into" the community and start marketing to members. That will get you booted by an administrator faster than you can hit the Submit button on your third post.

The people in the community who are there to learn or gain some kind of knowledge to solve a problem usually have some kind of pain point that brought them to the community. With this group, you need to help them after you learn the community's norms. Don't step on the influencers' toes, but be ready to give and give till it hurts. Whether it's a link to a competitor's site or an offer to have a tech person call to help clear up a problem, you must make an effort to ease this group's pain points.

By giving more than what you are taking within these communities, you will ultimately reap rewards. This giving can take different forms, whether helping a nonprofit by donating part of the proceeds of a sale of a product, offering free trials of your product or service, or offering free repairs to your products—even the ones that are out of warranty. Just make sure you understand how to relate to each type of community member before you start engaging them.

Communities Don't Want to Be Marketed To

This final point is probably the toughest for marketers to swallow. Communities hate to be marketed to. After years of push marketing from TV commercials and radio spots, consumers have finally found refuge in online social communities. These are places where they can talk about their passions and loves, uninhibited by marketing messages constantly pushed in their direction.

Social media exploded when consumers realized they had the power to come to online communities and talk to other people who had the same passions and hobbies, and to share their experiences. It exploded because marketers weren't in these communities pushing marketing messages or trying to direct how these community members should "really" be discussing their experiences with their products.

The moment a company sends a PR firm or a marketing firm into a social media community to represent it and get out a message, it loses all respect with the community. On a general level, most marketing firms or PR agencies tend to look at social media sites as marketing tactics instead of parts of an entire social media strategy. They neglect to do the proper research into rules, norms, and pecking orders of communities; they think it's about pushing out another press release, commercial on YouTube, or free coupon to try your product. Those are some of the fastest ways to fail in social media.

Communities want to share their experiences with you and their fellow community members. Encouraging that sharing is your best marketing message. It's something you can't pay for, and it's something you can't expect. However, it is something you can engage with and turn into a success for your social media strategy.

10

Come Bearing Gifts

In a lot of cultures, it's customary when coming to a party or event to bring a gift for the host or hostess. In fact, when you show up empty-handed, other guests might look down on you for not honoring this custom. You might even get a cold shoulder from a few other attendees because they perceive your actions as rude.

Now stop for a moment and think about your marketing actions in social media. You can't ignore a community's customs and expect people to embrace you as a new member. You might see some disapproving reaction in these situations:

- You came but weren't invited into the party (you just showed up at the door).

- You invited yourself into the party (you heard about the party and just told everyone you were invited and would be there).

- You didn't ask if it was okay to come to the party (the host said something about the party but never explicitly invited you, and you showed up anyway).

- *You didn't bring a gift for the hosts (you were invited, card an all, but you were just thoughtless).*

Basically, you are no better than Vince Vaughn and Owen Wilson's characters from the movie The Wedding Crashers, *only in this case, you will get tossed out instead of invited back to the party by the pretty bridesmaids. As I discussed in the last chapter, it's imperative that you understand the community you are dealing with so that when you come uninvited to the community, you come well prepared to add value to it.*

Understand What the Community Finds Valuable

By researching the communities you want to deal with when implementing your social media marketing strategy, you also begin to understand what exactly the people within the community find valuable. No community is the same, so no "one size fits all" sample pack of your product or service will serve as a gift the community will accept. This is why audience research is so important, sitting back for a few weeks observing what the community finds most valuable will allow you to tailor and personalize the gift you give them.

Think about it for a moment: If communities hate to be marketed to by marketers, why would coming into a forum and offering free samples of your latest product go over well with them? Just because your offline marketing team says that the free samples went like gangbusters at the supermarket marketing events they planned does not mean they'll go over as well in an online community.

However, communities—whether it's a group of bloggers or a forum of moms discussing how to deal with their children's food allergies—do find something of value. In fact, it might not be just one thing. It could be the opportunity to voice their own story on a major platform. It could the opportunity to show off their latest pictures in a newfangled online gadget. It could be a list of what not to combine their medications with. The point is, you don't know what the community finds valuable unless you sit back and listen to members' conversations.

Blindly throwing things into the community can lead to wasted effort. Many times what appeals offline doesn't cross over into the online world. Free supermarket giveaways work great offline because they're like an "instant" impulse buy, and when you are spending $100 or more on groceries, a free sample always appeals to shoppers passing by. But in this example, you're not dealing with a group of people who spend hours discussing their passions. It's a different community.

Social media communities aren't the supermarket. Sure, information about your product or service can circle the globe in mere seconds, but community members spend hours discussing and sharing their experiences with your brand, products, and services. To some members of these communities, those free giveaways are just like what "everyone else" can get. Community members who dedicate their time sharing expect a lot more when representatives from companies come calling. If you don't show up with the right gift, they just might slam the door in your face.

Valuable Content Is a Gift

When you are dealing with members of a passionate community, sometimes the right gift isn't a physical "thing." These members often find content more valuable than the product you sell.

Content can become a valuable commodity in online communities that are passionate about your industry, your brand, your product, or your service. This is because members have already experienced it and are sharing those experiences with other members. They've gone out and bought the new version of your software, or they've already gone to Best Buy and had that new Bluetooth-compatible car radio installed.. Now they want more.

Content doesn't have to be text on a web page, either, although that is one of the more simple ways to provide content that a community might find valuable. Videos, photos, and podcasts all serve as great forms of content. Putting up your latest slide presentation on a slide-sharing site about how someone can "trick out" your product and have even more fun with it can be a very powerful piece of content to share in a community. What's important is understanding what community members deem of value, not what you think is valuable.

All the money you have invested in your offline marketing pieces to create slick packaging or fancy pieces of literature is of little value to the online community. In a community of passionate brand loyalists, glossy brochures don't hold the power they do offline. Something as simple as an online site of recipes for your product can be the most valuable piece of content you produce—and you don't need a Madison Avenue marketing agency to produce it for you.

The bells and whistles of offline marketing tend not to cross over well as "quality content" to an online community. To give these communities with the "gifts" they are looking for, you have to engage with them, understand them, and then meet their need for quality.

Don't Expect the Community to Give Freely

If you are expecting members to give you something in return for your gift, you'll be waiting for a very long time. Members of these online communities are very skeptical of marketers and tend to have some serious aversions to attempts to be marketed to. When marketers come calling without establishing themselves as true members of the community, members likely will clam up or, worse yet, call you out.

Members of social media communities aren't dumb. They understand that eventually some kind of marketer will be part of their community. The approach the marketer takes is the relevant issue. If your approach is to give a free sample and then expect members to fill out a form to get that free sample, it won't happen in the droves that you believe it will.

For example, let's say your public relations team decides to issue a press release now that you've now entered the social media sphere and joined a particular online community. Your PR team wants to share the press release with the online community and attempt to engage members. One of two things will happen:

- You'll hear only the sound of chirping crickets.
- The audience will call you out for being a blowhard marketer.

Just because you come bearing gifts doesn't mean the community will freely give you what you want in return. Remember, it's not about you—it's about the community.

A Community Member's Time Is Just As Valuable As Yours

You are getting paid by your company to interact within the community, but remember that most of the other community members you are engaged with do not get paid to interact. They are giving up their valuable time to share the things they are most passionate about. They feel that the time they dedicate to the community is valuable and that they get something just as valuable in return.

If that equation ever becomes less profitable for the community member, his participation will wane and he eventually will look for another community in which he feels his time invested produces good returns. When communities become overrun by marketers who don't understand the value of the community members' time, the community will step up and ban any type of marketing, or community activity will drop off entirely.

When you are engaging members of these communities—whether it's a blogging community or a Facebook group—and you are asking them to do something in return for information, don't expect them to do this for free. Marketers need to keep in mind that they should reward or compensate members they engage with and those they ask for something in return. Whether they're completing a survey or just having a conversation with you, these members are giving you a piece of something they deem valuable—their time.

Acknowledging that fact can take you a long way in social media. It is paramount that you recognize that actively engaged members of a community aren't just another audience to dump your marketing literature upon. Furthermore, you need to keep in mind that the audience is full of real people who have lives and give their time to their passion or hobby. When you show respect for the community, your social media marketing strategies have a much better chance to succeed.

50¢ Coupons Mean Nothing

Almost any company on the planet can give a coupon. I can go to my local quick-mart on a Sunday and pick up the *Philadelphia Inquirer* and get whole ton of coupons for varying degrees of "cents" off the purchase of a product. Coupons are not special. They aren't unique, and they rarely sway me to change from a product to which I'm loyal to try another brand. I'm not alone.

Entering into a social media community with the idea of giving the same coupons you print in the newspaper won't get you very far. As with press releases, marketers need to realize that social communities are not another channel for coupon distribution.

For a coupon program to work, it must have some unique quality. In essence, it must make the community you are engaged with feel special. Making the community members feel appreciated for their involvement or engagement is crucial. If they can find the coupon elsewhere on the Web, there's nothing special there for them to hang on to or identify with.

You can make coupon programs work in social media communities in several ways:

- **Offer community-specific promotions**—You could reward people who engage with you on Twitter or MySpace with a special promotional code that's specifically tied back to that community. Name the code so that it is tied to the name of the community. Doing so further reminds community members that you were engaging with them on that particular platform.

- **Offer limited-time promotions**—Don't run a coupon promotion for an unlimited or undetermined amount of time. The value of that coupon to the community members goes down over time because eventually the coupon is no longer special. Community members know the longer a coupon is in circulation, the less likely it stays "special" to them. Coupons and coupon codes get passed around the Internet—some social media communities are dedicated to finding and promoting the latest coupon codes that are still working. When your "special" promotion hits one of these forums, it's no longer unique or special in any way.

- **Limit the coupon distribution method**—Determining how the community members get the coupon or promotional code is another way to make sure the specialness of the coupon stays intact. If you limit the way the coupon is distributed to either snail mail or email (instead of posting the code on a web page that anyone can access), the coupon tends to retain its specialness.

- **Don't tell the community the coupon is coming**—If you are rewarding community members with a special coupon or promotion, surprise them with the "thank you" coupon. Email or send it through snail mail. This shows you are going the extra mile and taking the time to give to them directly, to affirm that they really are special to you and your company.

- **Jazz it up**—Don't just make the coupon look like every other coupon you've delivered. Jazz it up—make it look unique. Include specific wording that thanks members for their participation in your project or engagement in the community. The community members will notice and talk about it as well.

Give When Least Expected

Community members don't always have to do something or engage with you in order for you to reward them. Of course, thanking community members by giving them a gift of some sort will be appreciated. However, you'll really get the attention of a community if you give when it's not expected.

Unexpected giving creates a whirlwind of buzz and appreciation. Saying, "Hey, thanks for sharing your experience in the XYZ forum—you've really helped us out", and adding a small token of appreciation, can go a long way. It goes even longer if that small token isn't one of your projects.

For example, consider the company Freshbooks, based out of Toronto, Canada. Rayanne Langdon is the marketing director for the company and an avid Twitterer for both the company and her own personal account. The Freshbooks community is an active one. One day Rayanne noticed that one of the company's followers had tweeted about being stood up on a first date. Rayanne didn't miss a beat. She tweeted back, "At Freshbooks, we'd never stand you up!"

She didn't stop there. She went to the follower's blog and found out where her office was. Rayanne proceeded to call a florist and have a bouquet of flowers sent to her for the next day. The buzz over what Rayanne did is still around today, the community knows that Freshbooks isn't just another company, and they know that Rayanne isn't just marketing to them.

Give Without Expectations

The final piece of the "come bearing gifts" puzzle is to not expect anything in return. When you give a gift to a person face-to-face, generally you don't expect anything in return. Dealing with online communities shouldn't work any differently.

When dealing with bloggers, for example, you build a rapport with them first. When that rapport is in place, you have an opportunity to send a gift or a free sample to bloggers you know would be interested. Tell them you'd love to hear their feedback if they have time to give it, but don't make their feedback a requirement of getting the gift or sample. Don't expect a blog post reviewing what you've sent them, and don't expect the feedback. Just give without expectations. It's when you give without expectations that you find the greatest rewards in social media.

11

Bloggers Have No Boundaries

Bloggers can be the most passionate community members out there. They are also creators, as defined by the book Groundswell, by Charlene Li and Josh Bernoff. Bloggers feel passionate enough about a certain subject that they are actually taking the time to create content around it. These are actively engaged members of a community, and they can be your best brand evangelists or your worst PR nightmare.

Bloggers don't have to follow any rules other than their own moral compasses. So if using other people's photos, defacing those photos, and then writing blog posts around them is okay by their own moral compasses, not much can stop a blogger from doing just that. In fact, that's how well-known blogger Perez Hilton makes his living, day in and day out.

Questions have arisen about the legality of how Perez Hilton goes about his blogging, especially when it comes to copyrighted material such as celebrity photos, but my point in bringing him into this conversation is to show that bloggers operate by a different set of ethics & rules— their own. There are still standard copyright and libel laws that bloggers need to abide by, but they don't have to follow a standard set of rules & ethics set up by a company or the company's legal department. For 90% of the blogs out there, no editors are in charge.

A blog can be set up in less than a day and is relatively cheap to set up. Blogs can even be free if an inexperienced blogger starts off on hosted services, such as WordPress, Blogger, or LiveJournal. If someone is angry enough at you, they can buy a domain, set up hosting, install the blogging platform of their choice, and start writing content about how bad your company treated them in less than 24 hours and for less than $100 for the whole year. And someone who doesn't have that kind of financial means can set up the free options in less than an hour.

When you begin to understand how easy it is to set up a blog, that bloggers have no rules to follow, and that bloggers are likely the most passionate creators out there, you also understand what a double-edged sword bloggers can be. Just emailing a blogger your press release can land you on "The Bad Pitch Blog," something no marketer or PR professional wants to happen.

Bloggers Are Not Journalists

A huge difference exists between a blogger and a journalist. It's safe to say that most bloggers are not paid journalists. Journalists have a code of ethics they must abide by, rules handed down by the publication they work for as well as advertisers the company has to worry about, and generally a fact finding and verification process is in place. Journalists also have a chain of command they have to answer to. From the editor of the publication, to the owner, to the advertisers, and finally to the publication's audience, journalists are paid to please a lot of people.

Most journalists are educated in journalism or a related field. They've gone through internships, started on unwanted beats, and moved their way up until they're finally writing about what they love. Journalists also have it ingrained in their very nature to be objective and fair with every piece they write.

Most bloggers, on the other hand, started down this road because they were incited, enraged, or just plain passionate about something. They didn't plan a real strategy when they started their blogs. They just wanted to share their experiences with the world, and a blog gave them ample opportunity to do so.

Bloggers are not obligated to be fair or objective, in that they don't have and editor or a legal team saying they need to be. Bloggers don't have to research, check facts, look for opposing views, or answer to advertisers who are upset by their stories. While most bloggers do feel morally obligated to present the truth and likely run by a stringent set of moral ethics, they really don't have to at the end of the day.

Journalists have a moral duty to check and recheck facts when it comes to contro-versial pieces because of the nature of the news business. For a journalist, having his integrity called into question is insulting and could be quite damaging to his career. If a journalist is labeled as biased or as repeatedly leaning to one side of an argu-ment, his future as a journalist can become very limited.

Bloggers don't have those same worries. Unless you see some kind of ad network on the blog, generally bloggers aren't getting paid for their efforts. Bloggers want engagement—people commenting on their blogs, linking to their content, and so forth. They want their experiences to get out there for the world to hear, and it doesn't matter whether their facts were checked.

Bloggers Understand the Power of Their Words

If you think you it will be easy to get bloggers to write about you just because you emailed them, you might want to rethink your strategy. Bloggers are very cognizant of the power their words can wield.

A blogger understands that words can influence not only the current audience, but also future audiences. Blog posts have the potential to rank well in search engines because those posts might contain fresh content about a poignant subject. So if the post gains enough attention from other blogs and sites linking to it, it has great potential to live on in the search engine rankings; it won't just affect the audience within a day or two of the post.

As blogging software becomes more adept at optimizing the infrastructures for the best search engine rankings, the propensity for blog posts to outrank your com-pany's static pages is greater. Bloggers understand this and aren't afraid to wield this power.

Bloggers also know that they have influence over other bloggers in their community. One of their posts can be furthered by another blogger, and that gives them potential to influence another whole audience with their experiences and information. If a blogger has several blogs or guest blogs on other blogs, the potential sphere of influence increases as the audience for the blogger increases. Bloggers jump at the opportunity to guest blog because it increases their sphere of influence and the power of their words to affect an audience.

It Doesn't Matter How Many Subscribers a Blog Has

"Oh that blog doesn't matter—it has only five subscribers!" If I had a dollar for every time I've heard something similar, I'd be a bit richer!

The number of subscribers a blog has publicly displayed is irrelevant to the power the blog has. The blog could have just five subscribers, but if those subscribers are family members and a journalist from the *New York Times,* the potential for a damaging situation is great.

Unfortunately, there's no way to know who's subscribing to a blog. It would be a godsend if there was, but you can't determine who is reading the blog. You also have to realize that the displayed number of subscribers doesn't take into account how many people have actually seen a particular blog or blog post, because it might rank well in the search engine or someone might have posted the link in Twitter as a shortened URL.

This is why relying solely on how many subscribers a blog has displayed is a bad marketing strategy in deciding whether to engage a blogger and build a relationship. Companies should look at a lot of other factors:

- Activity of the blog (comments on posts)
- How often content is posted
- Google page rank
- Technorati rank
- Search engine ranking for keywords

A Blogger Doesn't Need Your Love

One of the worst ways to start with professional bloggers is to tell them how much you "love" their blog. You probably don't realize how many times a week marketers email bloggers and proclaim to them just how much they love their blog.

Bloggers find this type of comment insulting and quite insincere, especially after they look at the title in your signature and see "Director of Marketing" or "Social Media Guru." They know perfectly well that you are trying to flatter them to get them to talk about you or your product.

Instead of emailing the blogger and starting off with "I really love your blog," try saying, "I really was intrigued by this piece of content you wrote" and including a link to the published post. This shows you've actually read the blog. That route shows a lot more sincere interest than false flattery, which a blogger really doesn't need.

Understand Bloggers Before You Approach Them

Bloggers will know if you don't take the time to actually understand them. If you just peripherally read a few blog posts and didn't bother to read through the conversation happening between bloggers and their audience in the comments, you are doing yourself and the blogger you want to approach an injustice. The name of the blog isn't the only relevant piece of information—the most recent blog posts or the blog posts ranking for your keywords give you clues into understanding what drives the blogger to continue producing content.

Looking at the categories of the blog posts, who the frequent commenters are, who the blogger frequently links to in posts, and who the blogger lists in the blog roll are all small keys to help you understand who the blogger really is. Just reading one or two blog posts isn't sufficient. Dig a little deeper and actually comment on the blog yourself, to get a feel for how to approach a particular blogger. As with businesses, no blogger is the same, and there's no cookie-cutter advice for approaching a blogger.

Establish a Relationship Before You Ask Anything of a Blogger

Just finding a blog you think you want to engage with and sending an email saying, "Hey, we want you to try our stuff," will get your email moved to the Delete folder. As with claiming you love a blog, sending a press release or samples to a blogger's doorstep smacks of insincerity and implies that you don't understand that social media is all about sharing experiences.

You can start to build a relationship with a blogger in several ways before you send an email. Start by reading the blog every day. If you find old blog posts that really intrigue you or spark your interest, comment on them. Be transparent about who you are—by that I mean make sure that if you are there working for XYZ company, make sure you sign it that way and leave your contact information and definitely don't drop a link to your website. Be honest and say, "Thanks for this blog post, Jim. I was going back through your blog and found this post relevant even today, especially in light of recent events in our industry." Sign your name and who you work for.

This is the beginning of building the relationship. As the blogger sees you are a serious member of the audience, she will start to reply to you in comments. It also doesn't hurt to link and reference the blogger's work in your own company's blog. Again, you have to be real about this approach—just linking to the blog for no real reason shows a lack of sincerity.

When you've got a good base of conversation going with the blogger through comments, send an email asking if she would like to be considered for future efforts with your company in gaining insight and feedback into your company's products or services. Taking this route helps strengthen the relationship you've been building with the blogger in a genuine way.

Although it may take some time to initially establish the relationship with a blogger, you likely will gain a serious ally for your future efforts. Only after you've established the relationship through transparent and upfront means can the magic really begin when working with bloggers.

Bloggers Are Their Own Community, and When They Unite, They Are Powerful

Bloggers talk—not just in their blog posts or on Twitter, but among themselves in their own communities. I can't count how many times I've emailed or IM'd another blogger in the search engine optimization (SEO) or social media industry about some lame press release I've received, asking that blogger if they got it, too.

Bloggers are a powerful community when they unite for a common good or if one of their fellow bloggers has been wronged. When word spreads from one blogger to another at the speed of light, it doesn't matter how much physical distance is between the bloggers—they go to work in the virtual world to share with all their audiences, to spread the word of what's going on and how it affects them personally.

No community is more powerful than the community of Mommy Bloggers. Upsetting one or two of these bloggers can result in a hailstorm of controversy, as Motrin found out in the spring of 2009. Motrin's campaign aimed at moms who transport their children via a "sling" offended a few prominent "Mommy Bloggers," and Motrin ended up with a serious black eye publicly. Motrin took down the commercials and videos on YouTube and ended its print campaign targeting these moms because of all the backlash caused by the Mommy Blogger community.

Give Link Love

Finally, give a little "link love" (giving a link back to the webpage or site you are referencing without expecting them to link back to you) where it's appropriate and doesn't seem like fake flattery. Recognizing bloggers for their efforts by adding a link to them in your own company's blog, publication, newsletter, or static website as a great resource on a particular subject can go a long way with a blogger.

Bloggers are all very aware of who's linking to them. Most likely, they will come to your own blog or website to see how and why you are linking to them. If it feels like it's more like a "bribe" to get you to link back to them, you've lost their respect. However, if the linking is done sincerely, it can further build your relationship—and possibly get the blogger thinking about working with you in the future.

It can also get bloggers looking into more of your company's content on their site, to see how they can integrate more of your information with theirs. That's a good sign that you're building the foundation for a great relationship with a blogger.

12

Every Business Is Different

No two businesses are the same. Even if you sell the same kind of products or services, you and your competition have different marketing approaches, target demographics, brand loyalists, ethics on how the company is run, and employees. A company's customers and its employees can make all the difference when comparing your company to the competition.

Just because Twitter is the latest, greatest, hyped-up thing on CNN doesn't mean that every single company should have a Twitter account and be out there actively tweeting. Nor should every company have a Facebook, MySpace, or YouTube account. Employing a certain mix and balance of social media marketing tactics in your strategy can produce success, but your marketing team must understand your audience in the social media sphere.

Should you be wise and secure accounts on the major social media sites? Yes. The last thing you want happening is your competition coming in and squatting on your brand name. Putting your basic information into these accounts is a great approach, but your audience might not be on these major social media platforms talking about your brands, products, or services. In fact, they could be having those conversations in small niche communities.

There's No Cookie-Cutter Approach

If a cookie-cutter approach to social media marketing did exist, the process would be more of a commodity, much as building websites has become. Any business can buy a domain name and hosting from companies such as GoDaddy.com and get a website up and running with little effort. Companies such as GoDaddy.com have made building websites a commodity by giving businesses easy-to-use options such as website templates in which they just choose a color, add a little content and a logo, and, "poof," they are now in business online.

But effective social media marketing involves research, strategy, planning, and measuring. The results of that research will vary for each company, so the most effective social media platforms and social marketing plans will vary, too.

Although the media hypes what's hot and what's not when it comes to successful social media marketing tactics, companies need to focus on specifically designing their own social media marketing strategy. Doing something just because the competition is doing it is not a wise strategy.

For example, you might find companies selling approaches to social media marketing in which you purchase a "package" that includes setting up a Twitter account, a Facebook page, and a blog. But how do you really know that package is right for you and for your audience? If these companies are offering to go even further and do the engagement for you, buyer beware. Social media marketing requires a lot of research, effort, and time; there's no fast-and-easy, prepackaged way around it.

See Chapter 45, "Putting it All Together," to learn put what you learn in this book into action.

Your Competition's Social Media Efforts

Just because your competition has a blog does not mean you need to develop one right away. You might find that mimicking your competitors' social media marketing efforts does not result in the same gains (or the same pitfalls) for your company. If you are focused on competing with your competitors, your real audience might be elsewhere talking about your company—and you will miss it.

Although you might have certain markets in common with your competition, your market research will likely show you that your audiences are different. For example, if your company sells tools primarily to female buyers, you wouldn't want to place your social media marketing efforts on sites that males more commonly use—even if your competitors are doing that. It would be a complete waste of time and money. You might not even know your audience's demographics or what social media sites they frequent yet, so do your research first and then formulate a plan.

Without doing research, and instead just following the sound of someone else's beating drum, you are blindly applying marketing tactics without a sound marketing strategy. Most important, just because your competitors are doing it doesn't mean you need to do it, too. No two businesses are alike, even if they are competing for nearly the same market share.

A Great Customer Service Department Is a Great Extension into Social Media

One of the best resources for learning about your audience is to ask your customer service people who are on the front lines every day. Your customers relate their experiences—both good and bad—to your customer service people. They likely have some inside information about the popular sentiment about your company, its brands, and its products or services.

Your customer service employees have a great gift of being able to listen and be empathic in a genuine way; otherwise, they wouldn't be working in customer service. Your social media marketing people need to have traits similar to your customer service employees, because their jobs are more similar than you might have imagined.

A great example of a company with top-notch customer service and social media efforts is Southwest Airlines. Southwest is known for having one of the best customer service departments in the airline industry. Its employees—including gate employees, pilots, and flight attendants—are always friendly, have smiles on their faces, and try to provide the best service to their customers. Southwest entered the social media sphere with the Nuts About Southwest blog. Its employees relate their stories about working for Southwest so customers can read about their perspective. This has helped humanize the airline. The success of the blog has prompted the company to venture into videos, photos, and even Twitter.

Southwest has seen phenomenal success with these channels because, at the heart of its business, it listens to its customers. It gives its customers various channels to share their experiences and engage with the airline and its employees. People in social media communities want to connect with humans, and Southwest is doing it well.

Southwest's approach to social media wouldn't necessarily work as well for other airlines, even though they are part of the same industry, because each airline services different customers and provides different levels of customer service.

Listen to Your Customers

Listening to your customers can do amazing things for your insight into building a successful social media strategy. If you listen to your audience, you can discover how different you are from your competition. Listening to what the social media communities are saying about you and your competition also gives you information about your products and services that you would have never gotten offline.

You can use many monitoring tools to help you listen to what your audience is saying about you. From enterprise-level monitoring tools such as Radian 6 or Techrigy, to free tools such as Google Alerts, companies can find relevant conversations and begin listening to what their customers are saying about them.

When you find these conversations and start listening to what your audience members are saying, you can help build a strategy to engage and interact with them. By listening, you learn what your customers really want. You might find that your products are fine but your service isn't, or vice versa. Maybe you overlooked something as simple as providing a quick-tips card with the packaging, or maybe you need to create an easier sign-up form. You'll never know unless you take the time to listen.

Listening to your audience is key, but you should also listen to your competition's audience. Although you don't want to mimic their strategy, understanding what their audience is saying about them can give you insight into the industry as a whole.

Your Brand Loyalists Can Make All the Difference in the World

Brand loyalists—people who are fanatically loyal to your brand and who recommend your company's products or services without promoting— are a golden ticket. Brand loyalists love you and everything about you. If you engage and interact with these brand loyalists, magic can happen.

As with your social media strategy, brand loyalists come in all shapes and sizes. No two are the same, so there's no cookie-cutter way to interact with them, except for how your legal counsel defines what can and cannot be said or offered.

Every company wants to have brand loyalists within a social media community. They share their experiences, their love, and the ways they use your products and services. Best of all, they do all this because they are passionate about your company. And they do it without expecting anything in return.

LEGO has brand loyalists. From bloggers to forum leaders, people who are passionate about LEGOs and what they can create with them have been active in social media communities long before the LEGO company became active in the social media space. These loyal brand advocates have shared with other avid adult fans their tips on how to best use these building blocks for children. They've shared everything from which block sets help make the best new designs, to how to create intricate projects.

When this social media engagement started happening organically, LEGO didn't think it was a really great thing. "At first, we didn't really like it and we were a bit concerned about the various information that started to appear on different Internet pages," says Tormod Askildsen, head of LEGO Community Development. "This was mainly because we weren't used to it and didn't know how to deal with it. But then we realized that we could actually benefit from it."

Engaging and interacting with brand loyalists can determine whether your social media strategy succeeds or fails. Identifying those key influencers and knowing how to connect with them in a genuine manner are crucial to your success.

Give Your Employees a Little Authority

Your employees are on the front line every day with your customers. They understand what makes them happy, what enrages them, and what turns them into "customers for life." Giving your employees a little authority to make decisions helps your company as a whole connect better with your customers, both offline and online.

If your employees feel that they have the power to take action for the customer, and that doing so can turn that customer into a brand evangelist, why not loosen your grip just a bit and give some authority to your employees? Whether they are engaging in a forum or on Twitter, give them the chance to connect with your audience and make the personal connection that members of social media communities are looking for. Your customers will soon be sharing the great customer service they received with other members of the social media community.

No predefined rules apply to this approach, either. Because every company's culture is different, giving authority to your employees could mean that you enable them to interact on Twitter on your behalf, offer special promotions, or take care of any volatile situations that arise in social media communities. Training your employees in your company culture impacts how they react and respond in social media communities. So make sure your employees are well versed in policies and procedures for interacting on social media sites before you set them loose with their newfound authority.

Be Open to Change

At one time, the hot topic in social media was Friendster; then it was Orkut, then MySpace, then Facebook, and now Twitter. In social media, the landscape is always changing. Audiences don't usually stay in one place on the Internet anymore. Community users often "cross-pollinate"—they are actively engaging and relating their experiences with other members in several different social media communities.

Companies need to be open to change. Every social media platform is different, and your audience is unlikely to stay in one particular forum. With the proper research, you can understand all the possibilities you can use in a strategy. Being open to changing those tactics can be a game changer. You might be on the cusp of creating something viral, so you must be open to the change it might require.

Not every change is the same. A company might need to begin by connecting its Twitter account to its blog while it establishes solid relationships via the blog. When those relationships are firmly rooted and the goals are being met, it could be time to be open to new opportunities in social media. No timetable exists, so the approach can differ significantly for each company.

The key is that every company is different, and marketers need to create social media strategies that are specific for them. Companies shouldn't use a cookie-cutter approach to social media and expect success (or, worse, expect not to fail).

13

Don't Fall in Love

One thing is certain, and that's change. When it comes to the Internet and marketing online, change is always happening. What was popular a year ago can be gone today. A powerful marketing tactic 6 months ago can lose its potency.

An important piece of the social media marketing puzzle is making sure your social media marketing efforts are optimized for the search engines. The link between search and social is "being found." It's also vital to understand how both search engines and social media platforms are constantly changing to meet the ever changing needs and desires of their users. We'll cover the subject of search engine optimization later on in this book.

Because search engines frequently change their algorithms to combat spam and to provide the most relevant search results and developers, you must be ready to change your search engine optimization (SEO) strategies. When it *comes to social media, keep in mind that programmers frequently create new social media platforms, applications, and widgets, so a change in marketing tactics for online marketing is inevitable, too. That's why you can't fall in love with one particular social media site. Change is always around the corner with online marketing, especially when you realize that the original web browser wasn't originally designed to be used with technologies such as Flash or Shockwave.*

The question marketers need to be asking is "What's the next platform on which my audience will be talking about my company?" For example, when Google started, it was a pure search engine. Years later, Google has moved from a search engine to a highly diverse group of web-based applications and is making a major push toward cloud computing—the capability to access shared services such as online storage, photo-editing tools, word-processing tools, and so on. In coming years, the web browser will likely become less relevant as new applications to access the Internet are created to work with Google's newly announced operating system, ChromeOS. Of course, that means more change for web marketers everywhere.

 Note

At the time of this writing, Google's ChromeOS was still under wraps. No official street date has been announced for the highly anticipated operating system (though many believe it will be released in late 2010). To learn more about Chrome OS, see Que's forthcoming *Using Google ChromeOS,* by Michael Miller.

When Tim Berners-Lee created the Hypertext Transfer Protocol (HTTP)—this was back at the dawn of the internet before the thought of broadband internet access was even a glimmer in anyone's eye—he likely never intended for applications such as Flash to be used through it. In fact, playing videos through a web browser probably was the furthest thing from his mind. He only wanted to share information with his other physicist colleagues. Mike Grehan (an online marketing thought leader who heads up Search Engine Watch, Click Z, and their companion conference series, "Search Engine Strategies") points to this fact about Berners-Lee's creation and what it's used for today. "It's like trying to shove an elephant through a keyhole; it just wasn't meant to be," Grehan says.

When you think about all the different ways that we can access the Internet—smart phones, traditional computers, PDA devices, and gaming systems such as the Nintendo Wii—the death of the web browser is not around the corner, but the reliance on it to connect to the Internet is lessening. We discuss this phenomenon in more detail in Chapter 42, "It's Not Just a Web Browser Anymore."

The Social Media Site You Love Might Not Be Where Your Audience Is

Although you might love Facebook and think it's a great place to communicate with your audience, you might find that your audience isn't on Facebook. When you look at social media technologies and sharing sites from your own personal view and think, "This would be a great place for my company," you need to stop and take a step back. You should perform objective research on whether your audience is really on that platform.

The social media platform(s) your audience uses might actually surprise you. Your audience might be using an old, very well-established forum that hasn't updated its platform in a few years and lacks all the bells and whistles that newer platforms offer. People are creatures of habit. If they are comfortable and find something of value, it can be tough for them to change.

The same holds true for marketers. You might be comfortable with a particular social media platform and, therefore, drive all your marketing efforts there. However, if your audience is on a different site, all that effort is wasted. Try not to fall into that trap.

Although you can certainly represent your company through your profile on a certain social media platform, keep in mind that your audience won't necessarily come searching for you on the platform you are most comfortable with. It certainly doesn't hurt your strategy to put your company's information and content into the profile you have on your favorite social media site. It's possible that some conversation about your company will develop there, but you still might not be hitting your target market.

People Don't Converse on Just One Platform

Nearly every week, some company announces a new social network or social sharing site. Just take a look at the archives of Michael Arrington's TechCrunch blog or Pete Cashmore's Mashable site (which is solely dedicated to reporting on social media), and you can get an idea of just how many new social media technologies appear every month. The sheer volume can be mind-blowing and intimidating.

The average Internet user, who doesn't keep track of the ins and outs of what's going on in social media, relies on friends to introduce different social media platforms and communities. In fact, users usually don't even attach the term *social media* to these communities. For the average user, social media sites are simply a place they visit to share with their friends and families.

People find the communities they become part of through a quick search in a search engine, recommendations from friends, or word of mouth. They start on one social media site, but eventually they branch out to finding a different community when they've become comfortable with one place and realize that they can share their hobbies and passions with other communities.

Through your research, you will find that the conversation is happening many places. That's because people aren't inclined to use only one social media platform after they've discovered just how much they can share with a global community. For instance, people aren't just using Twitter all by itself: Your audience might be chatting on Twitter; discussing the same thing in their favorite forums; sharing their personal information and passions on Facebook; uploading photos to Flickr; and then sharing those photos via Facebook, Twitter, and a favorite forum.

This type of cross-pollination can be tough to keep track of, which is why buzz-monitoring tools such as Techrigy and Radian6 can be valuable tools to have in your marketing arsenal. If you can't afford these enterprise-level tools, Google Alerts can help, but it requires a bit more manual work to keep track of the conversations happening across multiple platforms.

People often keep the same usernames across social media platforms or use something very similar if their original username is already taken on the new site. I started in online chat rooms and forums in 1992 with the moniker storyspinner. I've kept that same username, or the similar storyspinn, in all the places I hold conversations so that it's easy for my friends who also cross platforms to find me.

I also use the same avatar across all the social media sites I use so people can easily identify me. Using the same or similar username and avatar isn't just a unique thing to me. You'll often see this when you start researching and watching the communities in which the conversations about your company are happening. When people cross different communities to share their experiences, they generally act and speak in the same manner across all the sites.

If you start seeing the same person in two or three different travel forums and they are quite active in a community, you've likely found a major influencer. These people are dedicating a lot of time to sharing with not just one community, but a few, and their sphere of influence is magnified by moving from one platform to another. Other people notice this as well and tend to give these cross-pollinators a bit more authority because they believe that these influencers must have something of value to add because they are on multiple sites.

Your Audience Can Migrate from One Platform to Another

Over time, your audience might move. When social media sites upgrade or change features and community members don't accept or embrace the changes to make the community grow, the users tend to move on to a place where they feel comfortable. If the influencers move on, generally others in the community follow. This is another reason you should avoid falling in love with just one site.

Although humans are notoriously creatures of habit, we also love to feel comfortable. If change happens and we no longer feel comfortable, we will break habits to seek out a new place to find that comfort we previously had. This is why web marketers must be watching, listening, and actively participating in a community. If you are active in a community, you can stay abreast of migrations and understand why they are happening—and be ready to adjust your social media marketing strategy for that migration.

Sometimes these migrations happen slowly. Other times communities migrate rather quickly. If a new community appears or a competing social media site implements brand-new technologies that make communication and sharing much easier, community members will flock to that new platform—especially if the key influencers of the community quickly embrace it.

This is pretty evident when you look at how fast MySpace grew and then how quickly Facebook surpassed it (see Figure 13.1). Facebook offered more ways to connect and easier ways to share with friends—tagging photos, joining groups, and creating fan pages.

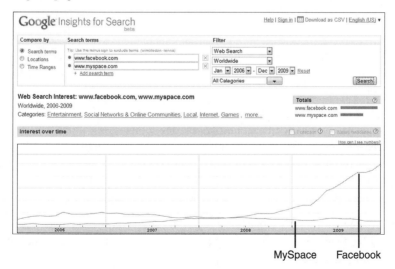

Figure 13.1   *A Google Trends Chart shows how Facebook overtook MySpace as the top social media platform between January 2006 and December 2009.*

I have to admit, I'm a reluctant Facebook member. I started in MySpace, and as I joined Facebook, I noticed a distinct difference in my friends between the two communities. My real-life friends—the ones that I see regularly—represented the majority of my friends on MySpace. On Facebook, I discovered that people from the online marketing industry and others involved with web technology represented the largest portion of my friends. I don't regularly see these people. That said, during recent months, I've seen my friends slowly migrating from MySpace to Facebook. I was curious why this was happening. When I asked one of my MySpace friends why he moved to Facebook, he plainly stated, "It's just easier."

Think Beyond the Web Browser

At the beginning of this chapter, I mentioned that the web browser might not be the way we will all communicate in social media sites in the future. That's why marketers need to start thinking outside of the proverbial box when it comes to marketing online. As companies sell more smart phones across the globe, developers are building applications that enable these devices to connect to the Internet. Some of these applications don't use the HTTP architecture of a web browser.

Smart phone apps such as the applications developed for Facebook, Yelp, MySpace, and Flickr, just to name a few that are cross platform (meaning BlackBerry, iPhone, Droids, etc.) are just another way to access the internet without having to utilize a web browser. As these types of devices are becoming more popular and integrated with every day life, we can expect to see fewer people accessing social media sites via a web browser.

 Note

To learn more about the exciting world of mobile marketing, see Cindy Krum's new book, "Mobile Marketing: Finding Your Customers No Matter Where They Are," published by Que. In it, you'll find hands on advice for marketing your business to mobile device users.

It's not just about phones. Programmers are developing applications that can access the Web without a web browser. Consider Twitter as an example. Although you can access Twitter via your browser through its website at www.twitter.com, desktop applications such as Tweetdeck enable Twitter users to organize, share, and communicate through Twitter without ever touching Safari, Firefox, or Internet Explorer.

We dive deeper into this subject in Chapter 42, but for now, remember not to fall in love with one technology—especially if it's tied to a web browser. It might not be around in the future.

What Happens If the Social Media Platform Disappears?

So what happens if the community you found does suddenly disappear? Or what happens if the service goes down for an uncertain amount of time? How much are you relying on just one platform for your social media marketing strategy? Falling in love with an unstable platform and banking your entire strategy on it can end up in failure.

When Twitter goes down, it makes the front page of CNN. On August 6, 2009, Twitter was the victim of a denial-of-service (DOS) attack, and the site was down for more than 2 hours. The DOS attack also impacted Facebook and MySpace.

Had this attack crippled Twitter for days, any company relying solely on it for its social media marketing strategy could've suffered adverse affects. The company's form of communication and channel for conversing with its audience would be gone without a contingency plan or another place to reach its audience.

If you use just one forum or message board (one that's owned and operated by someone else or another company) as your only form of communication with your audience, you could also fall into this detrimental situation. What happens if you find that the site has been taken down for nonpayment of hosting services, that the owner died, or that the original company that ran it filed for bankruptcy?

These types of events are very real and have happened. It's upsetting to the community members who have invested so much time and passion into the community. It's also detrimental to a strategy if that's the only place you relied on to communicate with your audience.

This is why social media marketers should look at a mix of social media tactics when creating their social media strategies. Falling in love with one type of social news site, such as Digg, or a particular forum is dangerous if you don't pay attention to the other places where the conversation is happening.

14

Don't Be Afraid to Throw Out What Isn't Working

Starting or implementing a social media strategy for the wrong reasons won't help your company. Also, just because your marketing agency thinks a particular tactic could work doesn't mean it's right for your company. Using a particular social media tactic just to keep up with your competition isn't the right thing to do, either. Many companies fall into the trap of continuing to use the wrong marketing tactics for the following reasons:

- The competition is doing it.

- Their agency told them it was a good thing.

- They saw a media report indicating the strategy would work.

- Money has been invested.

- The tactic worked before.

Continuing a marketing tactic without knowing whether your efforts are successful for your bottom line is like the blind leading the blind. If you just start engaging people in a forum without first establishing your end goals, your team will be blindly implementing a marketing tactic without knowing whether it can actually succeed. Continuing to engage the community without monitoring the effect on your company or measuring your success or failure can lead to wasted efforts.

Social media marketing has no rules. Just because you start a social media campaign doesn't mean you have to keep doing it the same way. Sometimes what you thought would be of value to a community won't be received well. Instead of continuing to waste money and resources, you should reevaluate what you are doing and tweak your strategy. If your campaign isn't returning good results, your customers might be subtly telling you that 'you need to find another approach.

How Do You Tell If Your Strategy Is Working?

Measuring and monitoring success with social media marketing is very subjective and fluid. A successful approach for one company might be a failure for another. Most of the time, you need to measure your success manually. Your social media marketing efforts will rarely result in direct action (such as a purchase of your product). Instead, social media affects the more intangible aspects of a company's marketing and branding. However, you *can* monitor and measure your efforts.

Monitoring is different than measuring. You need to use specialized monitoring tools that can tell you where people are discussing your company, your products, or your services. Furthermore, these tools can help you gauge the amount of buzz around your company and can even alert you to a potential problem on the horizon. Monitoring tools help companies respond to both good and bad situations in a timely manner.

Companies can use website analytics for measuring, but the approach has some drawbacks. Most companies are limited to seeing only their own analytics (meaning their own site's performance). For example, you could measure the success of a video that you post on your company's site, but you would not be able to monitor the success of the same video posted on YouTube. Although YouTube does provide a decent amount of data about your video, you still must manually port all those measurements into your own reporting structure to help measure success. Measuring social media is a lot more manually intensive than measuring other online marketing efforts such as search engine optimization (SEO) and pay-per-click (PPC) efforts.

Monitor, Monitor, Monitor

If you are planning a social media marketing strategy and having your team implement the engagement portion of that social media strategy, you need to use different tools to understand how far your engagement is reaching. Monitoring tools can help you locate where conversations about your company are occurring. They also can help you understand who the key influencers are in different sectors of social media.

Not falling in love with a single platform (such as Twitter or Facebook) will make your buzz-monitoring tools better serve your strategy. Buzz-monitoring tools can give you insight into where conversations about you are happening. Although you might believe the hype of Facebook and Twitter, buzz monitoring might find that your audience is really talking about your company on a very niche forum. These niche forums are an ideal place for finding key influencers to engage with, and the forums also enable you to tweak your strategy to hone in on your very niche market audience.

Some monitoring tools, such as Radian6, BuzzMetrics, and Techrigy, provide deep analysis into the monitoring data they return. These tools give you information about the demographics behind the buzz, other keywords used with the words you are monitoring, trends around the buzz, and, to some degree, a look into sentiment analysis (see Figure 14.1).

 Note

> Sentiment analysis is looking at not just what was said about you but the tonality of the conversations. Was it positive? Was it negative? Was it neutral? Sentiment analysis is in its infancy and remains very rudimentary, but it at least gives you an inkling of what direction these types of conversations are going in.

Currently, the technology behind sentiment analysis can be a give-and-take situation. Some of these tools enable users to amend their dictionaries, but others do not. With the ones that do not enable you to change definitions, you are limited to what the tool has defined as "good" or "bad." Sometimes this can lead to some false summations about the sentiment these tools present.

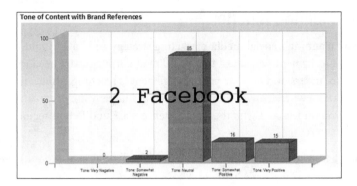

Figure 14.1 *Techrigy's sentiment analysis graph shows the general sentiment of customers as they talk about the company in social media circles.*

Let's say your company is a chain of stores that primarily specializes in fixing people's brakes, and you want social media to help you engage with your audience. You are primarily monitoring the ratings and reviews from your customers because you've discovered this is how you audience communicates and shares. A few of your customers have left reviews saying that when they had their brakes serviced at a particular store in your chain, they felt their brakes were "spongy."

The term *spongy* when it pertains to brakes is not a good thing. Unfortunately, some of these monitoring tools would not know how to interpret this comment and would file it into the "neutral" category of sentiment. Unless you look closely at the comments that the monitoring data returns, you'd incorrectly think nothing is wrong.

However, if the tool enables you to change the sentiment dictionary, the chain of stores that fixes brakes can change the meaning of the word *spongy* to negative. Being able to change the sentiment of this word within the monitoring reports would provide a more accurate reading of the conversations about your company.

Monitoring your social media marketing efforts can definitely help you understand how well your efforts are working and whether you should continue with them. Not everything you do in social media will get immediate traction from a buzz perspective, however. Sometimes building relationships and trust takes time, especially if you are just beginning to engage your audience in social media circles.

By benchmarking your buzz before your start your engagement (with the data you get from your buzz-monitoring tools), you can monitor how the buzz builds as you engage your audience. Not only will you be able to measure the increase of current buzz, but you also should be able to watch just how far and how rapidly your engagement tactics spread.

A lot of these buzz-monitoring tools also give you a "scent" of what other subjects people are discussing that relate to your own topics. These other types of words can be a great way to discover alternate, yet related conversations to join. You can use this information to shift gears, especially if your current social media tactic is not returning the desired results.

Measure, Measure, Measure

Marketers are held accountable for the marketing dollars they spend. When it comes to social media, marketers get a little edgy because it's difficult to determine the return on investment (ROI) of social media marketing. People have different opinions of what should be measured and how it should be measured; there's no standard way for every business. As with social media strategy, social media measurement differs for each company.

Unfortunately for social media marketers, many old-school marketers and corporate executives have been trained during the past 10 years that the ROI of online marketing is a click-to-purchase action. In social media, that action very rarely happens. The purchase eventually happens, but it's not an immediate action based on your social media efforts. For example, the traditional marketer or corporate executive views success as follows:

1. The searcher types "Dark Brown Minnetonka Sandals" into his or her favorite search engine.

2. The search engine returns a link for Zappos, listing those sandals at $49.99.

3. The searcher clicks the link and is taken to the Zappos site.

4. The searcher then purchases the sandals.

5. In this example, the company's SEO or PPC efforts were successful, with a clear ROI.

But is the following any less of a success?

1. A random person in Kansas tweets, "I really love Minnetonka sandals, but I'm having a hard time finding them near me."

2. A Zappos representative sees that tweet and starts a conversation with that person on Twitter.

3. During the conversation, the Zappos representative provides that person with a few links to look at (none of these have been tagged in the analytics as coming from the Zappos representative).

4. After discussing which ones the person likes with friends on Facebook and Twitter, the person finally decides on a light-brown (not dark-brown) pair of Minnetonka sandals.

5. The person then goes to the Zappos site and makes the purchase.

How do you measure that interaction?

Was it the influence of the Zappos representative or the discussion on Twitter or Facebook with friends that finally persuaded the buyer to purchase those Minnetonka sandals? Was it the personal way in which the Zappos representative interacted with that buyer on Twitter? Actually, you should be measuring all these things to determine whether your efforts are successful.

If you find that engaging on Twitter isn't resulting in conversation and interaction with your audience, maybe you should switch to FriendFeed. If you find that Facebook isn't creating the fans you are trying to achieve and influence, perhaps you should be trying MySpace, MiGentre, or BlackPlanet.

However, you won't know what's working or how your strategy needs to be adjusted unless you are setting goals and monitoring and measuring your actions. Measuring in social media isn't easy, and no one tool does it all. A combination of web analytics, manual interpretation and counting, a calculator, and a spreadsheet are most valuable when measuring social media.

If you set the right goals for your strategy, you will be able to measure what my coworkers (Nan Dawkins, CEO, and Nathan Linnell, Director of Analytics) and I at Serengeti Communications call the 4 I's of social media engagement, as defined by the Forrester Sequence (see *Marketing's New Key Metric: Engagement,* by Brian Haven [Forrester, 2007]):

- Involvement

- Interaction

- Intimacy

- Influence

 Note

For more information about Serengeti Communications' thoughts on measuring social media in this way, check out www.serengeticommunications. com/measuring-sm.

In the first two stages of engagement—involvement and interaction—a prospective customer establishes a tenuous relationship based on essentially an exchange of information. In these stages, branding and, to some extent, lead generation form the basis of measurement goals.

In the latter two stages of social media engagement—intimacy and influence—prospects (now customers) develop an opinion regarding the value of the brand purchase. As customers move further along the continuum, they share that opinion and, if the engagement experience has been strongly positive, might recommend, promote, or even evangelize for the brand. In these stages, companies can add direct sales to branding and lead-generation measurement goals.

Measuring these four pieces can help you determine whether you should change your strategy and tactics or whether you should keep pushing forward with the strategies you've set into motion.

What Are Your Success Goals?

An essential part of your social media strategy needs to be setting goals for success so that you know whether what you are doing is working. By setting success goals— for example, measuring involvement of your audience by the number of posts on your forum, comments on blogs posts, or videos watched—you can gauge whether your tactics are engaging your audience in the way you intended. If your engagement strategy isn't working—if it isn't reaching your desired goal you've defined as success—then it's time to reevaluate.

Not meeting these goals doesn't always equate to failure. Often companies are reluctant to put goals such as these in place with new strategies because they don't know how they will work. But to know whether something is truly working for your company, you must establish some kind of goal, especially if you are new to this process. If you aren't meeting the goals, you aren't necessarily failing. Missing your goals could be more directly tied to the tactic you've implemented. Perhaps that tactic isn't appealing to your audience in the manner you intended it to, and you should adjust your approach.

Adding these goals to your strategy can help save a lot of wasted time and resources. For example, if you set a goal to have a 10% increase in volume of buzz via blog posts and comments within 3 months of engaging the blogging community, and that isn't happening, you must either take a new approach or stop the engagement tactic.

If It Isn't Working, Stop

Maybe you've paid a lot of money to an agency to help you implement your engagement, or maybe your in-house team is right in the middle of your 6-month strategy. But none of that matters if you aren't meeting your goals. Companies get caught up in thinking that they have to continue down the same path until they totally implement the strategy. If you're not starting to see the needle move a little after a few weeks of implementation, you need to seriously consider a quick reevaluation.

Social media marketing doesn't require you to see a strategy through until the end. In fact, social media marketing is constantly changing. New tools and new ways to communicate and share are always appearing on the Internet. If one tactic isn't working as you hoped it would, a new one could be the right way to engage your audience.

Stopping a strategy to reevaluate and tweak your approach isn't shameful. In fact, smart companies do this all the time. Being open to change and different approaches is just another key to building successful social media strategies. Falling in love with tactics and not wanting to let them go when they are failing often leads to disappointment in social media strategies and fosters the belief that social media marketing is a fad and doesn't work. Don't be afraid to throw out what isn't working for you, your company, or your strategy.

15

Be Open to Trying New Things (but Don't Fall Off the Bleeding Edge)

New technologies are important. They help us constantly reinvent ourselves. Innovation shapes the Internet, as well as how many companies operate, and it can even lead to the evolution of an entire business model. Take Kodak, for example.

With the advent of digital cameras, technological advances in digital photography changed Kodak's core business. The company's primary business, manufacturing film for all types of cameras, became almost as extinct as the dinosaurs. Kodak had to reinvent itself by not only embracing these new technologies, but becoming a leader in advancing them. Film cameras might be pieces of our history, but Kodak is still part of our future.

Of course, companies shouldn't feel obligated to try every new social media site. For as many social media sites that launch in a week, just as many die slow, withering deaths. Although it's fun to try out the cool new "toys" on the block, it's not wise to bank your entire strategy on them.

Shiny Object Syndrome

One of my former bosses made a weekly habit of stopping by my desk or sending me an email saying, "Hey, Li, we need to implement this for XYZ client." He did this because he'd read about it on TechCrunch, SlashDot, or some other new-fangled technology blog that no longer exists (at the time, Mashable didn't even exist). My coworker and I would joke about this inevitable weekly debacle and call it his "SOS," or Shiny Object Syndrome.

My boss didn't research why we needed to use this tool or site; he merely heard about the latest, greatest fad and thought it would be a silver bullet to everything else that was failing. Utilizing, implementing, and engaging in brand-new tools and banking entire social media strategies on them can lead to disappointment for everyone.

Marketers need to do their due diligence in researching these new tools that appear on the scene. It is all too easy to get drawn into the excitement of a new technology being billed as the "New Twitter" or the "New Facebook." It's especially easy when enough media or superstar hype surrounds a new company or technology. Understanding how the tool enables its intended community to share and engage is essential to understanding how it could possibly fit into your strategy.

It might take time for a new social media site or social media tool to actually gain traction with an online demographic that it's targeted to reach. For example, Twitter didn't take off overnight. Twitter launched in 2006, but its major-name early adopters didn't embrace it until early 2007. Usage steadily increased through the rest of 2007. Finally, in late 2008, Twitter really began to take off (as Figure 15.1 demonstrates). It took time for users to embrace this new way of communicating with friends and followers. It has taken even more time for business to embrace it as a legitimate communications channel for marketers.

If you had included Twitter in your marketing plan in early 2007, you would have been very disappointed by its results. The Twitter community hadn't quite blossomed yet, no matter how much the early adopters were touting this as the next wave of communication. Relevant conversation about your industry, products, services, or brand probably would have been nonexistent at that time as well, unless you were a technology company, because many of Twitter's early adopters of Twitter were technology enthusiasts .

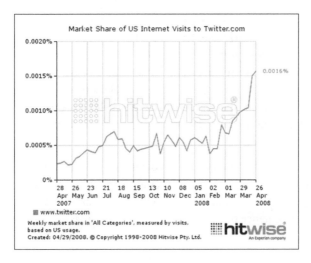

Figure 15.1   *Twitter's market share grew steadily in 2007–2008. Image courtesy of Hitwise.*

Early Adopters

Early adopters can be both a blessing and a curse, especially for new tools in social media. For example, Robert Scoble, a notorious early technology adopter who currently works for Rackspace, could propel the adoption of a new tool, social media site, or technology with mere mention in a blog post or one of his tweets.

By hiring Scoble, Rackspace itself experienced a bit of what the technology sector has dubbed the "Scoble Effect." Louis Gray, whose blog highlights "early adopters and technology geeks," points out that within 2 weeks of Rackspace hiring this well-known technology adopter, its stock rose (as shown in Figure 15.2).

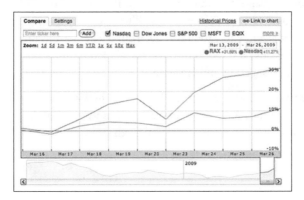

Figure 15.2   *How Scoble joining Rackspace might have affected Rackspace's stock value.*

Early adopters who promote social media sites and tools can inadvertently cause a negative impact. If an early adopter has a huge audience, as with Scoble, sometimes the tool or site cannot handle the influx of traffic and attention drawn to it. Often the site or tool is not ready for such an unanticipated rush of activity or adoptions and, sadly, either the site ceases to function or it becomes incredibly slow or unstable. If any of these consequences occurs, it can spell failure for both the touted tool or site and your own social media strategy if you banked on using it to produce successful engagements.

Although early adopters are great to follow for keeping an eye on what's emerging in the technology or social media space, they aren't the ones you should be following to find your best social media tools. Often you can find the best methods of engaging your audience by first listening to them and learning what sites and tools they use.

Fads of the Moment

Similar to those bell-bottom jeans my mother gave away when the fad wore off, but have since reemerged as fashionable, social media tools and sites can go through cycles. Communities go through ups and downs; new members join and older members leave without warning or explanation.

If a major influencer within a community leaves, this absence can create a vacuum within the community. Without the key influencer to carry on relevant conversation or engage other members, some community members move to new communities where they can find the sharing and engagement they once had with the previous community.

A similar experience can occur when new sites become popular. Key influencers have the power to bring new members to a community. However, if the new social media site or tool cannot sustain the community, it becomes a fad and the community migrates back to what's familiar. This illustrates why it's important to study your social media audience. You must determine whether the audience you are trying to reach is part of a stable and sound social media community or is part of a fad site that has popped up only recently.

As with the risks of investing time and resources in what the early adopters are touting, investing time and energy into a community's "fad of the moment" can be very disappointing for marketers in social media.

When Social Media Sites or Tools Fail

For anyone who has used Twitter since 2007, the image in Figure 15.3 is a painful reminder of Twitter's very public growing pains.

Figure 15.3 *An all-too-common error page that early Twitter users experienced*

If you were relying on Twitter as a major piece of your social media strategy in 2007, you probably would have pulled out a lot of your hair. Various surges in use and traffic on Twitter's network during summer 2007 through 2008 caused it to fail, resulting in users seeing the inevitable Fail Whale.

Thankfully, we rarely see the Fail Whale now. Even when Michael Jackson died in June 2009 and high traffic slowed many news sites, Twitter users weren't subjected to a single Fail Whale. Twitter has grown and greatly improved the scalability of its service.

However, when tools or sites fail repeatedly, a community can become frustrated and go in search of new social media tools to continue their conversations on. Plurk is one example.

Plurk is similar to Twitter in a lot of ways, namely the 140-character restriction on messages and the capability to send one message for all followers to see. When Twitter was failing on a consistent basis, people went to Plurk to converse, engage, and share.

Plurk wasn't having the scalability issues Twitter was having at the time because Plurk's audience was significantly smaller. Plurk benefited from Twitter's notorious Fail Whale by gaining community members for a short time. However, as Twitter regained its stability, the recently migrated Plurk users returned to Twitter, especially as new tools specifically created for Twitter started to take off.

If you were a marketer during this time and saw the migration of users to Plurk, you might have been tempted to put all your resources with Plurk without doing any further investigation. Identifying when popular tools or sites are failing and communities migrate to continue their conversations and engagements is just as important as spotting those technology fads.

It's important to research, watch, and understand your audience and the communities you want to engage for fads and technological issues that could drive them to temporarily seek out other modes of communication, sharing, and engagement.

The Edge Is Cool, but the Bleeding Edge Can Hurt

Being on the edge with these new social media tools is definitely a cool and fun place to be if you are a marketer implementing a social media strategy for your company. However, the bleeding edge isn't a fun place to hang out. If you fall off that edge, it can really hurt your company—especially if your entire marketing budget for social media has been invested in something that doesn't take off.

Taking the time to investigate, research, and understand the new tools and how your audience will potentially use them can prevent you from falling off that bleeding edge. Community members can adopt tools and use them the way they were intended for use by its creators or they can adapt the tools to use them in ways that better suit their needs. It's vital to your strategy to understand how the community has adapted to using these new tools so that your strategy can implement them in the same way and thus, engage the community.

It's also important to make sure that you keep a close eye on the measurements you've put in place with these tools and establish firmly set goals. This will allow you to see whether this new, bleeding edge tool (if you choose to try it out) is really working for you. It can also help you determine if and when a community's tool preference has changed and save you time, resources and money by ceasing to use the new fangled tool.

III

Social Media from the Inside Out

16

Everyone in Your Company Has a Stake in Your Social Media Strategy

Before the Internet, companies didn't need to worry about outside forces such as customers, or even employees, impacting their PR efforts, marketing, or advertising. Marketing efforts were very isolated, and a specific team of experts crafted brands and messages about products, services, and brands that consumers simply consumed.

Marketing was a very insulated process during those times. Companies relied on either internal staff experts or Madison Avenue agencies to research their demographics, figure out what appealed to them, and craft a message around that information. The thought of consumers, let alone company employees who didn't have any interest in the marketing department, interacting with brands would not have entered their minds.

With the advent of the Internet and the creation of social media sites, the rules of marketing, public relations, and advertising all changed. Not only did the consumer have *a voice, but employees who weren't in marketing unwittingly became unpaid spokespeople for the companies they worked for.*

Striking a balance with your employees and getting them to comprehend that their actions on social media sites affect not just your company, but other companies as well can impact how you implement your social media strategy. Failing to factor in a contingency plan for a misstep by an unknowing employee can send what was destined to be a successful venture into a deep chasm of failure.

Who Owns Your Social Media Strategy?

Chapter 19, "Define Who Owns the Conversation," is dedicated to this topic because it's vitally important if you want to get your social media marketing strategy right. You need to define who "owns" your social media strategy from the onset, to prevent miscommunication, avoid stepping on employees' toes, and to ensure that everyone is on the same page when it comes to implementation and messaging.

Social media is a hot topic, and everyone wants a piece of it. You might find that many departments within your company or outside agencies will claim to be social media experts who should be planning and implementing your strategy. However, no one department or type of agency is the expert in social media.

A combination of skill sets will make your team's social media efforts succeed or fail. If you stack the team with only public relations people, you'll likely miss the search optimization component of social media. Put too much emphasis on searching and gaining links from social media marketing, and you'll miss messaging and turning evangelists into your best allies. If you forget about your customer service team or tech crew, you might experience major infrastructure issues when you finally implement your plans.

Not All Social Media Users Are from Generation Y

With the prices of computers continually falling and access to broadband becoming increasingly more affordable, broadband Internet–connected computers and devices are the norm. According to Forrester, three out of four Americans are using some sort of social media service (in *The Growth of Social Technology Adoption*,

2008). That means a lot of your employees are not just on the Internet—they're also actively engaging in some type of social media community.

Whether via a connection from work, home, the library, the local coffee shop, or even free public Wi-Fi, just about anyone can get access to the Internet and all the ways to communicate with likeminded individuals who share the same passions. With each passing month, all these social media platforms continue to grow their user bases. Undoubtedly, some of your employees are on them and are being very social within these communities.

Having a website and keeping it updated can seem a bit daunting to the average Internet user, which is why social media sites have such appeal. They are easy, quick, and simple to understand and get comfortable with. They offer great ways to discuss, share, and engage—something a typical static website cannot do. This is why user-generated content through social media sites has grown at such a phenomenal rate and why the creation of static websites has slowed.

Your C-Suite Needs to Get Involved

You need to make everyone in your company aware of your social media strategy efforts, including your C-suite executive staff. Their actions in social media communities, even if unrelated to the company, can impact anything that you are planning to implement in social media.

Most C-suite employees are well trained in understanding how their actions can impact the public perception of their company. However, something as minor as communicating in a forum on fishing because it's a hobby they love can impact a company that sells memory chips for computers.

Generally, C-suite executives are reluctant to get involved in social media because it lacks control—namely, their own. They can't control what's being said about them, so instead of addressing the negative (for example, complaints about poor customer phone service) they ignore it or push it off. To that end they are also missing out on the positive things people are saying. The executives could be missing out on just how much an audience has embraced a new feature, product or brand. However, companies whose C-suite executives embrace social media and get involved with it find that it gives them a much better perspective of what their customers are thinking.

GM's Vice Chairman of Global Product Development, Bob Lutz, is a perfect example of this. As Li and Bernoff highlighted in their book, *Groundswell*, Lutz was the one who took the initiative to start their blog, "Fast Lane" (http://fastlane.gmblogs.com). From decision to implementation, the blog took three weeks to put together and launch. Lutz's first post received more than 120 comments. Not only is this an amazing feat for a company in an industry not known to rush and adapt to changes, but it also shows that people actually wanted to hear what GM had to say, even if the spokesperson was a C-suite executive.

GM's blog didn't radically change anything for GM financially or for its products. However, as Li and Bernoff rightly point out, it changed the way that GM communicates with its audience.

Every Position in Your Company Can Adversely Affect Your Social Media Strategy

Companies that are venturing into social media need to first understand that anyone who receives a company paycheck can affect the company's strategies. From the CEO, to the ticket sellers and collectors, to the janitorial staff, *employees are involved in your social media strategy, regardless of whether they've seen your social media strategy.*

Ticket collectors? Really?

Yes, even the people who collect the tickets at the gates to your events can have an impact. The cook in your company cafeteria, the woman who answers your phones, and the guy who delivers the mail to your office every day can affect your social media strategy in ways you probably haven't considered.

Although they don't participate in creating the strategy or attend meetings discussing your research, employees can have a significant effect on the outcome, even if you or they don't realize it. It's important to not only plan contingencies for your social media efforts, but also put in place policies for employees and their actions on social media platforms.

Your employees must understand how their online actions can ultimately affect what your company is attempting to do. Even Facebook updates have an effect on how a company is perceived. Consider an example from the Philadelphia Eagles.

In March 2009, a part-time employee of the Eagles lost his job because he voiced his opinion on Facebook about Brian Dawkins leaving the Eagles to go to the Denver Broncos. The Eagles didn't discuss the situation with the employee. They simply fired him because of his Facebook post.

Unfortunately for the Eagles, the firing of this employee spurred a hot debate and a lot of hammering from the media. Fan discontent was already high after Dawkins left the Eagles for a competing team, but the firing of one of its employees for making a Facebook post that the organization found disagreeable fanned that discontent. In the end, the fired employee looks much better than the Philadelphia Eagles (they look like the big bully). Making matters more interesting, Brian Dawkins offered to give his visitor passes to the fired employee when the Denver Broncos played the Eagles in 2009 in Philly, which brought the whole situation and debate to light again in the press. Talk about a total miscalculation and no contingency plan. The Philadelphia Eagles certainly didn't plan on one Facebook update giving them a black eye.

Companies should implement policies about how their employees reference their employers on social media sites. If the references are negative, the policies should clearly define the repercussions.

Your human resources department shouldn't be doing this task alone. Your online marketing and social media teams should help define these policies. You can't be an iron fist, but almost every employee on your payroll will be smart enough to understand that they shouldn't be saying negative things about their employer on public forums. We discuss this more in the next chapter, "Plan Social Media Policies for Company Employees."

Get Employee Buy-In

Getting buy-in isn't easy, but most people want to do the right thing. So instead of coming down with an iron fist and demanding that your employees take down their blogs, help them understand that their words have influence. Just because you hand your employees a paycheck doesn't mean you have ultimate authority over what they do in their off-hours.

You can benefit from working *with* your employees who are active and influential in social media communities instead of working *against* them. You might even discover an occasional gold mine in what your employees are doing outside the office. Wouldn't it be better to work with that gold mine instead of to board it up for no one to access?

Everyone has hobbies. Most people love to share their experiences about those hobbies, and going online is one way to do that. Your employees could be joining MySpace, Twitter, or Facebook to converse with long-lost high school friends, old fishing buddies, or other Girl Scout leaders. They could be avid community leaders in forums you would have never even thought existed—and in these communities, they are the authorities. If they are savvy social media users, they are probably aware of ways they could actually help your company.

The Internet gives anyone a voice through these social platforms. Because of the ease of voicing opinions on social media platforms, you need to both be prepared and plan contingencies, and also get your entire company to buy into your own social media strategy. Keeping employees abreast of corporate messaging and endeavors in social media communities can help prevent accidental missteps that can send your social media strategy into free-fall.

Have a Social Media Champion

Beyond implementing policies, the online marketing or social media team should be internally championing your efforts on the different platforms. They should be talking to all your employees about social media, as well as perhaps how they can casually help with your strategy.

Getting this type of buy-in from within your own walls and understanding that all your employees affect your social media strategy makes your strategy stronger and gives it a much better chance for success. Your social media champion can also discover employees who you never realized were so involved in social media and bring them into your corner. This makes them potential allies and evangelists, which can be helpful when you first step into certain communities.

Introduce training sessions for all employees on how to use not only the social media tools and sites that you not want to be prominent in, but also sites that you feel have a significant impact on your bottom line. Having your social media champion internally educating your employees makes controlling what's going on less of a factor. When employees are educated about how to use social media and their company's social media strategy for these sites, they can be more of a help than a hindrance.

17

Plan Social Media Policies for Company Employees

As discussed in Chapter 16, "Everyone in Your Company Has a Stake in Your Social Media Strategy," just one seemingly innocent post or update in a social media community can send a great strategy straight into a tailspin. Taking the time to put social media policies in place before you implement your strategy can be a saving grace to help you avoid any snafus that employees might accidently create.

Social media policies should not be iron-fisted and strict or so limiting that your employees will want to circumvent them. You must understand how social communities work to create policies that are suitable for both your marketing efforts and your employees.

Although you don't want accidental snafus derailing your corporate social media strategy, you also don't want rebellion among the ranks in your company. This is especially true if your employees are active in social media *communities that might be beneficial to your company. You need to strike a careful balance between employee rights, both on and off the job, and the company's marketing strategy and efforts.*

At-Work Access to Social Media Sites

This topic can be a sticky one. A lot of research points to employees being more productive if they have access at work to social media sites such as YouTube, Flickr, Facebook, and MySpace. Yet companies are fearful of employee abuse, which can cause decreased productivity and bandwidth issues. Also, security issues abound from employees accidentally divulging proprietary information or misrepresenting the company. And as with everything else on the Internet, misuse of social media tools can lead to virus and spyware infections that could compromise corporate equipment and networks.

Regardless of whether your company plans to be active with social media marketing, you need to address all these issues. If you are actively engaged in social media marketing efforts, at least some of your employees will need at-work access to social media sites. You will need to implement policies for their use of those sites. If you are not yet ready to start a social media campaign, you will need to decide whether your employees—those that are part of your marketing team, as well as everyone else—can access social media sites from your corporate network.

If your company currently has a rule in place banning social media sites (possibly based on the early days of social media when YouTube and MySpace took the Internet by storm, resulting in a company stranglehold on the sites employees can access), it could be time to revise that rule. Companies that are actively engaging in social media but are severely limiting their employees' own movements could be casting a negative light on themselves. It might smack of hypocrisy if your company is utilizing social media for marketing gains but you do not enable your employees to utilize social media to help engage, share, and interact with the same communities.

For example, Dell previously restricted its employees from accessing certain social media sites. However, with its successful foray into social media marketing and a better understanding of how conversations about Dell between customers and employees positively affect its bottom line, Dell opened up. Early in 2009, Dell lifted the restrictions on Internet access for all employees, not just those in the social media strategy area of marketing. Although Dell does monitor traffic and Internet usage, it questions employees about their Internet usage only in the severest of abuse cases. The results have been positive for both Dell and its employees.

Severely restricting your employees' use of the Internet can create resentment among employees who see your marketing team accessing sites they cannot. That's not good for company morale or to get employee buy-in on your efforts to launch a successful social media strategy.

If your company is concerned about proprietary information being leaked or about network infiltration by outside users, you can address these concerns and then reevaluate whether you can open up access to all your employees.

- **Work with your tech team**—Advances in security during the last few years can help you avoid outside threats. You might need to adjust protocols, install new software, or change a policy that was enacted 4 years ago when the technologies weren't as advanced.

- **Educate your employees**—Give them short seminars to understand and identify sensitive data that they need to be careful discussing in open public forums such as social media communities. When employees are educated and informed, it creates a more open and less resentful climate when implementing your social media strategy.

Educate and Train Your Employees About Social Media Sites

Educating your employees about social media and your policies regarding discussions in those communities is not only a wise thing to do, but it's also a money saver. If your employees understand how their actions affect your company's efforts, you can help prevent situations in which you might need to call in an expensive crisis management team.

Wouldn't it be more beneficial to hold a company-sponsored lunch once a week or month to share how your company is working with Twitter, Flickr, or YouTube? The price of buying a few pizzas before you launch your social media campaign can save you tens of thousands of dollars that you'd need to pay another agency to help you clean up an accidental misstep of an employee saying something on Twitter that he shouldn't have.

Zappos believes that controlling social media and employee access to it is the wrong approach. The company believes and instills in its staff that education is the key. So far, this has worked wonders for them.

As mentioned by Zappos CEO Tony Hsieh at both conferences and in interviews with industry magazines such as *Fortune*, Zappos' employees go through training on Twitter before they can actively tweet as a Zappos employee. Through this education, Zappos employees not only understand their professional boundaries, but they also know how to interact and handle situations with customers that could come up while tweeting or posting on Facebook or another social media platform.

You need to educate your employees that not just their friends see what goes on in these social media communities. Employees are often under the false impression that the photos they share, the experiences they post in forums, and the videos they upload to niche video-sharing sites are seen only by those community members. Nothing could be further from the truth. The spiders that search engines send out to "crawl" the Internet eagerly consume, file, and distribute results of all kinds of consumer-generated media posted to these social media sites.

Another element to make employees aware of is that other community members can have "not so nice" intentions: Others can steal photos or videos meant for only a select few to see and post them on other sites. Such was the case for a New Jersey woman who posted somewhat compromising photos on her Facebook page for only friends to see. One of the people she trusted as a friend stole those photos and attempted to blackmail her with them. This situation demonstrates how it's not only harmful to the individual, but potentially harmful to a company or brand, especially if this woman is either branding herself, or an identifiable person related to a brand or company. If the photos were compromising enough, it could also reflect negatively on the type of people that work for a company.

It's a smart approach to train your employees to make wise decisions about the private information they are sharing on these social media communities, not only for your company's sake, but for their own personal well-being. It's important to educate them that friends on the Internet aren't exactly the same as the friends they have in real life, and that simple conversations can be misconstrued and cost companies thousands, if not millions, of dollars.

Don't Let HR Set the Policies Alone

Your human resources department is a great resource to help you build and implement a policy that affects employees. That's one of their specialties, and it's definitely smart to include them in the policy-creation process for employees' social media use. HR specialists also know and understand the laws regarding employees' rights when implementing these types of policies.

However, it's not wise to make your human resources department solely responsible for this type of policy creation. Although they are familiar with HR issues, they might not be familiar with the lingo employees might use in social media communities. Your HR department also might not be familiar with what can be shared or experienced on the social media sites you intend to engage with or that your employees are already engaging with.

When creating social media policies for your company that address employee use, access, restrictions, and implementation, the best course of action is to include people from all areas of your company. Doing so helps you cover all aspects—from technical to administrative. Your tech team might have issues with bandwidth, your operations team might need access to different sites than your marketing team, and your customer service team might have some great stories they want to share but they aren't sure how or even if they can. You can include all these topics, and reduce the chance of overlooking something, if you have a diverse team putting the policies together.

Involving Your Legal Department

Although Human Resources knows and understands the laws governing policies for employees and social media, you also want your legal team or consultant review the policies you've put in place (as discussed in Chapter 7, "Bring Legal in Early"). Your legal team will be well versed in what you can and cannot dictate to your employees. They'll also be able to help ensure that any repercussions for misuse of social media are fair and properly applied. The last thing you want to do is go through the motions of putting these policies and repercussions in place but then not be able to implement them because of a legal issue you didn't know about. As you might imagine, ironing all this out early also saves you in the long run because you will know that you are standing on solid ground when handling employees who violate your social media policies. If your legal team helps you put these policies in place and you have clearly explained these policies to your employees, it's less likely that your employees will violate them.

It's better to get the guidance of legal experts for all these policies, especially if your company has offices in different states and countries. Different states might have different documentation requirements, enforcement requirements, and so on, so it's best to let your legal advisors sort all this out.

 Note

To learn more about working with legal counsel to produce your social media marketing campaing, see Chapter 7, "Bring Legal In Early."

Off-Hour Social Media Activities

When your employees leave the building for the day, most of them want to forget the company when they close the door behind them. That's not really saying anything bad about you or your company—it's just reality. When employees are on their own time, they might think that anything they do in social media communities is fair game. And often they are right.

However, for some of your employees, their off-hour actions on social media sites might have a direct effect on your company's social media efforts. And depending on what those employees do or say, it could also have an effect on their continued employment with your company.

Many social media sites include employer information in the profile members are asked to complete. If your employees put your company name in their profiles, they are now tied to you and are unofficially representing you in this community. Their actions in these communities can now be tied back to your company. This is fine if the employees aren't doing anything that will harm your company's image. However, if your company is in the fast food industry and an employee is now supporting a group that promotes banning fast food chains because they are the root of child obesity, you might have a problem.

Domino's Pizza had such an issue in late summer of 2009 when Domino's employees created a firestorm while using social media in a way that was terrible unbecoming to the company. Not only was this embarrassing for Domino's, the employees found themselves in a lot of legal trouble. In a nutshell, a few Domino's employees shot video of what they do when they make customers' food and then posted those videos on YouTube. Even though the filming of the actions was done while the employees were at work, uploading those videos to YouTube was most likely done from their homes, away from the workplace. This demonstrates the need for companies to address social media activities both on- and off-the–clock, not to mention the need for companies to clearly outline the consequences employees might face even if their off-the-clock activities affect the company in a negative way.

Another issue with company employees and social media sites is that social media sites can divulge a lot of private information. Many applications on Facebook request access to the information members have put in their profiles. Even if employees have limited access to just family and a few close friends, granting access to these applications gives them full access to your employees' profiles. If they've put sensitive photos, videos, or any content into their profiles, these applications now have access to it.

Let's face it—we all just check the "I accept" box when we are signing up for a new service or installing new software. It's very rare for us to read through the entire terms of service (TOS) for any service, not to mention a social media site. While accepting the TOS basically clears the community or application developers, it still leaves a lot of users not realizing the potential negative impact that sharing such information with these communities or applications could have on both their personal and professional lives.

For example. certain applications in Facebook allow users to join their Flickr accounts and put their photos from Flickr into their Facebook photo albums. This is a great way to share photos you've already uploaded into Flickr with your Facebook friends. However, what most users fail to recognize is that when you upload your photos to Facebook—according to Facebook's terms of service—you are giving Facebook permission to utilize any photo you upload to help Facebook promote it's services without being compensated for that usage.

Using this example, let's say a professional photographer uploads images to Flickr and puts the copyright license on those photos. If the photographer then imports those photos over to Facebook, that copyright doesn't transfer to Facebook, which means the photographer is now granting Facebook the right to use the photographers images without any compensation or acknowledgement.

Companies need to look at and address many issues related to their employees and their use of social media. This can be intimidating to most companies, but every company thinking of implementing a social media strategy needs to address this issue with its employees.

18

Personal Ethics Matter

In general, we are all guided by our own moral compasses. Almost everyone has a genuine sense of what is "right" and "wrong." Our parents, teachers, preachers, leaders, and society in general have molded our compasses. Stark differences can arise in what is viewed as right or wrong across cultures or religions. But as neighbors in a global community, most people try to follow the compass of being nice to their neighbors.

Businesses also need to have moral compasses. Putting themselves into social media communities shines a huge spotlight on their ethics and philosophies. They must reflect those ethics and philosophies in their actions within the social media communities. If their actions are not in line with those ethics and philosophies, community members will not hesitate to call them out on the discrepancies. You can talk the talk, but if you aren't walking the walk, the community members you are trying to engage won't respect or trust you.

Members in these communities can "smell a rat," so to speak, a mile away. If you are just there for primarily monetary gains—getting people to buy things or trying to get them to link to you—and you aren't being honest about your intentions, it will be very apparent to the members of the communities.

Members could view your actions as immoral and might even dig into your previous actions in social media communities. If you've shown the same pattern of action in other places, members will announce it to the world and point out what a misguided effort your company continues to engage in.

Others' Personal Ethics Can Affect Your Social Media Strategy

Conversations in social media communities are happening with or without your presence or engagement. If your company isn't involved in social media, you are in effect allowing those social media community members to influence how people perceive your brand, products, or services. Without your involvement, members of the community can only judge your company by what other members post. How a community or individual community members relate and share experiences can greatly affect the opinions that are formed. If you aren't participating in these conversations, you are blindly and unknowingly enabling others' personal ethics to define the perception of your brands or your company.

Each community has its own moral compass as well. The group as a whole defines the ethics and actions that it will and won't tolerate. Many communities are self-policing and will call out members who aren't acting or engaging in a fair manner. "Negative Nellies" and trolls will always be present in communities, but the communities are smart enough to ignore these types of people or give them the boot. However, if key influencers in a community have a gripe or your company has wronged them, the way they relate those experiences (as well as their own moral compasses) will have an effect on the opinion of other community members.

It's also important to clearly understand how communities and ethics combine. Be sure to thoroughly research your plan if you want to bank your entire social media strategy on allowing social media communities to run the conversation without any involvement from your company—and plan for both successes and contingencies. For a perfect example of someone else's moral compass affecting a company's social media strategy, we can look to Skittles in March 2009.

Skittles decided to implement a social media strategy in which it turned its home page into a "flow" of different social media sites talking about the term *Skittles*. The first social media tool it chose was Twitter. Initially, Skittles was lauded as being "brave," "cool," or "funky" for engaging in such a unique campaign. Unfortunately, Skittles neglected to consider other people's ethics before implementing this social media tactic.

When Mashable featured the story about Skittles' tactic, it spread like wildfire across the Twitter community (see "Skittles Receives an Extreme Social Makeover," by Stan Schroeder, at http://mashable.com/2009/03/02/skittles-social/). All you had to do to get on the Skittles home page was put the word *Skittles* in your 140-character message and your tweet would appear. The home page had no filters—nothing to prevent people from spamming or using vulgar language in their message and having it appear on the page. I wanted to include a screen shot from the site, but the language some posters used was just too vulgar to print. Use your imagination.

Skittles the brand did not own the Skittles Twitter account: No one from Skittles was holding conversations in Twitter, and a firestorm resulted. People abused the fact that they could get their posts on the Skittles home page so easily without any filters.

Others were critiquing Skittles for not thinking through the idea. Skittles is a candy company that markets to kids, and every package of Skittles shows its URL. That URL was now showing vulgar, racist, and obscene messages on the home page. What parent wants his or her child seeing that? Eventually, Skittles started monitoring posts and put a stop to the free-for-all.

As for fallout, Skittles never publicly mentioned how all of this turned out as most companies do not like to publicly admit to their failures when it comes to unsuccessful forays into social media. From personal experiences I know a few parents who won't allow their children to go to the Skittles site, and I know "they talk" to other parents.

Everyone Wants to Be a Star

Let's face it—everyone wants to feel special occasionally. Social media communities enable ordinary people who don't have the star power of Oprah or Madonna to feel special in very easy ways. By sharing thoughts and experiences with communities in a consistent manner, ordinary people can become stars in very niche communities.

When what you are sharing starts to resonate with a larger community, the "star" factor begins. As word spreads that either the community or the influencer is someone people should be listening to, their influence or "star power" rises. Many people who enter social media communities don't realize that this can happen to them. But when it does, it's hard not to crave the continual attention.

As I've pointed out before, most people want to do the right thing and follow that moral compass. However, when they start to gain power and influence within a community and are considered a thought leader, moral compasses can become skewed. Marketers need to keep this in mind when looking at the community influencers they want to engage for a portion of their social media strategies. When engaging these "stars" and relying on them, companies are, in essence, trusting their images to the stars' personal ethics.

Researching your influencers is imperative. You must understand the reach of their words, the effect of what they say, and how they reached that influencer status. Did they become a thought leader by ruthless and immoral tactics? If they have a reputation for being mean and calculating, do you really want to have your brand associated with this "star"?

Controversy and Drama Aren't Always the Best Tactics

Although controversy and drama are definitely traffic drivers, they are not usually the best tactics to implement within your social media strategy. Constantly creating some sort of situation that causes controversy can result in a certain "labeling" for your brand or company. Only if you are a gossip columnist is this a good thing.

Gossip websites TMZ and Perez Hilton both are notorious for lacking a moral compass and for causing much controversy and drama, which is expected from this type of industry and the content they produce. Such drama and controversy isn't expected from companies who provide products or services. Banking your social media strategy on creating controversial situations can make your audience question your company's philosophies and ethics.

If you represent a company that provides services to your clients and you have a blog, carefully consider who blogs for you and the tone of their writing. If your bloggers aren't writing content that reflects your company's philosophies and ethics, you need to fix that. If your bloggers are creating content that continually creates controversy, such as calling out the competition or referring to members of an industry in an unprofessional manner just to drive traffic to the blog, you might want to rethink that strategy. Although traffic is great, it could leave an unwanted impression on future clients about the way your company operates and its ethics.

Bloggers love it when a lot of traffic comes to a blog post, and your team can mistakenly believe that controversy and drama is the way to shoot to the top of your industry. Unfortunately, companies that implement this tactic will see that it backfires more often than it succeeds. The perception of ethical behavior is very important, and the question becomes whether you want to sacrifice your company's moral compass for the sake of the traffic that controversy and drama can bring.

The Internet Amplifies

The Internet is a powerful tool for marketers and consumers. This can be a blessing and a curse. When planning a social media strategy, marketers must keep in mind how the Internet can amplify a message, whether it's their own message or someone else presenting a message about them that they have no control over.

Messages on the Internet take mere seconds to travel across the globe. Someone in Japan can form an instant opinion about your company within moments of a community member in Florida posting an experience with your product. When three other people chime in that they had the same experience, that message is amplified. If the poster's opinion is that your company operates opposite of your philosophy, a bad reputation will be amplified on the Internet.

Keep in mind that the good also gets amplified on the Internet. Most people don't always want to be complaining, griping and angry. Most of us like to hear and see something good that makes us smile or laugh. If you don't incorporate into your strategy a possibility of whatever you've created going viral—whether it's good or bad—you could be disappointed and encounter angry audiences who question your company's ethics. Think about what happened recently when Oprah announced a coupon for the new Kentucky Fried Chicken grilled chicken – which was a good thing. KFC was overwhelmed by the popularity (not just by TV, but Twitter, emails and blogs) and later angered customers by not honoring the coupon.

Although the Internet is a very powerful tool, its ability to amplify messages is definitely a double-edged sword that marketers must factor into their social media strategies.

We're All Human

Overall, marketers need to keep in mind that we're all human and most people want to be treated that way. Community members on social media sites don't want to be treated as just another "channel" upon which to have their messages sent— that only upsets community members and makes them question the company's morality and ethics.

It's imperative that everyone on your team who will be influential in representing your company's efforts on your chosen social media sites completely understand your company's philosophies and ethics. This enables them to uphold those ethics when they are representing you to these community members, and your employees will be less likely to cause the unwanted drama or controversy that can occur when a company's actions don't match how it represents itself.

19

Define Who Owns the Conversation

Social media marketing has become such a hot topic of conversation and one that some consultants consider a gold mine. Many consultants claim to be the social media experts—the only ones who can design and implement your company's strategy. However, don't assume that any one consultant or firm can handle every aspect of your social media marketing campaign. In marketing, public relations, search optimization, tech teams, and even customer service, everyone has a role in your strategy—not just one department in your company.

If you want an agency to help you build your strategy, look to those agencies offer more than just advertising, SEO or PR services. Social media marketing requires a lot of experience across multiple media. PR agencies that claim they can implement your social media strategy tend to look at social media as just another channel to try to control "spin." SEO agencies tend to see social media as just another place to gain links to your website. And pure marketing or advertising agencies tend to see social media as just another place to slam your ad or commercial.

Although a company can use social media to control spin, gain links, and place advertisements, these are not the primary or only goals of social media. As we've discussed throughout this book, social media is about the following:

* *Conversation*

* *Sharing*

* *Engagement*

All three concepts require your company's involvement—you can't entirely farm them out to a third party.

Everyone Can Have a Role

Relying on one department or one type of agency to plan and implement your social media strategy can limit your potential success when entering the social media space. Companies shouldn't limit themselves by believing that their PR agencies can handle their social media strategies just because they claim they can do it all. Particular disciplines, such as public relations and search marketing, often have very limited scopes of how social media should be used (such as a spin control method).

Many different departments should have a role in your social media strategy. If you are looking to an agency to help you plan the strategy, look for one that has a broad range of experience. You want to be able to pull the best from different disciplines. Everyone can have a role—from research and planning to engagement. Just be sure to use your existing resources to your advantage.

If you are choosing an agency, look at what other social media projects the agency has helped its other clients launch. If the agency has done only Twitter accounts or ambassador programs and little else, you should be asking, "Why?" Obviously, this kind of agency is approaching social media in a cookie-cutter way. Just because a strategy works for one client doesn't mean it will work for your company.

Remember, every client and every audience is different. Agencies that are selling a single type of social media expertise, such as an ambassador program, or that are suggesting they write your social media content might not have the best strategy in mind for your company. For example, just because an agency says it can drive lots of votes on Digg doesn't mean it can offer the services you really need. If an agency is offering little else in the way of strategy, you might want to seriously rethink working with that agency. The best approach pairs the services of a specialty agency with talents your own staff provides. Again, include internal resources from a variety of departments—marketing, public relations, search optimization, customer service, IT, and so on.

 Note

One caveat: I was a full-time SEO expert for many years before I settled into creating, training, and helping implement and measure client social media strategies. I also have a deep technology background with a public relations degree, so I understand different perspectives of who owns your conversations.

Marketing

Your marketing team understands how to craft your message in a way that can appeal broadly. Creating pieces such as commercials and brochures, labeling, and so on is what they do best. These professionals understand what's needed to draw customers to your company, brand, products, or services.

Most marketers learned the classic way of marketing, which includes among other things, the line of thinking that a company must push a message to customers a certain number of times to truly reach them. Marketers carefully craft and push a message to the company's desired demographic, hoping to convert at least a portion of the audience to real customers. In this form of marketing, there is no "conversation."

This worked when the only media available to the customer and marketing were print, TV, and radio—push marketing was the only marketing game in town. The trouble with classical marketing is that although it was effective before the Internet, the game has entirely changed now that much of a company's marketing efforts occur online and in social media circles.

With the advent on the Internet, customers began to have more control over the companies, brands, products, and services which they want to become intimately involved with. Instead of having access only to carefully crafted marketing messages, the potential customer base wanted to have conversations with other people around the world about products and brands. They wanted to discuss a company's products or services, research buying decisions, and share their experiences without having someone marketing to them.

Although your marketing department might be in charge of your social media strategy, it can be a serious misstep for only that department to implement your strategy. Instead of engaging in conversation, you run the risk of "marketing to" a community that will run marketers right out town. Community members want to have a conversation about the brands they love, not listen to the same old marketing messages they get in brochures and see in TV commercials.

When your marketing team learns the ins and outs of social media, they can help your company craft its marketing message, as well as assist you in honing your capability to include this messaging in your conversations without alienating your potential customers. Your marketing team can help you create effective social media marketing plans and make sure your branding is consistent with other company messaging—something many companies forget when entering to the social media space.

Public Relations

Public relations is notoriously about control and spin. As a blogger, I have received many odd press releases from PR professionals who appeared to be sending them to just about anyone with a blog—me included. It seemed as though these PR agencies thought every blogger on Earth needed to know about their company's news, even if the blog had nothing to do with the product or service the PR agency was shilling. Unfortunately for these PR agencies—and for your company, if you decide to hire a PR agency to handle your social media campaign—social media isn't just another outlet for PR efforts. Treating social media this way can have disastrous results for your social media campaign.

When it comes to spin control, your PR team (or an outside agency, if you've decided to go that route) won't be able to control much of anything that happens in social media. The discussion can't be controlled directly, but you can participate in those conversations and possibly influence the final outcome in a positive manner.

Many public relations agencies think entering the social media realm simply requires setting up a Twitter account and then announcing you've entered the social media space. Such was the case for Pizza Hut. In April 2009, Pizza Hut decided to enter the social media realm by having its public relations agency announce to the world they were hiring a "Twittern." What's a Twittern? Apparently, Pizza Hut was looking for an intern to run its Twitter efforts, and its PR agency thought this was a great way to get some spin for Pizza Hut. The problem was that Pizza Hut and its PR agency made this more like a stunt than a true conversation. When that press release hit the *New York Times,* Pizza Hut was following only 19 people and had only 20 "tweets," all promoting something Pizza Hut was doing (see Figure 19.1).

Figure 19.1   *An ill-fated Twitter campaign run by Pizza Hut*

Pizza Hut surprisingly intended to hire an intern to run its Twitter account. Someone who has no investment in the brand and no education in its messaging would be representing a global brand on a global platform.

Pizza Hut also erred by expecting its "twittern" to reach college students. Had the company done its research, it would have realized that the company's time was better spent on Facebook—real social media conversations were already happening in a Facebook fan page. Sadly, Pizza Hut wasn't engaging in those conversations.

For PR agencies, success is measured in press mentions and spin. The PR agency thought Pizza Hut would look "cool" because it was hiring a "twittern," and Twitter was the hottest social media tool around. But to most people on Twitter, it appeared that Pizza Hut was just pushing its marketing messages to the community.

Coincidentally (or perhaps not—the public can be the final decision makers here) while Pizza Hut was looking for the "Twittern", Domino's was all over the news for the two employees who filmed themselves doing disgusting things with the food they were making for customers that I highlighted in Chapter17.

Search Optimization

For many search optimization professionals, social media is all about the links and traffic it generates for a client's site. Those links lead to search engine rankings, which are the golden goose to an SEO. SEOs use social media profiles, blogs, videos, and social news sites to help promote their clients in the search engines. SEO efforts can be a legitimate part of your social media campaign. However, it doesn't always happen that way.

In search optimization, "black hat" is a term for people who use underhanded tactics in an attempt to manipulate search engines, such as Google, Yahoo!, and Bing, into ranking a site higher in search results. Black-hat SEO, also known as "spamdexing," employs a variety of sleazy tactics, such as creating link farms, keyword stuffing, and article spinning, to get a site unfairly ranked by a search engine while diminishing the relevance of search results. Search engines are always on the lookout for sites that employ these techniques and kick offending the sites off their indexes and possibly ban the offender from the search engine's rankings.

"Gray hat"—if such a thing really exists—is a mix of the "good" and the "bad," meaning that legitimate SEO practices are used for illegitimate means. Gray-hat tactics can still get you banned from the search engines. In social media, it'll get a lot of people really angry at you, too.

I served on a social media panel with a search optimization expert at one of the more popular search conferences, and I was floored when he said during a Q&A session, "I don't care about ethics or that my methods are gray hat; all I care about is making money." If you see or hear professionals call their tactics "gray hat" or say they aren't concerned about ethics, you should think twice about hiring them if they don't make contingency plans if their "gray hat" tactics backfire for their clients. Unfortunately, not all SEO agencies honestly explain how they use social media, so make sure to research their methods.

SEOs definitely have a place in your team because they understand the workings of the search engines better than anyone. And good SEOs know how to strike a balance between following ethical SEO practices and making money. They can help you secure your name across all social media platforms, think about proper domain names, and optimize your blogs and profiles around what's most important to your company's image.

Be wary of an SEO company that looks to only Digg or other social news sites, or even relies too heavily on just one social media tactic as your social media strategy. If SEOs claim they are great at social media because they have "power diggers" on staff, take a second look at their methods and what they are defining as success.

Customer Service

Your customer service team definitely needs to have a seat at your social media strategy table. Chapter 20, "A Great Customer Service Program Is a Natural Extension into Social Media," describes in more detail why it's such an important piece of a social media strategy.

The people on your customer service team hear your customers relating their stories on a daily basis. They know how to communicate in real conversations with your customers—perhaps better than anyone in your company. They hear both the good and the bad about what people think about your company, brand, products or services, and even the people who work for you. Leaving the professionals from this team out of the mix just because they might not have any kind of marketing background is a serious misstep. They can provide invaluable information that can not only help in your research, but also aid in sculpting a successful social media strategy.

IT Department

Your IT department needs to be included in your social media team because it can help you with the technical foundation of your strategy. It's imperative that you know your technical capabilities before you get too far down the road in investing in a social media strategy that your IT department can't handle. Get your IT department's opinion, and make sure the right systems are in place before you wade hip deep into social media.

Your IT professionals will be far more willing to suggest alternatives to make your social media strategy work if you've included them from the beginning. If you put a social media strategy in place without consulting them and then suffer from technical difficulties, your IT staff will likely be resentful. In essence, you're asking your IT department to fix something that shouldn't be broken, and you might even be asking them to be "miracle workers."

Your Team—the Individuals

A very important piece of this "who owns the conversation?" topic is the individuals of the team you put together. As a company implementing a strategy, you need to define who owns the conversation from the start.

If you have employees tweeting for you, do they tweet as their name? Or do they tweet as a hybrid, perhaps their name and your company's put together? What happens when an employee leaves the company or the team? Who owns that account?

This topic has become very touchy as social media becomes more influential in our society. As your company makes inroads into the social media communities, relationships with the members of those communities will begin to develop. If you have just one person representing your company within social media circles, community members will develop a relationship with just one person and not your company overall. Should that person leave your company, you might lose most of all of the progress you have made. If that person leaves your company and takes a position with the competition, matters could be even worse.

Spreading the responsibilities of engaging members of social media communities across your social media marketing team or even across your company can help to alleviate some of that "one-person" attachment. It also helps to spread the resource load especially if you have to deal with absences of staff members quite frequently.

Make sure to plan for personnel transitions and clearly define what happens to the accounts those employees managed. Social media can end up, unwittingly, being a personal branding mechanism for your team members. If members of your social media team use their status within your social media efforts for self-branding, your social media strategy might do more for the employee than it does for your company. That's why it's important to lay the ground rules for employee participation in your social marketing strategy. Zappos, for example, educates its employees who want to use Twitter on behalf of the company. Zappos trains its employees how to best represent Zappos in the way the company feels it should be represented. Also, Zappos requires that employees include "zappos" as part of their user names. If the employee leaves Zappos' employ, the account can no longer be used to send tweets. This clearly establishes the employee as working on the behalf of Zappos.

Everyone Needs to Be on the Same Page

Finally, but by no means least important, make sure that all these teams are talking to each other. For a social media strategy to fully succeed, you have to break the silos that exist among marketing, public relations, customer service, search marketing, and IT. Conversation and dialogue must occur among them so that everyone's message is congruent and no one steps on anyone else's toes.

Discussing your plans ahead of time can produce amazing results. For instance, if your marketing department is producing a commercial that they think has nothing to do with social media (but actually does), perhaps your PR department will recognize its social media potential and will get it onto YouTube. Your search team can make sure that commercial video is optimized around your brand and targeted messaging, your public relations team can help promote its release, and your social media team can share it with the community they are engaging with and ask them for feedback and ratings.

Social media has begun to force companies to break down those silos. Your departments are no longer isolated, nor should they be. Just as social media creates conversations and sharing of experiences between companies and customers, it should be creating conversations and dialogue between employees and departments.

20

A Great Customer Service Program Is a Natural Extension into Social Media

Companies around the globe are known for their great customer service. Southwest Airlines, Zappos, and Whole Foods are three companies that I consistently hear have great customer service. These three companies have implemented the fundamentals of their customer service practices as part of their social media strategies.

Southwest Airlines has the "Nuts About Southwest" blog in which employees from all parts of the company share their stories about working with Southwest. The company includes Flickr and YouTube streams, and is very active and responsive on Twitter. Zappos enables (and, in fact, encourages) all its employees to create a Twitter account and communicate with customers via that channel after they go through training on the ins and outs of Twitter. Whole Foods is very active on Twitter as well, helping its customers find products in their stores, interacting with them, encouraging them and holding actual conversation with the community about issues around Whole Foods.

Many companies with great customer service departments have realized that social media is another medium for them to provide great customer service. Social media enables people to interact directly with a company and offers yet another avenue for the company to provide customer service. When deciding whether to participate in social media, companies with solid customer service know that restricting their direct interaction to phone conversations via traditional customer support methods is unnecessarily limiting. Instead, proactive companies join and encourage conversations on social media platforms.

They Don't Just Answer Phones

Other employees in your company might be under the impression that your customer service employees only answer the phones. Although that might be the physical action they do to earn their paychecks, they provide so much more to your company. Without your customer service department, your company won't be seen as "human"—the customer service department is the heart of your company.

Whether your customer service team consists of 2 or 2,000 people, its team members are vital to keeping that connection between company and customer alive and well. Your customer service reps are a unique breed of problem solvers within your company. They are constantly put into situations in which they need to solve issues your customers have with your products or services.

Along with being problem solvers, they are advice givers. Through their interaction with customers, they learn the ins and outs, and tips and tricks that other customers have used to either enhance or improve their experiences with your products.

Finally, and probably most important, your customer service representatives are ad hoc counselors, listening to and consoling customers who have just had a bad experience with your product. They listen, console, and help repair your relationships with those customers.

Your customer service representatives already know how a social community works, so they are probably one of your best resources to tap when implementing a social media strategy that involves direct engagement with an audience. They know and understand your customers on a one-to-one basis better than any other department in your company.

It's worth repeating—your customer service team does so much more than just answer the phones.

Empathy Is Important to Conversations

Having empathy is a great gift that customer service representatives need to effectively work with your customers and the issues they encounter with your company, brand, product, or service. To relate to the customers on a one-to-one level, as they do on a daily basis while manning your phone banks, they need to develop and hone that empathy skill.

The online environment is very similar. The people you select to engage in communities on a one-on-one level with your audience need to have that same empathy. They need to relate to both positive and negative conversations in a way that represents your company in the best possible way. They need to encourage the positives and help turn the negatives into positives, and who does that better than your customer service team with the customers they empathize with on the phone?

Although your marketing team and public relations experts might be uniquely skilled at creating marketing pieces and crafting the messages, you need to relate to your audience. Social media communities tend to rebuff these types of overtures from companies if they feel it's a marketing message. However, social media communities are much more likely to embrace your company's involvement if members of your team show them true empathy. If you listen and respond, your social media experience will be far more rewarding. The two most important things you can say (and truly mean) when fielding a complaint are "I hear you" and "Thank you for sharing your experience with me—it helps us become a better company."

They Know How to Listen

In previous chapters, I've emphasized the importance of listening to your audience before jumping right into social media marketing. Listening gives you an opportunity to learn not just what people are saying about you, but also how people communicate about you in these social communities. For example, are they more prone to tweet out to their friends the latest link to your blog post? Or will they create a slide share that shows how to use your product more effectively? Understanding the "how" is just as important as the "what" and the "Where". You also learn the ins and outs about how a community forms, as well as who are the key influencers, followers, and trouble makers.

Listening is what customer service representatives do best. Someone who calls to speak with customer service usually wants someone at the company to listen to their story, and that's what customer service representatives do so well. They are adeptly trained to listen to not just what customers are saying, but also what they aren't saying. Although someone might be complaining about one thing, another issue could be the heart of why they called. The customer service representative is skilled enough to discover that and help resolve the real issue.

Having customer service representatives on your team is crucial to implementing your social media strategy. They can help you uncover underlying issues that might not be so obvious to others on your team. Although marketers and public relations professionals are trained to address the obvious good and bad situations, customer service representatives are trained to listen and to uncover the underlying issues that could bubble to the surface and later turn into severe issues you hadn't antici-pated.

Many companies tend to downplay the role that the customer service representa-tives play within the marketing efforts of a company. I say that if you don't build your foundation with a great customer service staff, having a phenomenal product is irrelevant—you'll be fighting an uphill battle with your customers. The customer service representatives are on the front lines on a daily basis. They're listening to your customers and getting a feel for how customers view your company, which is something marketing can't achieve with a focus group.

One of your social media strategy's best moves is to recruit a few customer service representatives to help you implement your social media engagement where it involves one-on-one contact with members of various communities. Their skills are invaluable when it comes to listening, so involve them from the research phase.

They Know How to Share

Along with knowing how to listen, customer service representatives are keenly adept at knowing how to share with the customers on the other end. They are acutely aware of how much they can share and when it's the right time to share it.

Whether your customer service representatives are relating their own personal experiences or letting customers know that they aren't alone, they can put cus-tomers at ease and begin to build a bond of trust. This same process can occur on a social media platform. When people share in a social media setting—whether it's through photos, videos, or even stories about their experiences with a product or service—they are giving a little piece of themselves, and community members rec-ognize that. Your customers are going out on a limb. When people are willing to give of themselves without expecting anything in return, it is usually met with respect, and a newfound trust begins to build. This becomes the bedrock of founda-tions within social media.

Conversations are built upon the sharing of information. You could be offering a new tip or trick you've discovered for improving the use of a product or service, or maybe you found a way to get from point A to point B faster and without a lot of hassle. In any case, you are giving up a piece of content that you deem valuable for the greater good of the community. Customer service representatives know how to do this because they do it every day with the customers they speak with on the phone.

Sharing isn't always about a "secret" way of doing things. It can be as simple as sharing a link to a website that has been valuable. Sharing directions on how to improve a recipe or a project, or sharing how to improve a golf swing or take a photograph in low light is a great way to start conversations and build relationships in social media communities. As simple as these things seem, they could be the "golden goose" that members of a social media community have been searching for. The next time an opportunity comes around in which they can help your company, they will be much more willing to share their time and resources.

They Can Give You Insight

If you ever want to really know how your customers think your products are performing or how your sales staff is representing your products compared to what the customers understand, your customer service department should be your first resource for information. These professionals can give you insight into things that a focus group—for which you pay tens of thousands of dollars—can't give you. Your customer service representatives receive unbiased feedback from your customers, which is something that a focus group won't provide.

These people take the brunt force of angry customers with relative ease. They can most likely tell you whether the newest release of your software is lousy or awesome just by the number of calls they get from customers who've installed the latest version and have either a horrible time upgrading or just have general questions about what the new upgrade includes.

As I stated earlier, customer service representatives are keenly skilled in uncovering the underlying problems of a situation. What's on the surface might be only the tip of the iceberg if a major problem is about to arise. Customer service representative have insight into these issues because not just one customer will be calling about it—numerous customers will. Their insight can be invaluable.

Including customer service reps in your social media team can add that skill for uncovering the "icebergs" within the communities you want to work with. Your reps can listen, start conversations, and build relationships that provide incredible insight into the true "feel" of what's going on. This kind of insight is invaluable when you can find out whether your marketing is really having an effect on the people who are using your products or services.

Customer service representatives on your social media team are invaluable for listening, sharing, and gaining insight into the dynamics of communities. Not only are they a great barometer for how community members feel and what they are saying about you, but they can also be your "psychics" into whether storms are brewing that you might not have otherwise known about.

Final Thoughts

In today's social media communities, engagement is key. Those one-on-one conversations and relationships that are formed require key skills that your customer service department likely is already very well attuned to. To ignore a rich, reliable and already trained resource would be a serious misstep in your social media strategy. Just because your customer service department might not have marketing experience doesn't mean members of your customer service team cannot become valuable resources or even members of your social media team. Don't count them out!

21

Interns Make Coffee, Not Social Media Strategies

I was an intern a few times in my life, and I can say that I ported my fair share of coffee carafes in those days. But I also learned a lot from those who were (and, to this day, still are) my mentors. Internships enable interns to learn about the workings of a real company and how it relates to their current educational course. Companies with interns are getting somewhat "free labor" and are also gaining insight into the younger generation's perspective. Interns can help companies complete tasks that their employees currently don't have time to complete or that aren't high on the priority list.

However, I've unfortunately encountered more than a few companies that ask interns to plan or jump-start their social media strategies. These companies mistakenly believe that because their interns come from Generation Y, they are just the people to plan and launch their social media strategies. That could be one of the worst moves a company can take.

Sure, interns today are some of the most plugged-in individuals in history. They grew up on computers, cellphones, and Nintendo Game Boys. They text their friends more than they call them. And forget about email—that's too old-school and time-consuming for this generation. However, just because they are so plugged in and use social media platforms such as Bebo and Facebook to communicate with their friends on a regular basis, doesn't mean they know how to utilize these sites for marketing purposes.

As you'll see throughout this chapter, interns are a great addition to your social media strategy. However, think carefully about how you integrate them into your social media team. How much access do you really want to give these interns to your marketing processes when they are leaving in just a few months? Think about not only your social media strategy's future goals, but also what happens if you have an intern who learns your company's social media strategies and then moves on and uses that knowledge for a competing company's benefit?

They Don't Know Your Brand

Interns coming into your company for the summer likely know as much about your company and your brands as they can find on the Internet, where this generation consumes the majority of their information. If your company is well known or has major brands, you likely have a Wikipedia page the interns can read and learn the company history in an hour or less. However, knowing your history doesn't mean they know your brand.

Brands can become iconic and hold meaning. Unless interns do the kind of in-depth research that is required of any marketing plan from the beginning to become successful, they've probably only scratched the surface on knowing or understanding your brand and the value it brings to your customers.

Add to the mix the fact that interns generally are with a company for only 8–12 weeks during the summer, and you can start to understand why looking to them to develop a social media strategy is not such a wise decision. Interns just don't have enough time to learn the ins and outs of your brands, your messaging, or your customers' perspectives to be able to build a successful social media strategy.

However, interns can be part of the equation. They can give you insight into how their generation uses these social media sites. They also might be able to point you in the direction of several social media sites you might not have been aware of. They can be part of your team, but it's not a wise decision to make them the leaders of your social media strategy.

They Don't Know Your Ethics or Philosophies

Along with not knowing your branding, interns don't know the inner workings of your ethics or philosophies. Although these ethics and philosophies might be written in the HR manual the interns get on their first day, the interns don't have a grasp on how those ethics and philosophies relate to the job they will be assigned to do for your company. As for any new hire, learning how your company operates takes time.

Understanding how your company's ethics and philosophies were formed and how they affect your current business would probably take half to three-quarters of the time interns are slated to be with your company. Fully understanding your ethics and philosophies is a must for an intern (or anyone else) to represent you in social media communities and to build a strategy for your company.

Without understanding how your company operates from a philosophical or ethical point of view, interns are much more likely to make a serious misstep in representing you in social media communities or take a different direction (one that isn't consistent with your identity) when planning the strategy. Interns are young, and although they might have a decent set of personal ethics upon starting their internships, they aren't the business ethics upon which your company is built.

How you converse with customers, the value propositions you share about your products and services, and even how you want the general public to perceive your company all come from your ethics and policies. When your interns arrive, they likely know what they've seen from the outside, but that perception can be derived from false information. If you set them loose in social media, they can make serious missteps if they don't have a solid foundation in your company's philosophy and ethics.

They Have No Real Vested Interest

Unless you are promising your summer interns a job after they graduate, they have no real vested interest in your company beyond their last paycheck or college credits. Interns are generally more concerned about getting back to school, hanging with their friends, and figuring out how they will get through the next semester.

In the beginning of their internships, interns will likely be gung ho about helping out. But as their time with you approaches the end, their focus will waiver to the next adventure in their lives. That's not saying anything bad about interns or your company and the way it operates. It's just common intern behavior.

Consequently, do you really want to put a major piece of marketing in the lap of someone who will eventually leave and who, therefore, has no real vested interest in seeing the plan successfully implemented? They're excited and appreciative when they arrive, they eventually settle in, and then they'll start the process of leaving. Unless you guarantee them a position after they graduate based upon their performance with your company during their internship, they won't be motivated to invest a ton of time or brain power in helping you attain social media success.

Would You Let an Intern Plan a Major PR Event?

If you had a public relations intern for the summer, would you have that intern research, plan, launch, and report on a major new product? I'll bet you wouldn't place the success or failure of your new product's launch in the hands of an intern. Interns might be part of the team that pulls together a great PR event for the product launch, but you would leave the heavy lifting to your experienced PR experts.

If you wouldn't let interns plan a major PR event for your company, why would you leave your social media marketing strategy in their hands? Just because they have a Facebook page? That's akin to letting them plan your event because they've done a mock launch of a product and their professor gave them an A for it.

This is the real world—real dollars, and real success or real failure. You pay your experts substantial amounts of money for a reason. They are experienced, are proven, and know the pitfalls and shortcuts to put the event together successfully. An intern just doesn't have the proven track record.

Just as you wouldn't leave your PR event planning solely in the hands of an intern, don't be tempted to do that with your social media strategy, either.

Global Platforms

Even though a company might be a local company, launching a website opens it to a global community. People from all over the globe can visit a website for a limousine company in Limerick, Pennsylvania. The company or site might not be relevant to someone in Australia, but anyone can still form an opinion about the limousine company because the website is on a global platform.

Because of social media, a company's concern is no longer just static websites being seen globally. Anything that is posted on a social media site is seen globally. People from around the globe have more of a chance of seeing conversations about your company via social media sites than they do of finding your static site through a web search.

Social media sites such as Facebook, LinkedIn, Travelocity, and Twitter are global platforms to which your company, brand, and product or services are being exposed. Do you want to place the social media marketing efforts your company is implementing solely in the hands of someone with extremely limited experience in marketing on global platforms? Again, an intern can be an extremely insightful and helpful part of your team, given the proper guidance. Most likely, interns can understand the ins and outs of different social sites better than anyone else, but they still need that expert guidance to pull it all together.

Global platforms can significantly affect the perception of your company. One wrong miscommunication on Twitter or Facebook, and you can have a major problem on your hands seen by not only the local media, but also global customers.

It's important to recognize the talents and skills of your interns and incorporate them into helping you implement your social media strategy. However, it's just as important to recognize that social media marketing isn't a fly-by-night marketing medium. Instead, social media marketing is a global platform that enables customers from all over the globe to converse and engage with your brand.

They Might Know Facebook, but Do They Really Know Marketing?

Interns take a lot of classes, from Marketing 101 to Public Relations and Law. Interns are likely checking their Facebook pages every few hours to connect with their friends and family through wall posts, tagged photos, and postings in the groups they belong to. They are quite savvy when it comes to these social media sites and *their* use of them, without proper training, Interns really don't think much beyond how they connect with their friends on these types of sites. They don't think of the sites from a marketing perspective. Unfortunately, most marketing and PR classes taught today still do not include online marketing, so the thought of using Facebook, a blog, or Flickr to market to a demographic can be quite foreign.

Sometimes interns can be a little reluctant to think about using social media sites for marketing. They've been raised to ignore marketing. Most of Generation Y has become "banner blind"—they ignore blatant marketing attempts in the places where they hang with their friends. They consider marketing in social media sites an annoying intrusion. How eager do you think interns will be to deliver these unwanted conversations?

Can They Relate to Your Target Market?

Because interns are new to your business—and possibly the business world itself—it's very unlikely that they will have the experience needed to be able to listen, understand, and empathize with the communities you want to engage with. Therefore, it's very unlikely that interns can create and implement your social media strategies. In addition, how can your audience truly relate to interns who lack experience with the product or service?

If you want to build true, foundational, and respectful relationships in these communities, you need to have a team of people from your company who can relate to your target demographics. For example, if you are selling a trendy body spray, interns might be effective in the engagement parts of your social media strategy. But if you are selling scrapbooking supplies, interns won't be the people you want leading up the charge or being the voice of your strategy, because the primary demographic of scrapbookers are mothers.

They Are Gone Before You Know It

Interns are like the summer winds—fun, delightful, refreshing…and gone before you realize it. For this reason alone, relying on them to research, plan, and implement a social media strategy is an unwise decision. They come into your company in May and are gone by mid-August or sometimes sooner. That's an incredibly short amount of time to get anything substantial established, let alone be able to measure it for true success or failure.

 Interns won't be around long enough to both build and sustain the kind of relationships that need to be made in social media communities to have a successful venture into social media. By the time they've discovered the community, watched, listened, and made a few engagements with community members, it's time for them to return to school.

If you've brought interns into the engagement portion of your strategy, make sure you are up front about who they are and how long they will be around. The last thing you want is the community developing a solid relationship with an intern, only to see the intern leave, graduate, and then land a job with a competitor.

2

Branding and Messaging Need to Be Consistent

When it comes to branding and messaging, your marketing people are the experts. Look to them for direction in creating the best messaging that reflects both your company's philosophies and how you should present your products or services to the public. However, companies need to remember that offline and online marketing work differently. The offline audience can view brands very differently than an online community.

Most likely, that means you will need different messaging to relate to, engage, and help identify with online communities. But just because you need a different way to relate your message to these online communities doesn't mean that your core messaging and branding needs to change. It is critical that your online and offline messaging and branding be consistent.

Knowing that everyone in your company has some role in your social media strategy—whether or not they are *aware of it—is another aspect of branding and messaging you need to plan for. Companies don't usually educate all their employees on their marketing messaging, nor do they articulate the goal of the messaging to all employees. Having everyone in the same boat when that social media strategy embarks is important if you want to avoid straying off course.*

Does Everyone Know Your Message?

You should educate everyone in your company about your marketing efforts, especially your social media strategy and the messaging that you want to present to the public. If your social media marketing team doesn't know what your marketing communications team has planned to launch, how will they be knowledgeable when they are representing you in these online communities?

You don't want to appear clueless in an online community. Your social media team must know about outside marketing efforts, as well as all branding and messaging for your products and services. Failure to make all this consistent won't bode well for your respect or authority with members of the online communities you want to engage. Your efforts will look totally disjointed and similar to "the left hand doesn't know what the right hand is doing."

For example, if some portions of your company are extolling one virtue of your product or service, and your CEO is saying that your company is considering a revamp of that product or service, there is bound to be some confusion in your social media strategy. The social media communities you interact with are likely to think that your CEO is out of touch, or that your marketing team is force feeding a product or feature on them that the company knows has problems.

The members of your social media team aren't the only ones who need to know the direction of your marketing messages. Everyone in your company should be educated because it helps create a level of camaraderie, and almost everyone in your company is online in some manner. Having all employees on the same page about how your company should be represented can help prevent accidental snafus from bringing your social media efforts to a screeching halt.

For example, earlier in this book, I discussed the firing of a Philadelphia Eagles employee over social media use the company found unacceptable. If the Eagles organization had laid down some rules about acceptable use of social media by its employees, they might've been able to avoid the sticky situation that ensued. Instead, the Eagles organization came out of it appearing to be a corporate bully.

Thinking that only your marketing department or your social media team needs to be aware of your marketing messages and branding can be a huge misstep when it comes to implementing a social media strategy. If your employees don't have a Facebook account or MySpace page now, they will within the next year. Social networking sites are often the gateways for most Americans to enter a social media community. Do you really want them putting information in their profiles about where they work and having that message conflict with the messaging you've put in place to promote your company?

Does It Jive Online?

As I've mentioned throughout this book, successful offline marketing often doesn't translate nearly as well—if at all—in the online environment. People within online communities have become advertising blind (they ignore the ads, the banners, etc. shown on sites) and very skeptical of any attempts marketers make to infiltrate their communities.

Mass-marketing messages just do not have the same appeal to people within online communities as they do to someone driving in a car and listening to the radio or seeing a billboard. Online communities are special because they discuss niche topics, their members choose to be there, and the people who inhabit these communities feel a special bond that makes those individuals feel important. If your marketing team comes into the forum or community with the same message they push to everyone, it just won't jive with this type of online audience.

You need your A game when entering a community that you want to engage. No one-size-fits-all approach is effective in social media. Messaging must be on target and your branding must be consistent. However, your approach must be unique to the community, not just a general approach you might take if you were pushing it to a mass audience watching a sporting event.

Your marketing department might think that giving away free samples of your product is a great way to get people to engage with you in online communities. However, if these community members can go to their grocery store and get that same sample, your approach won't help you build a relationship with those community members. In this example, your marketing efforts are saying that members of this community are no different than anyone else you are pushing your message to.

As discussed in previous chapters, online community members invest a lot of time in sharing their experience with other members. Social community members are making an investment of not only time, but also emotional connections. This makes them different than the average shopper pushing the cart up and down the aisles of the local grocery store. Your message needs to jive with these people but still relay the ethics, philosophies, and purpose of your company's products or services. You must achieve this careful balance to make your marketing messages jive both online and offline.

Stop Siloing

Larger companies are notorious for siloing their marketing efforts into specific departments, with each department performing a specific duty and knowing its boundaries. If those boundaries are overstepped, internal political issues can arise. Your company has some issues to overcome if internal stakeholders are more concerned about controlling their territory than seeing a strategy succeed. When departments do not talk to each other about the strategies they are planning to implement, it limits the strategy's full potential for success. One department might "own" a particular strategy and be the experts in that area, but other departments might be better equipped to implement aspects of the strategy. Before you delve into a new social media strategy, you must iron out these issues.

 Consider an example of your public relations department planning a special event to promote the launch of a new product or service. If your public relations department hasn't talked to your marketing department about the messaging of the product and who it's targeted for, how will the PR department really know who it should speak to in the press, beyond the traditional media? Perhaps they should contact influential bloggers and social community members.

Now take it a step further. Your online marketing department might be clueless about this event and start marketing online about the messaging and new product launch. If your PR department hasn't informed marketing of its intended PR strategy, and marketing puts out an ordinary press release, you've just missed out on several key opportunities to increase your exposure for the PR event.

First, your PR department's release should be optimized for search engines by including major keywords. Your online marketing department should work with the marketing department (assuming they are different groups) to determine what keywords would give your company the best search ranking. Second, your company could launch pay-per-click (PPC) campaigns to promote the PR department's event for the launch of the product or service. Third, your online marketing department could design high-impact pages on your site to help successfully market and promote this product's launch.

Forgetting about the social media team can also have a significant impact on this event. Your social media team can get the word out about the launch, creating buzz in online communities. Your social media team also can help make sure the event is listed in event-sharing sites such as MeetUp, Yahoo!'s Upcoming, and Eventful. That team can also help you determine where you can make the best impact for this event. Could it be photos, videos, or even a podcast?

If your company is siloing its efforts, you'd never know unless someone starts looking at how each department interacts with one another and what effects each department has on the overall plan. When it comes to social media marketing, siloing can actually hinder your efforts because one hand won't know what the other is doing.

You should also consider your customer service department in this example. Customer service representatives will be interacting with customers asking all sorts of questions about the new product or service. They will be hearing from angry and upset customers who just bought the old version and might now have to pay for the new one, too. If your PR department doesn't consult your customer service department before the product or service launch goes live, your customer service department could be blindsided and overwhelmed by what your customers do next.

If you see territorialism and bickering over what department's budget will pay for the hours in a multidepartment effort to make your social media campaign more effective, you need to remind everyone that success depends on companywide buy-in and support. Too much infighting will slow implementation of a strategy and bog down the rate of success for your social media strategy. Not just one person or one team will make a social media strategy successful. Everyone working together across departments makes it successful.

A single department can develop tunnel vision and see success only from its perspective, which can limit your potential success. Other departments can contribute to your strategy and help propel that strategy into another realm of success.

Everyone Needs to Know

For some departments, sharing what's going on doesn't come naturally. The old ways of marketing and communications enabled the siloing of information, meaning that some departments shared with other departments only on a "need to know" basis. That worked in the old days of TV, radio, and print advertising, but unfortunately for those stodgy old marketers still stuck in the past, it doesn't work that way in the new world of online marketing, especially with social media.

In contrast, marketing within social media actually promotes the sharing of information. Therefore, it's important that you educate everyone in your company about your current branding and marketing message efforts—especially your social media team. If your social media team isn't aware of a PR event to launch a new product, how will the group know how the PR department wants to promote the event? If the PR department promotes it one way and the social media team promotes it another way, your efforts will look disjointed and your teams will definitely look as if they don't communicate.

Consider your other employees. With three out of four Americans utilizing social media sites, inevitably employees who have nothing to do with your marketing efforts will be on a social media site. If they've filled out their profiles and indicate that they work for your company, wouldn't it be nice if they, too, were touting your current promotions—even if they work in the mailroom or the warehouse? By not having each of your employees positively connected to your marketing efforts, you're missing an opportunity to possibly have an employee make a personal connection with a potential customer or audience member.

Not every employee needs to know the ins and outs of your marketing strategies, but you should educate all employees about your current efforts to market your company, brands, products, and services. If the opportunity arises for an employee not directly involved in marketing or branding to point an interested social media audience member to the right community or person on your social media team, it's certainly worth seizing.

Most of your employees want to see your company succeed. That can spill over into their nonwork lives, such as representing your company outside of their working hours on the social media sites they are involved in. They might not be directly involved in your planning for social media, but you should be planning to educate them on the basics of your marketing efforts.

It's Not Just Your Site That Needs Branding

When it =comes to marketing online, some companies think only about consistency between their websites and banner ads. Unfortunately, some companies don't carry over this consistency to their social media marketing efforts as well. As social media consistently becomes a more permanent part of the online marketing equation, companies must start thinking beyond just their websites when it comes to branding.

You need to consider everything from having your company logo used as an avatar to carefully choosing what's listed in your profiles on social media sites—it's all part of branding your company and helps build trust and establish authority in social media communities.

Members come to trust logos. From the blue oval of Ford to John Deer "Green," people understand and relate to logos and avatars that companies choose to represent them in a less personal way. They also help people remember your company and your ultimate message. "Have a Coke and a smile" is a message that sticks in my brain from years ago, along with the company's familiar red-and-white scripted logo. I know it, I trust it, and when I see it—whether it's on a can, bottle, or soda fountain—I know I'll get a Coke .

If potential customers don't remember your logo and branding, they are less likely to remember your company, let alone recommend your product to a friend in an email, point it out to a fellow shopper in a store, or write a review, no matter how much they trust you.

An excellent example of branding beyond a website is Jeep's efforts on Flickr (see Figure 22.1). Jeep started several groups on Flickr for Jeep owners to share their photos of their experiences at "Jeep Camps" or other various get-togethers with fellow Jeep owners.

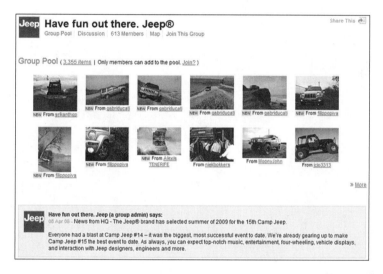

Figure 22.1   *Jeep carries its website branding across its social media campaign.*

Jeep clearly brands its efforts with its familiar green Jeep logo. Jeep's profile and groups are clearly branded with its "Have Fun Out There" messaging. When people see or promote these groups, they know and instinctively trust that Jeep is engaging in this community.

No matter what your logo or messaging is, make sure you are consistent with its use across all your channels, both offline and online. Most important, make sure you take full advantage of the entire might of your company by getting everyone onboard and aware of those logos and messages, as well as their intended impact.

23

Be Transparent: Trust and Readership Must Be Earned

Pretending to be someone you aren't is probably one of the biggest taboos in social media. Having someone pose as a genuine reviewer, tweeter, or friend, or using bots to artificially inflate online vote results is the fast track to getting your company labeled as dishonest. Online communities are especially sensitive to this bad form, and when you've upset one group, more are sure to follow. Although you might think Marketing 101 teaches honest behavior, a surprising number of "experts" suggest behaving dishonestly.

- Writing fake reviews

- Posting comments under fake names

- Adding hundreds of friends (such as models, sports stars, and so on) to your friends lists

- Implementing bots to vote up content on sites such as StumbleUpon, Digg, and Mixx

- Using ghost writers for blog posts

- Using ghost tweeters for Twitter accounts

- *Posing as a customer in forums and message boards*
- *Posting fake or factually incorrect content that incites audiences*

Employing such dishonest tactics could cause irreparable damage to your brand or company image. For example if you are "found out" for having someone write fake reviews for your national hotel chain, people are less likely to trust any other review they see and then less likely to book rooms at your hotel. You might think you are fooling the audience by engaging in these tactics, but social media communities are smart. And when they figure out you've implemented one of these tactics in the community, you will lose all trust and any authority you've managed to gain through manipulating them.

Tell Them Why You Are There

Companies should join and participate in social media communities. You will earn a lot more respect and gain more credibility with the community members if you tell them right from the start who you are and why you are joining the community. Posing as a customer or being secretive about your motives in the community will get you nowhere. Inevitably, you'll slip, and when you do, you'll ruin your chance to form true relationships that might help your social media strategy succeed.

Approaching the administrators of the community before you start your actual engagement might be the wisest step. Doing so allows the administrators to give you a few pointers to help you avoid violating unwritten rules of the community. The community administrators might also be willing to verify that you are indeed a representative of the company you claim to represent, which is a huge boon to your credibility with that community.

When you are up front about who you are and why you are joining a community— whether it's a photo group on Flickr, a forum, or a group on Facebook—amazing things can happen. When you have established trust in the community, you'll likely find that the community members will be open and accepting of your participation. You might even see that these community members really want to engage with you and help you, which won't happen if you are working under a false identity.

Fill Out Your Profiles

People are curious about other people in their community. Community members will first look at your profile before engaging in conversation with you. If your profile lacks information, community members will likely be very wary of you from the start.

Fill in information about your company, as well as your personal information (or information about the person who is handling the account). Let people know how they can contact you outside the community. Don't be afraid to add a link to your site. Although you might not gain search engine optimization benefits by adding the link, community members will still click on these types of links to find out more information about you and your company. Filling in this information does the following:

- Builds trust around your actions in the community.

- Enables community members to feel safe in directing others to you for more information about your company and brands.

- Helps make community members more comfortable coming to you with questions, concerns, complaints, and compliments.

- Helps you when things go wrong. When something bad happens with a product or service your company provides, this added trust you've built in social media communities will help you weather the storm. In fact, community members just might come to your rescue.

Brand Yourself from the Beginning

As discussed in Chapter 22, "Branding and Messaging Need to Be Consistent," branding in the context of social media is very important because it helps community members identify with your company. Customers relate to logos and avatars, and eventually come to trust them. You also want the community members to identify and remember who you are—and they do that a lot easier with an image or a logo, rather than with just text.

Your branding must be in synch with both your traditional online activities (website and banner ads) and your social media strategy. You want community members to remember the branding that they have come to know and trust through their relationship with you. It's also important that community members be able to identify and interact with your brand when they aren't online (unless your entire presence is online). Whether it's sending an email recommendation to a friend, pointing someone to your product in a store, or having someone write a review, if members of a community can't identify your brands, they won't perform these activities, no matter how much they trust you.

Everything you do online and offline must be consistent—from your avatar to the way you speak about your product, service, or brand. What you say online must mirror what your company says in TV commercials, radio spots, and print pieces. Your branding and messaging become another big piece in the trust factor of building relationships online. Although members of the community hate to have messages jammed down their throats, they still want to be able to trust that you are who you say you are. The best way to earn that trust is to make sure your branding is right from the start.

Act As You Would in Person

A common fallacy is to think that your online persona can be totally different than your real-life persona. The problem with this is that "real life" always gets in the way. Although people tend to be disingenuous on dating sites, this has happened in online communities as well. However, being fake always shines through. Somewhere along the line, these people slip up in their "story" and are outted in the community. People in the community then stop and think, "Would I really want to be friends with this person in 'real life' if they treated me like this online?"

This also applies to a company's efforts in social media communities. Companies are likely held to higher standards because they are working as a group instead of as individuals. There's a bit of a fallacy that groups are more ethical because many people are working as one entity, and one person can't ruin the whole bunch. If one person is an influencer and has a grudge or axe to grind, his or her influence on the community as a group can be very harmful and cause the group as a whole to act together. Of course, this "pack mentality" can also work in your favor, too, if a key influencer is pleased and shares his or her opinions with the group. As you can see, it can be a double-edged sword. Unfortunately, this shows how one person can ruin a company's reputation in an online community within mere seconds of clicking the Submit button.

A good rule of thumb is to make sure you are treating the people you are engaging in online communities the same way you treat your customers who walk through the doors of your establishment or call your telephones. They're basically the same; the only real difference is the way in which you are communicating with your online contacts. Don't brush off online community complaints because you cannot make eye contact or hear the anger in their voices.

You Have to Earn Their Trust

The online world can be a very finicky place. People can misinterpret, misconstrue, and misread information. The first step in earning trust is to be honest from the onset and very transparent about who you are and what your intentions are.

As with offline relationships in a face-to-face environment, we must establish trust in the online environment. Offline, we look for certain cues to help us determine whether a person seems trustworthy. If someone fidgets too much or doesn't look you in the eyes when speaking to you, you might feel less inclined to trust that person and might wonder if he is hiding something.

In online communities, members look for different cues that point to the same traits (such as honesty vs. dishonesty). An online community member might use these cues to judge your trustworthiness:

- Is your profile filed out?

- What does your profile say about you and your company?

- Does the information in your profile jive with what this community member already knows about your company?

- Do you engage with members of the community in a manner that positively reflects the company?

These are all cues that online community members look at (plus a lot more) to gauge whether you are "for real." If something seems even remotely off-key from the tune you've been singing, the trust is gone.

People Are Cynical

On more than one occasion, I've heard about special sessions or panels at conferences that teach companies how to write fake reviews for social media sites such as Yelp, TripAdvisor, or Amazon. Companies often receive misguided advice telling them that to get stellar reviews, everything has to be squeaky clean and golden. However, most Americans are too cynical to believe a list of reviews that are all 5-out-of-5 stars.

People who rely on ratings and reviews are much more likely to believe a review that has a few bad or "not so stellar" reviews in the mix along with many good reviews. Pop into the mix a few replies from a very transparent business addressing the not-so-stellar reviews with logical or "we are addressing these issues, thank you for bringing it to our attention" type replies, and you've just earned major respect and authority with the audience reading the reviews.

Americans have a tough time believing that everything is lollipops and sunshine when reading reviews because we've been trained to expect the worst. When we're presented with 5-star stellar reviews that start with "The manager Nancy said...," our radar kicks into overdrive. We find it difficult to trust others, especially online, so gaining people's trust in online communities takes a lot of time and effort. Making sure you aren't faking anything is a step in the right direction when working with such cynical groups.

Avoid Ghost-Written Content

If members of a community even catch a glimpse of impropriety suggesting that your team or your company isn't really producing your content, they will be on a mission to prove to the world you've been dishonest.

Ghost blogging and ghost tweeting is a practice in which companies hire agencies or individuals to perform underhanded deeds that are designed to make your company look good in the eyes of the online community. This can include tweeting, posting Facebook updates, adding friends to your MySpace account, adding fake photos to your Flickr account, or writing blog posts—all under the guise of being legitimate. As you might imagine, this practice is risky and a bad idea. If anyone gets wind of your company implementing these types of tactics, you will lose all respect, trust, and almost any opportunity of becoming successful in social media.

For example, if your company makes unique candies and you are trying to engage customers on Twitter with posts being handled by an outside third party, how will this third party know what kind of candy molds you have in stock to make a certain shape or style of candy? That's simple—they won't. The third-party company would have to come back to you, ask you that question, and wait for your answer to tweet it back to the person who asked. What happens if you are on vacation for a few days when that question comes in? You've lost the golden opportunity to engage with a very viable potential customer.

Let's say you have a ghost blogger on staff—someone who writes blog posts to build up content on your website's blog—and the byline was attributed to the president or CEO of your company. Now imagine that the president or CEO was giving a keynote address at a major industry conference that included press in the front row, as well as a Q&A opportunity at the end from the audience. One of those audience members asks a question about a blog post your CEO wrote that contradicts what he just spoke about in the keynote speech. Your CEO didn't really write, read, or edit the post, and your ghost blogger has no way of knowing what your CEO thinks or might say in public that could contradict what "his blog" says.

Looking to the outside for help in planning a strategy is a wise move. However, those outside companies shouldn't tweet, blog, or post for you on a regular basis for a fee. Building relationships with online social media communities requires real people from your own team who know your products and services the best.

Third Time Is a Charm

To wrap up this chapter, I want to highlight one of the more notorious cases of not being transparent and paying a huge price. Some years ago, Walmart and its PR company, Edelman, launched a blog called "Wal-Marting Across America," which was suppose to tell the story of a couple who traveled across America in their RV staying in Walmart parking lots. They had a blog where they logged the adventures of their journeys (see Figure 23.1).

Figure 23.1   *Wal-Marting Across America's now-defunct blog*

However, these weren't really just "two people" who loved RVing. They were the sister of an Edelman employee and her boyfriend, who was a professional photographer for a major East Coast newspaper. When this was reported, both Walmart and Edelman were taken to task for such a flagrant attempt to trick the public with a marketing tactic. It even hit the front page of MSNBC in October 2006.

Walmart's second attempt at social media didn't fare any better because the company still didn't understand that it couldn't control social media communities. In this lame attempt, they launched a social network aimed at teens called The Hub.

Unfortunately for the would-be members of The Hub, Walmart wouldn't let them join unless their parents approved it, permitted their children to message other members, and screened all posts. In addition to other restrictions community members do not have to endure elsewhere, it's no wonder that after launching in July 2006, the community was closed in October of the same year.

Finally, Walmart began to listen, and its "Checkout" blog has become a decent success. Similar to the "Nuts About Southwest" blog, which is written by real employees of Southwest airlines, Checkout enables Walmart employees to tell their stories and make announcements. One particular blogger got to announce that Walmart would be selling only BlueRay players going forward, which pretty much spelled the death of the rival HD DVD system.

It took three attempts for Walmart to exhibit transparency and build trust. Walmart has billions of dollars in its reserves. Not every company has that kind of money at their disposal to "waste" on such costly mistakes and foolish moves to try to manipulate an audience.

24

Audiences Trust Icons and Avatars

In Chapter 23, "Be Transparent: Trust and Readership Must Be Earned," I mentioned that branding with your avatars and messaging builds trust in social media communities. In this chapter, we look at this a little more deeply.

Icons and avatars (the terms are basically synonymous within social media communities) are images that help portray who you are. They provide a simple but effective way for people to visually identify with you beyond the text information in your profile. People eventually trust them as a symbol of an established relationship. Community members will also quickly note changes in avatars, especially if you frequently converse with them.

If your avatar is the same across all your social media communities, people who also cross-pollinate social media communities will easily identify you and trust that you are the same person with whom they have an established relationship in another community.

Choose Your Avatar Carefully

When you are first establishing your presence in social media communities, think carefully about the avatar you choose to represent your company. It's the first visual impression you'll make upon the community members you want to engage. As with a first date, first impressions matter. Decide whether that icon of Happy Smurf is the first thing you want people to identify with you, your company, or your brand.

Assuming that you are representing your business, the most logical approach is to use a form of your company logo. If you are representing an established brand instead of a company, use the most recent logo your brand is using in its messaging. If you are an individual representing yourself, you have a bit more freedom. But again, think about how this avatar will affect how people perceive you.

Sometimes using a photo of yourself is a great idea. You really can't go wrong with a professionally taken headshot for your avatar, but be careful of candid photos. What you might think is an innocent photo of a fun night out could offend someone so much that they won't interact with you. You might be unaware that your photo could offend some cultures or religions.

For example, you might really like a particular character from a movie, such as Tigger. You believe that Tigger represents you in a cute, bouncy, and fun way. However, if you are trying to establish a professional and authoritative presence in a community, using an animated avatar of Tigger most likely won't help you establish the authority you want to achieve. Also, be careful about using a copyrighted image or character in your avatars unless you have permission to use it.

Avatars create an emotional connection to other community members and contribute to the overall impression your company makes, regardless of whether that perception is accurate. Thoroughly investigate all your options before choosing an avatar, and ask a few colleagues to share their opinions about your avatar options. This quick check can be very helpful in the long run. Remember, your goal is to make a good first impression.

Your Employees' Avatars

Although you cannot control what your employees do on their own time, it's helpful to implement policies about avatars and icons, especially if employees list your company as their employer in their profiles. If employees are easily identifiable (spokespeople or other well-known positions) and they don't identify your company in their profiles, you could have another issue to address.

Although such employees aren't representing you officially, they are still making an impression on the community. In this case, a Tigger icon or avatar wouldn't be bad.

However, an avatar of a photo of your employee in a sexually suggestive pose could have some damaging effects.

Educating your employees about social media and its potential effects on your company is probably the first best step you can take. Working with your employees to establish policies around issues such as these can go more smoothly when everyone understands what's at stake.

It's a different situation when your employees are representing you within a social media community. In this case, they are directly interacting with community members on your behalf. Although you want to give them a little leeway to express themselves individually, you still want them to represent you in a way that is in line with your marketing and messaging. Some companies have merged a photo with a logo to clearly identify who the person is working for and also let community members know that this is a real person at the keyboard, not just some robot or automated account from the company.

If you have multiple team members representing your firm across many communities, having everyone use the same logo as their avatar can confuse community members. It also can hinder the trust- and relationship-building processes. If community members see multiple people with the same avatar, they could wonder who is really representing you, and who to go to if they want information. Enabling your team members to establish their own identities while representing you in the form of a more personalized icon or avatar will help in creating the connections you need to build solid relationships in social media communities.

Community Members and Their Avatars

It's important to take note of the people you are engaging with in these social media communities. Although your avatar can say a lot about you, their avatars can tell you more about them. Sometimes an avatar offers a clue to the type of personality you are dealing with and what that person considers important. Sometimes it can also give you an idea of how open or closed a person is.

Those guesses are all just generalities and supposition, but people's avatars are often a clue to what they are really like. If members are really proud of their families, you will most likely see photo avatars of them with their families. When community members comment on their avatars and say, "What a cute family," you can bet that touches them and makes them proud. This illustrates why it also pays to research the community first. The avatars people use can help you understand the community and the influencers in those communities.

Avatars are an easy way to identify members of one community who cross over to other social media communities. Humans are creatures of habit and are somewhat reluctant to change. Members of one community who interact frequently with each other are likely to congregate in other communities, and they often use the same avatar everywhere. The avatar a community member uses is the most easily identifiable feature of that member no matter what online social community they are in, this is why people tend to keep the same avatar across social media communities.

Another side benefit of watching and learning before jumping into a social community is that you can spot trends happening in these communities via the avatars people are using. Sometimes community members change their icons slightly to show support for a cause, highlight a special event, or even get into the current holiday spirit.

Consider an example from summer 2009, when the Iranian elections caused turmoil and political conflict about who was declared the winner. Protests ensued, unrest erupted, and support from around the globe appeared in many different ways. Twitter was one visible example: Members of the Twitter community changed their avatars to be shaded green, in direct support of the opposition in Iran, who claimed that color for its campaign.

They Remember

Because icons are meant to be visual cues, members of a social media community can easily commit them to memory. You might even see people refer to other community members by a nickname that comes from their icon, instead of by the moniker or username they have chosen.

People talk offline about the neat avatars or icons they see people using, especially if they've seen it somewhere else other than on the user's profile. People sometimes choose to use artwork as their avatars, which increases the likelihood that other community members will remember them. When you implement your company's social media marketing strategy, remember that community members distinctly recall avatars. Along with the messaging you are crafting, you should be thinking about your visual impressions to these audiences. If you are a marketer, you'll want to make sure they remember your branding.

If your company features many products or services but your main purpose for engaging in social media is to promote one particular product, consider using that brand or product's photo as your avatar. Although using a company logo isn't a wrong choice, a more effective choice is to use the particular brand's logo to help reinforce the experiences and passionate feelings your audience identifies with that particular brand.

When Should You Change Your Avatar?

Changing your avatar is sometimes appropriate. If you are working in social media marketing on a more personal level and you are using a photo of yourself, it's perfectly acceptable to change your avatar to new photos that reflect your current look. If you have a few pictures of your current look, switching them frequently keeps things fresh, especially when the face of the person really isn't changing.

However, companies being represented online by multiple people should think carefully before changing avatars. Companies want to establish a brand or presence, so maintaining a consistent look and feel is important.

If you make changes to your branding or logo (especially if those changes affect your marketing message), you should change your avatar, profile, or icon that you are using in the social media communities because those icons should reflect your current branding efforts.

Having Fun and Being Creative

Have a little fun and be creative with your avatar or icon. Individuals have more leeway because they don't have a published set of company philosophies they need to abide by, as companies do.

Companies also can be creative and can join the fun the entire community is having with their avatars. If the community is supporting a cause that is directly in line with your company's beliefs, consider investing a little of your graphic art team's time to modify your avatar to show your support for that cause.

You can also create holiday-themed avatars for your engagement in social media. This shows that the company has a "human" side and that you are willing to join in the community for more than just marketing purposes. Joining the community in something as small as an icon change can help build trust and relationships in these communities.

IV

It's Not About You

25

Give Up Control
and Drop the Ego

Traditional media agencies have typically controlled the marketing messages and their dissemination to the public, so it's difficult for them to embrace that marketing in social media is a totally different ballgame. Comparing traditional marketing to social media marketing is akin to comparing golf to rugby. Golf involves little or no contact (unless you get whacked with a golf ball). Rugby, on the other hand, involves full contact with opponents who can smash your face into the grass. Think of social media marketing as a game of rugby, without the striped shirts and sweaty jocks.

The idea of control in social media is a fallacy because you can't control what other people think, hear, see, or say. How they interpret your message and relate it back to their communities is also totally out of your hands.

The idea of managing your reputation within the social media environment is another fairy tale that public relations and marketing firms like to spin to their clients. It's an easy sell, too. A PR firm types in certain keywords and gets a listing of results from a search engine or a social media site, and they've got the client hooked. For example, see the listing shown in Figure 25.1 for the term "Comcast."

Figure 25.1   *Search results aren't always your friend.*

Comcast will most likely *always* be impacted by the item that (highlighted by the box around it) is currently ranking in the seventh position on Google search results. Because this is consumer-generated media, Comcast cannot control how many people see the video of its technician falling asleep on a customer's couch, nor can it control how many people rate it, comment on it, link to it, or embed it in their blogs.

However, Comcast can do something—and has done so with how it's perceived in social media circles. Frank Eliason, the primary voice of the "Comcast Cares" account on Twitter, has been working tirelessly to improve the company's image when it comes to customer service via social media. He's done so by conversing with people who have issues with all different types of Comcast service. He has actual conversations with the community as well and isn't pushing a marketing message.

Frank's efforts for Comcast have become so successful there are now other Comcast employees helping Frank with this effort. Recently, ComcastDete replied to me on Twitter about a tweet I sent regarding my move and transferring my Comcast service. Now that's proactive customer service!

Comcast is managing its relationships with people in social media communities, as it does in Twitter, as shown in Figure 25.2. That is the essence of social media marketing—managing relationships.

Figure 25.2   *Frank Eliason of the "Comcast Cares" Twitter account builds relationships with customers on Twitter.*

Some companies eventually realize that they don't have much control over how the public interprets their messages. Unfortunately for many companies, their egos get in the way and they focus on "getting rid of" or "quieting" the person who's been saying "bad things" about their companies. Taking that stance only makes others perceive them as "Goliaths" in a David versus Goliath situation. However, if you know the story, it took only a small pebble from David to take down the giant Goliath.

Control Is a Fallacy in Social Media

No matter how much you think you can control your social media message or how much your marketing or PR department tries to convince you they have it under control, neither of you is in control. Control is just a myth that companies believe will help build their brands.

Although companies might control how the marketing messages are originally placed in the public spectrum, public opinion determines how people will perceive the company. Until social media marketing, determining whether the public believed the message the company was sending about a product, a service, or even a brand was apparent at the cash register or in focus groups. Now companies can see how the actual audience is receiving their marketing messages. This enables companies to interpret public opinion and discuss it with the community even before a sale is made. However, the company has no control over that public opinion.

This type of buzz or talk happens organically. One person might start a conversation about how much he liked, loved, or hated a product, and the conversation just gains legs of its own. This is especially true if other members of a community have had similar experiences. No marketing or PR department can control conversations such as these—and if they tried to, the company would receive considerable backlash and more bad press.

Companies have a hard time grasping that they don't have control over these types of conversations or consumer-generated media because they're thinking about the old way of advertising. In the old way, companies had complete control over their messaging and how they were perceived. They could repeatedly push out that message without worrying about customer feedback. Aside from customers directly contacting them, no public record existed of customers' opinion about the messages. Everything centered on the companies and the messages they put out.

It's Not about You

Part of navigating reputation management is a term called *ego searches*. This term focuses on keywords that matter to a company and what ranks in the search engine results for those keywords. This could be a company name, a brand, a product or service name, or even the name of someone prominent in the company. A lot of companies pride themselves on ranking number 1 for their key terms, and rightfully so. However, what about all those people who don't even know who you are?

Although your company might be ranking in the top spots of different search engine results, more than a few conversations going on about your industry, or the category of products or services you offer, don't include your company name. These conversations won't ever rank in a search engine for your company's name, brand name, or product or service offering unless it is part of the name.

Consider a karaoke song–producing company. As an avid karaoke singer myself, very few "brands" stick in my mind of who produces the karaoke versions of the songs I sing. When I look up a song, I generally look up the song title attached with "karaoke" or "karaoke version." I don't ever use "Sound Choice" or "Pop Hits Monthly" because it's not about them—it's about the song I want to sing.

Figures 25.3 and 25.4 show recent results of a search for "Toes Zac Brown Band Karaoke" in Google Search and "Toes Zac Brown Band" in Google Insights. Only one karaoke company ranking appears for this result in Google, but the trend is rising for this song. People are interested in it and want to find it. The only social media site nominally capitalizing on this term is MySpace, with the video from Zac Brown Band's MySpace page.

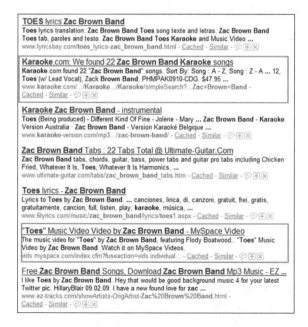

Figure 25.3   *Google Search Results for "Toes Zac Brown Band Karaoke."*

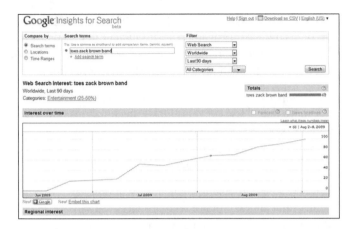

Figure 25.4 *Google Insights for "Toes Zac Brown Band" Showing a Rising Trend for This Song.*

What if the karaoke song–producing companies had used this information and produced a social media network or community that focused on genre or band songs that were available in karaoke? Could you imagine the type of traffic and revenue if they had?

Customers Now Own a Piece

Whether companies like it or not, customers now own a piece of them. When customers purchase a product or a service from your company, they have the ability to affect your bottom dollar. In essence, they own a piece of your bottom line.

The advent of ratings and reviews brought a whole new aspect of social media marketing to the forefront of what companies need to be looking at and caring about. If a company marketed a poor-quality product, it used to take a few weeks or months for the public to find out through TV, newspaper, or radio news reports. By that time, the company marketing the poor product most likely had already recouped whatever investments it had sunk into the production and marketing of the product or service, so the reports and subsequent sales drops didn't heavily impact the bottom line.

Unfortunately for companies who are manufacturing low-quality products or giving poor customer service, those days are over.

Sites such as Yelp, Angie's List, TripAdvisor, YahooTravel, and even Amazon can actually make or break a product, service provider, or destination spot. For example, if your company is in the travel industry, arbitrary conversations about you also occur in communities that aren't even related to travel. The scope can be so wide that you cannot cast a full net. The best thing you can do is attempt to manage the relationships that you have and that you can establish in social media communities.

Knowing what people are saying about you in social networks is vital, but responding to each of those conversations can be impossible. The key is to recognize consumers' power—recognize that they do own a piece of your company. Acknowledge it, embrace it, and use it to the best of your ability. Ask the customer to help you.

You Can't Control When Conversations Happen

Conversations about your company can be difficult for your own staff to manage without looking self-promotional. The moment you look self-promotional, you've basically lost all credibility, trust, and authority within the community you are engaging.

Trying to force a conversation when either the timing isn't right or customers just aren't the interested makes your company look like one of those lame marketing companies entering the social media space.

Community members talk about subjects as they arrive. You just can't enter into a community and say, "Hey, I'm here now, let's talk about me." It just doesn't work that way, no matter how much your CEO or Chief Marketing Officer (CMO) might think it does. Taking that approach can result in community members giving you a cold shoulder or possibly even banning you for "marketing" instead of participating.

It generally doesn't take long for conversation about your industry, category, brand, product, or service to form, especially when you aren't forceful about it. People are generally inquisitive. If you are new to the community and start engaging with its members, the evitable question of "What do you do?" will arise, and that's the perfect opportunity to start a conversation in a natural manner.

You Can't Control What's Discussed

The other part to this control equation is that you can't really control the conversation topics in social media communities. Try as you might to seed a conversation with a blog post or video on YouTube, you can't control the viral aspect of word-of-mouth conversations.

Although a blog post review on a blog you solicited to test your product might be initially about your product, you can't stop the community from talking about either how the competition stacks up against you or how great or bad the audience's experience with your product was.

To demonstrate how you can't control the conversations around your product, service, or brand, consider the ShamWow. Famous from late-night infomercials, this product is a "super chamois" that is supposed to soak up gallons of liquid in a relatively short amount of time. Although the company would really hope people are talking about the ShamWow's amazing feats in absorption, instead the conversations are about its pitchman.

Figure 25.5 shows the search results for "ShamWow." From blog posts to YouTube videos, people are talking more about the pitch man, and putting up user-generated content about him, than talking about the actual product itself.

Figure 25.5 *Google Search Results for "Sham Wow."*

It's important for marketers to realize that companies can't control messages in social media. You can craft the message to the best of your ability, hone it, fine-tune it, and send it out for public consumption. However, the audience is really in control in these social media communities, in how much value they put into that message, how they interpret it, and how they propagate that message to their own social media network. That's something no marketer or PR company can control.

26

You Need to Be All "Ears"

You've probably heard the old adage that you were given two ears and one mouth for a reason. As a child, I heard that adage often from my grandmother, but I never really understood it until later in life. It becomes more poignant when working with social media communities— although, in this case, our ears are our eyes because of the mode of communication that drives social media communities.

When it comes to delving into social communities, being humble works best—not shooting off your mouth and announcing your arrival with guns blazing. No one likes a show-off or a know-it-all. For example, in the offline world, you might represent a giant pharmaceutical corporation that controls a budget that is larger than the gross domestic product (GDP) of a small third-world country. You might think this makes you important. However, in

*social media communities, you are actually less impor-
tant than the mom who has taken the time to share her
experience of raising a child with autism. Just because
your company sells a drug that can help children with
autism doesn't mean people will automatically listen to
your message if you announce your presence to a social
media community. You won't have an immediate band of
followers. Building networks takes a lot of listening and
understanding to uncover the difference between what
people say they want and what they need.*

People Want to Be Heard

Dale Carnegie says in his little "Golden Rule Book" that the most beautiful sound to
people is hearing their own names. The same is true in online communities. People
want to be heard, and they want acknowledgment that they are being heard. That's
why listening is so important (as is dropping the ego). If you are too busy talking
about your company, proclaiming how it knows everything about the products you
produce, and announcing your new venture into social media, you'll never hear the
audience and what they really need from you.

In 2006, Dell created a blog to better interact with its customers. Instead of writing
articles about how great Dell products and services are, Dell realized that customer
service was the key issue (followed closely by exploding laptop batteries) that it
needed to address. Jeff Jarvis, a popular blogger (BuzzMachine.com) and columnist
for *Business Week*, had by this time coined the term "Dell Hell." The many comments
that appeared on social community forums and blogs was overwhelmingly negative. To respond to all this negativity, Dell launched a blog (operated by Lionel
Menchaca) and waded into the blogging world just as the issue of exploding batteries in Dell laptops was at its height.

Dell realized it had a huge issue on its hands well before the exploding notebook in
Osaka, Japan, hit Endgadget. In 2006, the company went beyond just listening to the
feedback through the website and phone lines, to actually using social media sites
to gauge what its customers were saying about Dell (see Figure 26.1).

Figure 26.1   *Lionel Menchaca, Dell's chief blogger, address the laptops catching fire on Dell's blog.*

Following is an excerpt from Dell's original blog announcement:

> Before we established a presence in the blogosphere, we had been read-
> ing your thoughts on Dell. Some posts were good, some were bad, but
> the most concerning were those that were from customers who had
> outstanding support issues. In April this year, we decided to do some-
> thing about it: We began monitoring blogs to find customers who
> needed help from Dell support. We use a mix of common tools like
> Technorati and de.licio.us along with some internal apps to track these
> efforts.
>
> (Dell Customer Advocates in the Blogosphere, July 25, 2006)

Since that time, Dell has taken its social media strategy to an entirely different level.
Dell launched IdeaStorm, which enables customers to submit their ideas for new
products. Dell also uses its Dell Outlet Twitter stream not just as an RSS feed, but
also as a conversation engagement tool. Dell has learned that listening to the customer in social media is one of the most important things it can do.

You Learn the Lingo

You might call your products one thing and refer to what they do or how they perform in a very specific way. This creates a reserved vocabulary known only to the
organization's insiders. Your audience likely has no clue about this company-specific
vocabulary. Your customers refer to your products in a way that is most comfortable
to them. It works by word-of-mouth first; then it travels to the Internet. It's important for companies to know how their customers refer to them and their services.

For example, my Pennsylvania hometown isn't far from where Yuengling Lager Beer
is brewed. In Schuylkill County, we're pretty proud of the fact that we're home to
America's oldest continuously operating brewery. At one time, Yuengling was sold

only in Pennsylvania, New Jersey, and New York. However, Dick Yuengling, the current owner, expanded that sales area and also expanded the line of beers Yuengling brewed. In the early 1990s, the company began brewing what has become the very popular Yuengling Lager.

Being from Schuylkill County, we never called it "Yuengling Lager." To us, it was always just "Lager." People from around the county would travel in all directions from Schuylkill County to see how far they could go and still get a Yuengling Lager by simply asking for a "Lager." As the years went on, the lingo for "Lager" meaning Yuengling Lager spread geographically. Each year, you could go a little farther north, east, south, or west and get a "Lager."

The same is true for any product or service. If your customers are nicknaming or shortening your brands, product, or service names, it's because they feel comfortable with them, like them, and want to easily share them with other like-minded people. McDonald's became MickyD's, Coca-Cola became Coke, the Tampa Bay Buccaneers became just the Bucs, and Buffy the Vampire Slayer became BotVS in forums and blogs alike.

It's possible that the lingo your customers use is very different than how you and other members of the industry refer to your company or products. Something as inane as "LOL" (Internet shorthand for "laughing out loud") is a perfect example of comfortable lingo. Lingo is an easy way for audiences to converse with like-minded people, and the only way you learn what lingo your audience is using is by taking the time to listen to the conversations taking place in social media communities.

Listening Can Help You Avoid Disasters

A few years ago, Kryptonite (a bike lock company that catered to the bike messenger industry) encountered a situation in which a customer discovered a flaw in his new bike lock. Chris Brennan, a network security analyst and bike enthusiast, posted a warning on www.bikeforums.net stating that Kryptonite's new U-Lock was not secure because it could be picked open with only a ballpoint pen. (These threads have since been removed, but the website features a directory of videos on the subject.) Unfortunately for Kryptonite, the company either wasn't watching the forum or chose to ignore it. Not only was this issue newsworthy to *Wired* magazine and *Engadget*, it also made the front page of the *New York Times* in September 2004.

Videos of how to pick these locks spread across the Internet from video share sites to blogs. The word was out to not trust Kryptonite bike locks. In an interview with *Wired* magazine, Chris Brennan said Kryptonite's response to rush a new product to market instead of replacing the faulty locks customers had already purchased was a "slap in the face."

"They're looking to profit from a series of mistakes they made," Brennan said. "They need to replace their faulty product." He also added that he wouldn't purchase another lock from Kryptonite because he no longer trusted the company.

 Note

For more information, see the article "Twist a Pen, Open a Lock," at www.wired.com/culture/lifestyle/news/2004/09/64987.

Brennan sharing the video and his experience with Kryptonite was powerful. Had Kryptonite been paying attention or addressed the claim when it arose in the forum, the company might have averted the firestorm that ensued and nearly destroyed it.

Listening to your customers can help you in ways you might never fathom. Customers are very willing to share their ideas and experiences with you and members of social media communities.

The added advantage to listening to your customers interact in social media communities is preparation. Often you can catch wind of both good and bad situations with your products or services before the stories hit the mainstream press.

Social Communities Are Your Best Focus Groups

By listening first, you can learn so much more than "tainting the pool," so to speak, by announcing your arrival in a community. Listening can open your eyes to so many possibilities that you would never have known about, as well as help you avoid taboos and things not to do or say. By observing a community, you learn the lingo and also discover what your audience really thinks about your company.

Traditional focus groups can be quite flawed. People know they are being brought in for a reason, either to test something or to give their opinion about something. People want to be "right" and will always try to please the person or company by answering the way they think you want them to answer. This really doesn't happen with social communities.

Communities share their experiences—good, bad, or indifferent—with one another. They share tips and tricks on how to use your product or service. They share other forms of media about your product—maybe a photo or a video of how to use it. This can be a totally uninhibited way to learn what people are thinking about, sharing, and saying about your product.

Focus groups can cost your company many thousands of dollars to set up and run. Making matters worse, traditional focus groups often result in responses that are only moderately reliable. However, monitoring social media communities costs far less and likely saves time and resources. You do need to plan for your resources to monitor the social media communities that are discussing the topics that interest you. That means you need to do your research into where those conversations are happening. Then it's just a matter of listening to what those communities are saying.

Don't Just Hear—Listen

Hearing and listening are very different activities. Listening involves comprehending and understanding what the other person is saying. By listening, you get beyond the surface of hearing, which helps you get to the audience's pain point and find out what is most important to them.

It's similar to when someone says to you, "Did you hear that new Bon Jovi song?" Sure, you likely heard it on the radio a few times and you can immediately say, "Yes." But then your friend says, "Did you listen to the lyrics?" Now you have a totally different scenario because listening to the lyrics means that you had to actually understand them and comprehend them, instead of just whistling along to the catchy melody or tapping your foot to the funky beat. The hearing and listening scenarios are similar in social media communities, too.

When Dell began listening to all the complaints about its customer service, it didn't just hear "Your customer service sucks." The company listened and tried to understand why people were saying that customer service was poor. Dell learned that Dell product owners were frustrated by being transferred to help desks in India and talking to technicians who have hard-to-understand accents, which made their issues even more frustrating to resolve.

If Dell had only heard "You suck" or "Your customer service line stinks," it might have thought a number of things were wrong before even stumbling upon the fact help-desk operators were difficult for Americans to understand. However, when Dell listened to its customers and learned that the language-barrier issue was repeatedly discussed in blogs and on forums, the company began shifting help-desk calls back to the United States.

By listening through social media channels—whether using the Direct2Dell blog or Idea Storm, or just listening to complaints about its customer service line on blogs and forums—Dell was able to decrease the negative sentiment around its products and customer service. As Lionel Menchaca stated in his interview with Geoffrey Livingston's Buzz Bin in July 2007, "closing the loop [listening to customers' feedback and actually doing something with it] is the most important aspect of digital media for us."

A Different Vested Interest

Your customers have an entirely different vested interest than your CEO, your marketing team, or any other employee in your company. Although you have employees who are committed to your company's success and are proud of the products and services they are responsible for, their vested interest is entirely different than your customers'. Your customers' view of what's important, what doesn't work right, and what's truly valuable about your product can be totally different than what your company views as valuable.

A social media community is an excellent place to gain this knowledge. The people in these communities share without expectation. They might have agendas, but they generally aren't political in nature (unless it's a political forum), compared to those of your employees, aimed at getting more budget dollars for their departments. Social media communities have a vested interest that's totally free of that, which means their vested interest is their free time or the money they earn to purchase your product or service.

Your audience doesn't have to share their experiences with your company with other people in their free time, but they do. They don't have to buy your product when money is a bit hard to come by, but they do. They are investing time, energy, sweat, and maybe even a few tears in your product or service.

If you don't take the time to listen, you won't have any idea just how valuable your product is to your audience. You won't understand what vested interest your audience has in your company. Is it the time they spent putting together recipes using your product to share with others, or was it the expense of all the other ingredients along with your product for making the recipes they are now showing off in videos on YouTube or photos on Flickr? If you don't take the time to listen and instead just assume, you could end up insulting the very people in the community who could be your biggest advocates.

As my grandmother always told me, "God gave you two ears and one mouth for a reason."

27

Your Customers Know Your Products Better Than You

You might be the creator of your products or services, and you might think you know everything about them. If so, you're likely fooling yourself. And you might push marketing to your consumers about how wonderful specific features of your product or service are, but your customers likely aren't talking about those features in the social media communities.

This happens because users can value features differently than you might expect.

In social media, you must discover what the end user finds most valuable. Your customers use your products or services in their everyday lives. They might know a trick or two that you didn't think of when you sat down with your marketing team to create your latest marketing strategy. Your customers know the faults and limitations of products and services because they are spending money to purchase them and are using them in their everyday lives.

You can say that your product has been field-tested and that it has gone through tests for endurance, tolerance, and use. However, all that testing matters little if one person in a social media community says, "It might have been tested for endurance, but when I used the product, it failed." Your customers might be using your products in ways you never even considered. Unfortunately for you, it doesn't matter that a customer might be using your product in a way that you define as practical. All that matters is that the customer has used your product and is reporting its failure on a social media site. That particular user's experience will speak louder to a group of avid users in a social media community than any marketing claims to the contrary. You need to listen to your customers. You might just learn a thing or two about your own product or service.

Customers Know Things You Don't Know

Although you've invested a lot of money into product research, development, and marketing to create the perfect product or service that people will want to buy, the people buying your products are using them in ways you might not expect. People adapt product and services they like into their everyday lives in ways you can't predict.

Take for example Avon's popular product "Skin So Soft" oil. When Skin So Soft was first introduced to the market by Avon, its intended use was as a skin softener. It became one of Avon's top selling products and to this day is still one of their top selling products.

Over the years, other uses of Skin So Soft have made their way from "wives tales" to common popular uses. One of the most famous is as a mosquito repellent. As a child I can remember my mother (who by the way is very active on Facebook!) slathering us up in Skin So Soft to ward off those pesky mosquitoes. Eventually Avon listened to its customer base and started to include this fact into some of its marketing. By embracing it's customer's ideas Avon found another market to which it could appeal—the mom's wanting to protect her kids from itching all summer long (not to mention some avid anglers and hunters who swear by its mosquito repelling abilities).

The reality is, you don't know how your customers will use your products or services. You don't know how they will embrace and repurpose your marketing, either. Because your product might be used in a way you'd never imagine, part of your social media strategy should involve listening and learning.

You need to decide whether you want to acknowledge the other uses of your products. You don't always need to acknowledge these alternative uses, nor do you need to work them into your marketing. However, you should be very aware of how your customers are adapting your products or services to fit their needs.

There are a lot of other uses for Avon's Skin So Soft oil. It's even blogged about as shown in Figure 27.1. From removing head lice, to being and ant killer, it's likely that Avon won't incorporate all of these uses into its marketing efforts. But if Avon even went to the step to either highlight the blog post that the *eHow* author Meagan Morris wrote (http://www.ehow.com/about_5451826_uses-avon-skin-soft-oil.html) or comment on the post, it could influence both Avon's current customers and the *eHow* readers in a very positive manner.

Figure 27.1   *eHow author Meagan Morris write about several uses for Avon's Skin So Soft oil beyond softening your skin.*

Understanding and accepting that you might not know everything about your product or service is tough. However, if you listen, you might learn that your customers' alternate uses of your product can inspire your company to create new lines of products, improve faults, correct issues, or even find a new niche market for your product or service.

Your Employees Know Things You Don't Know

You and your employees might not realize it, but employees can also be a wealth of knowledge in knowing how people are using your products or services. If your employees are active in social media communities outside of work and identify themselves as being employed by your company, members of a social media community will share their experience with them.

Your employees might not be involved in marketing, product production, or even customer service, so they might not share their information or experiences with anyone at your company. Everyone in your company has a stake in your social media efforts, but you might miss opportunities such as these every day if your employees aren't involved with your social media strategy.

The majority of your workforce is not in executive management, so they are likely far removed from the major decisions that propel companies into success or oblivion. But this can be a good thing for your social media strategy and your company, because higher-ranking, more powerful members of a company tend to intimidate the average consumer. High-ranking power creates one of three reactions in the average consumer:

- **Pure worship**—Apple CEO Steve Jobs is a good example

- **Complete hatred**—Donald Trump is a good example

- **Discomfort**— Not everyone knows how to act around "high-powered" people.

Because most people want to interact with people on their own level, your employees have an advantage over your executive management team when it comes to being successful in social media.

Your staff can relate on a one-on-one basis with your customer base better than any of your senior management can. Customers feel they can relate because they are on the same level as the person at the other end of the keyboard or phone, if your employees are representing themselves as just employees of your company. Relating to the "average Joe" is easy when customers also consider themselves to be average Joes.

When consumers or audience members relate to your employees on this level, they tend to be more open and trusting. They tell your employees more about the ins and outs of your product than they would ever share with a member of your senior staff. Customers do this because they might distrust authority or, in a worst-case scenario, they might not like a member of your senior management team. Your employees can learn more about your product than you'd ever know, which is why you need to make sure that all your employees understand what you are trying to accomplish with social media and that you ask for their help in executing your strategy.

Don't Be Afraid of Mashup

You've might have heard the term "Mashup" a few times in recent years, but it's possible you don't know exactly what a mashup is. Essentially, a mashup is a mix of two or more products. Often, these mixes are subpar, but some are extremely useful or at least interesting enough to reach cult status—or "go viral," as you'll often hear. Some examples that come to mind are:

- Google Maps mixed with Real Estate Information became Zillow.com

- Diet Coke and Mentos Experiments became EeepyBird.com Viral Videos

- Apple's 1984 television advertisement for the Macintosh plus Hillary Clinton became the Vote Different YouTube Video (http://www.youtube.com/watch?v=6h3G-lMZxjo)

Sometimes when companies learn how customers are using their products or services, they immediately go into "all defenses up" mode and try to squash the consumer movement through cease and desist orders—some even go as far as lawsuits. In the world of social media, taking this action can spell a PR disaster for your company.

The Internet has changed the idea of total control over your products and services, and even the marketing around them. Your customers and your audience own and control a piece of them, even though they are not compensated for it.

Consider the mashup example from above of the Eepybird guys—Fritz Grobe and Stephen Voltz—who took the Internet by storm in 2006 with their mashup of Diet Coke and Mentos. Their video, a choreographed fountain show using Diet Coke and Mentos, was shown on Jay Leno, David Letterman, and many morning shows, and was featured on video-sharing sites such as YouTube, blogs, and forums around the world (see Figure 27.2). In a word, it was cool.

Figure 27.2 *The Extreme Diet Coke and Mentos Experiments video by the EepyBird guys has been viewed nearly 12 million times.*

Mentos thought it was cool, too. The company embraced this mashup phenomenon and even sponsored a contest asking its customers to submit their experiments with Mentos and Diet Coke. In interviews, Mentos stated that it valued this free publicity at as much as $10 million in free publicity that it didn't have to shell out for and in turn to its marketing bottom line. However, Coke didn't initially embrace this mashup, saying to the *Wall Street Journal*, "We would hope people want to drink [Diet Coke] more than try experiments with it."

Eventually, Coke came around and embraced this mashup phenomenon, but it was long after the initial buzz and free publicity had died down. The company lost the opportunity to prove to its customers that Coke was still "it."

Give Them Ownership

When the first message boards appeared on the Internet, giving people the capability to create their own content about anything they liked or didn't like, companies lost their grip on total control and ownership of their brands, products, and services. Not until a few years later did consumers and companies realize the power that this held for both sides.

Consumers feel empowered that they have a stake in the products they love. Some create new marketing ideas without expecting compensation. Some create mashups. Some become evangelists just because they feel they their experience with the product or service enables them to do so. All these examples are forms of ownership. Companies need to not only be aware of it, but also embrace and encourage it.

Yes, this involves an element of risk, because consumers can say something bad. But as stated in this book, people will say something bad online or offline. It will happen. By encouraging your customers to claim some kind of ownership of your products, services, or brands, you foster a sort of "Ugly Baby Syndrome"—a baby isn't ugly if it's yours.

Your customers will want to help you. Your audience will want to give you feedback to improve your product. Your audience, if given the opportunity, will want to be part of something bigger so they can say to their own communities, "I was part of making that." We all want to belong. It's rare to find a person who just wants to live out life alone in a cave somewhere on the edge of a desert. By embracing that your customers and audience want to be part of something bigger and allowing your customers some form of ownership, you are creating opportunities to reach more people and make your company better.

28

It's All About the Idea

Everything we know started with an idea—an idea to make it easier to communicate across many miles, an idea to make illuminating the dark easier, an idea to make it faster to get from point A to point B. Without these ideas and people acting upon those ideas, we could still be living in caves, and hunting and gathering our food. Humans thrive on ideas, and communities thrive on expanding those ideas and making them realities.

Every day on the Internet, hundreds of thousands of people have ideas that they share with like-minded individuals in social media communities. Before the advent of message boards and forums, it was pretty tough to communicate one idea to a global community. However, with one post in a community forum, someone on the other side of the globe can share an idea in mere milliseconds. By sharing these ideas, cultures, communities, and even individuals are becoming more skilled at actualizing these ideas because the community helps improve them.

Wikipedia is a great example of this process in action. Wikipedia is a public database of sorts in which anyone can create or add to a definition or explanation of nearly anything imaginable. Want to know the history of the *Titanic*? Wikipedia has an entry for that. Want to know the win–loss record of any of the Iron Chefs? Wikipedia has an entry on that, too. Wiki users are encouraged to flesh out entries with facts, citing books, magazines, and web sources. Ideas start with one person, but the community as a whole helps actualize ideas (if they're worthy) and improves on them.

 Note

Wikipedia isn't without it's flaws though. The "authenticity" is always called into question as the information provided isn't verified by a fact checking entity. Because of this, most educational institutions have banned using it as a source for papers and research citations.

Small businesses often get their start via social media. An entrepreneur might use social media to seek advice from other like-minded individuals. Perhaps the entire idea was borne out of an experience on a social media site. Many ideas that become business models are culled from discussions in small-business forums that can help solidify a business plan, or from niche-industry communities and bloggers that can help inspire marketing to reach potential clients.

Everyone Has Ideas

Even the most remotely located individuals on the planet have ideas. They might not be able to share those ideas easily, but they have them. Sharing ideas is critical for pushing societies forward. It's key to creating new products and services that improve communities. It starts with a little encouragement after the sharing of an idea. An idea can start from something as simple as a post reading, "Hey, I have this idea to improve…." If the community members respond with encouragement and suggestions for refining the idea, a business model or a new product can spring forth very quickly. From there, it's off to the races—a plan is born, a product is launched, and a brand becomes an icon.

Although everyone has ideas, the social media communities have truly become the incubators for developing these fledgling ideas. Whether the idea centers on improvements to a service or a product, or on ways to market a product or service, the encouragement and feedback given in social media communities can help ideas grow into reality. Social media communities foster this type of development because of the ease of communicating with like-minded individuals.

You Might Not Have the Next Great Idea

The key theme throughout this book is that social media, and marketing within social media, is not all about you. I've discussed how you need to lose your ego and that you don't always know your product as well as you think you do. You really need to be open to the possibility that your customers might often know it better, and they communicate that through their interaction and sharing of experiences in social media communities.

The same holds true for the next great idea for improving your product or service, or even for marketing to your audience. Those ideas might not come from you. They might come from your audience members, who are sharing their ideas on how to improve, mashup, or integrate the things they already love about your product or service. The key is to not only listen to your audience about these ideas, but also encourage them and foster an environment that helps these ideas flourish.

Before becoming the Federal Chief Information Officer (CIO) of the United States of America, Vivek Kundra understood that the best ideas commonly come from the community. He also realized that these ideas could be better implemented and improved upon through the community when he was Chief Technology Officer (CTO) of Washington, D.C. While in this position, he turned to Peter Corbett of iStrategyLabs, and they launched the Apps for Democracy program.

This program enabled the community to develop ideas utilizing the city's 311 open Application Programming Interface (API). The program encouraged the community to build applications, websites, portals, and other ways of accessing the city's 311 data into useful applications that could benefit both Washington, D.C., and the people who lived and worked within it. At the end of the program, prizes were awarded for the various ideas that were turned into applications, websites, and so on. The results were amazing.

From applications that enabled people to report potholes on city streets via iPhone, to ways to help fix the city's parking meter issues, the program was deemed an overwhelming success. These two example applications weren't even the winners. One of the winners was an application called iLive.at, which enables visitors to enter their address (Washington, D.C., only) to get information about the area. From crime, to demographics, to transportation, and more, users can find out in one very neat and concise display everything that Washington, D.C., knows about that particular residence.

These applications were developed only because Kundra realized that he alone didn't have all the great ideas. He alone couldn't get all these ideas developed and launched into actual working programs that could benefit the taxpayers of Washington, D.C. Understanding both of these circumstances—especially that he wasn't the sole provider of great ideas for Washington, D.C.—he fostered an interactive social media community with the help of Peter Corbett and iStrategy Labs that encouraged the ideas to blossom into reality.

The Next Great Idea Could Be Your Boon

As demonstrated with the Apps for Democracy program, Washington, D.C.'s boon wasn't just one idea—it was several. Not only was the parking meter application a hit with people who had to park in D.C., it also helped uncover a major issue with how the parking meters got fixed. When parking meters were reported as broken, it took an average of five to six days to have a meter fixed.

Something interesting happened when Apps for Democracy was launched and Shaun Farrell developed the Park It DC application for the contest (see Figure 28.1). Washington, D.C., learned that it had a contract with a vendor to repair broken parking meters within 24 hours of the report. With that knowledge, the city went back to the vendor to address this underperformance issue, and now the parking meters are being fixed within the contracted time frame.

Figure 28.1 *Park It DC was an application written as part of Washington D.C.'s Apps For Democracy program.*

The idea that could become your boon might be something as simple as those coffee sleeves that prevent your fingers from burning when the coffee cup is too hot.

You need to be open to ideas that aren't your own—and, most important, you need to be listening to the conversations where these ideas are being discussed.

For most business-minded people, accepting that the next big idea might come from someone other than you or your company can be hard. However, encouraging members of a social media community to share their ideas for your products, services, or brands can help bring success to your social media strategy more quickly.

Embrace the Out-of-the-Box Thinkers Who Contribute

When Washington, D.C., launched its Apps for Democracy program, it got many out-of-the-box ideas. One could argue that every idea was "out-of-the-box." As Corbett explained at the Open Government and Innovations conference in Washington, D.C., in July 2009, the applications entered into the contest were all interesting and definitely not straightforward, government-type applications.

Development Seed (a D.C.-area communications company) created one app called Stumble Safely that married the Washington, D.C., 311 data in a way most people wouldn't have considered. The program crosses local crime reporting with locations with valid liquor licenses (see Figure 28.2).

Figure 28.2 *The Stumble Safely application was created for the Apps For Democracy project.*

Some might think this program is designed to avoid being arrested for a DUI. However, it's more than that. The Stumble Safely app helps people avoid dangerous areas when they are out late at night, possibly after having a few drinks. Social media embraces this type of out-of-the-box thinking. No one can be right all the time or have all the best ideas. Sometimes it takes the most "out there" idea to spawn some of the best ideas for improving existing products or creating new products.

Sometimes Even the Simplest Ideas Work

The winner of the Apps for Democracy contest was DC Historic Tours. The app helps visitors (and natives) plan tours of historic sites around DC in an efficient manner. It was so simple and fun that it just "worked." Sometimes that's all you need—a very simple idea that you can't see because you are too close to your products or services. An outside set of eyes can see the simplest and easiest routes to improvement or the next level of success.

Unless you are tuned into the social media communities that are talking about you, your industry, or your products or services, you will likely miss these conversations that can result in some simple but powerful ideas. Perhaps the idea is as simple as adding a pink version of your product for the month of October in honor of breast cancer awareness and donating a portion of the proceeds to the Breast Cancer Research Foundation.

The idea is simple, but you might've missed it unless you were paying attention in social media forums. Sometimes ideas are spawned from the simplest conversations if you're listening. Sometimes listening to what people are saying even when it might not relate directly to you product or service can be results in those ideas that just work.

29

Your Content Must Have Value

If you are just putting content on your site to rank in the search engines, don't expect that content to be of much value beyond the ranking you've attained. Search engine optimization (SEO) experts often suggest that you create blogs, web pages, or even forums just to claim dominance in the search engine rankings for your most valuable keywords.

Even if you rank well by implementing some of these SEO marketing tactics, what good is it if the person clicking on the link sees your content as totally irrelevant and not valuable? All you will have managed to do is align the term worthless to your search engine ranking and your site (at least, for that keyword).

Value is one of the central components to creating content that will get audiences to interact with you in social media communities. Without value, you will get the inevitable "So what?" Getting that "So what?" means that

you aren't engaging or even piquing the audience's inter-
est. You're just another schmuck marketer attempting to
sell another bill of goods to the community you are trying
to engage.

If you listen to what the community finds valuable and
design your content around that, you'll get a lot more
interest from the audience you are trying to reach. By cre-
ating valuable content for your audience, you give mem-
bers of a social media community a reason to think,
"Wow, someone's actually listening to me and giving me
what I need." People are amazed when companies actu-
ally take the time to listen and create things their audi-
ence requests.

The End User Decides the Value of Your Content

The person who is reading your blog, engaging with you on a forum or message board, watching your video, or looking at photos in your photo group on Flickr is the person who deems whether that content is valuable to him or her. You cannot make that decision for anyone. For example, if members think that your video is only a marketing piece without any value, they'll do one of two things:

1. Stop watching before the end and move on to find more valuable content

2. Comment on how bad the video is and then move on to other more valuable content

Unfortunately for most marketers, most people perform the first action, and the marketers don't get the opportunity to understand why the viewer didn't find the content valuable. At least with the second action, marketers can begin to understand why either the content offended the viewer or the viewer didn't find it valuable. If you are producing content, don't fear those negative comments—embrace them and learn from them.

End users can assign value in many different ways, but generally your content is either filling a need or easing a pain point for them. People tend to talk more about content and share what they find valuable with others when the content fulfills their need or solves a problem.

You might make assumptions about your audience. However, don't assume that your audience's needs are similar to your own. It's vital to research the communities you want to engage and create content for.

Just because your product has a certain feature doesn't mean it's filling a need. Audiences won't necessarily find all your product's features valuable. However, if you write a blog post about how to utilize your product to achieve a specific result, then you are creating valuable content for customers. That means your customers will probably share that information with their friends who also use your product.

A good example is the ShamWow, which is a chamois that supposedly has superabsorbent features that make it superior to all other chamois on the market today. As the company's spokesman says in the product video, "It's made by Germans, and you always know they make great stuff." The company makes this same claim in product literature and marketing pieces (see Figure 29.1). As a consumer, I could care less who makes it or how great the company claims it is.

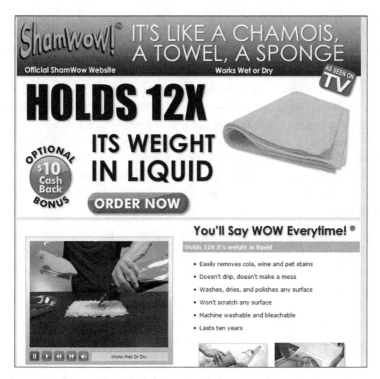

Figure 29.1 *Is the company that markets the ShamWow missing out on social media marketing opportunities?*

I think the most valuable feature about the ShamWow is the part of the video when soda is poured on the carpet and the ShamWow soaks it all up, including the liquid down into the carpet padding. That's valuable because it hits a pain point with me, having spilled many liquids on my carpet. I've shared the video with friends and family and said, "Isn't that cool? It soaks up everything down to the carpet padding!"

The company that makes ShamWow doesn't really tout this as one of its features, but maybe it should. The fact that it even brings up the brown color of the soda is another feature that someone could find valuable. It could do the very same thing for a glass of wine spilled on carpet, which would be valuable to wine drinkers.

Listen to Your Audience to Produce Valuable Content

The key to producing valuable content for social media communities is to listen to your audience. The focus might be something that is slightly removed from the actual purpose of your product or service. This valuable content might also come in the form of instructions for using your product in a way that you hadn't originally intended. However, by listening to your audience, you will be able to pick out topics, themes, and issues for which you can create valuable content.

For example, consider a company that sells prom gowns. Although this company might think its main target audience is teens, that assumption might not be true. First, if the company created a blog devoted to prom gowns, that blog would have limited value because the audience is talking about prom gowns only from December to March (according to Bill Tancer's research in his book *Click*). Second, just talking about a particular design isn't really valuable and unique content. The audience can find that content on many other fashion blogs. So what would they find valuable?

If you listened to the conversation in social media circles, you'd likely find that comparing styles to the trends on the red carpet, as well as integrating those comparisons with photos and videos, would be highly valuable to your target audience. Focusing solely on the prom gowns on the racks of your store is valuable only to your company. However, your audience will be much more interested in content that answers the question, "Can I buy a dress that is similar to the one Drew Barrymore wore to the Emmy Awards in September 2009?"

What You Deem Valuable Could Be Worthless to Your Audience

You might think that your PDF spec sheet of the 20 top features of your product or service is the best thing since sliced bread. You've spent hours designing the marketing look and feel around it. You want to make sure that it's on your website and is put into every sales packet that goes out. You believe this is the most valuable piece of content to sell your product.

Unfortunately, you aren't thinking from the end user's perspective.

A list of specs and features doesn't help end users if they can't figure out how to use your products or services. Companies often mistakenly believe that adding more bells and whistles to their products is what customers find valuable. However, most customers don't use the bells and whistles that have been added because the company thought they were cool. Customers use the product the way it gives them value—and, most of the time, the bells and whistles aren't what provide the value.

Listening to your audience discuss the best features of your product should give you insight into how to give them valuable content. It can also help you improve your marketing efforts to reach more people. Using this kind of knowledge can be a tremendous boost to your social media marketing efforts.

Content isn't just about text, either. Content can take many forms. A simple video showing how to use the basic features of your product can become an invaluable resource to a new customer. And after watching the video, your audience will talk about how easy your product is to use. They might even share it with their friends, which can lead to additional sales.

Audio can be just as compelling because your audience might not have the time to sit and read your blog or watch a video. However, they might have time to download a podcast and listen to it on their drive to or from work. In this case, podcasts can become a very valuable resource to the audience that is short on time during the day, but has time on their commutes to listen to an interview with an expert about the latest research in your field.

Although you might think that the content you're providing to your audience or customers is very valuable, you should take the time to listen to them in social media communities. However, be prepared if you come from a traditional marketing background in which slick ad pieces or literature was your way of communicating. You'll find that those don't work or aren't welcomed in social media communities, and your audience will let you know that right up front. Audiences aren't afraid to tell you if your content is just plain crap—or is truly the best thing since sliced bread.

Valuable Content Is Portable

If it's important to make sure that your content is valuable, then making sure that valuable content is portable is essential. By "portable," I mean content that is easily sharable. Allow your content to be placed in Facebook or MySpace, shared via

Twitter, saved on bookmarking sites, or even sent via email to friends. If your audience finds value in what you are providing, they will want to share the experience with their friends.

You will need to do your due diligence to determine the best ways to make your content portable for your audience. Every audience is different. Some like to use social bookmarking services, and others like to use Twitter to spread the content they find valuable to their audiences. Others might find that submitting your content to social news sites is the perfect way to share their experiences. You should research this first instead of putting up buttons on content that cover every single social media site under the sun as applications in Figure 29.2 show.

Figure 29.2   *Share This type applications which overwhelm users actually hinder people from sharing your content because they have too many choices.*

Giving your audience too many choices for portable content is a sure way to kill the portability. When people are faced with too many choices, they end up not sharing it. Research what tools your audience uses (social bookmarking, social news, and so on). You want to make sure your content is ending up where others will find it valuable.

Although it might seem really cool to have a Share This button on your content that enables users to choose everything from Mixx to Bebo, your visitor will likely take one look at a screen such as this and blink, hit the X, and not bother to share it—you provided too many choices. Do you know if your audience is really using Bebo? Why present that as an option and waste both your time and your audience's by presenting options that aren't valuable or viable?

Take the time to research where your audience posts valuable content for sharing. Select the top three or four social media communities and use those as options to share. You'll see that your audience shares content to these sites more often than if you offered many places to share it.

30

Sharing with Others Is Key

Tim Berners-Lee invented —the protocol that enables us to surf websites—to create an easy way to share information with his fellow colleagues via the Internet. At its core, the Internet is about sharing. Whether its recipes, comics, health information, events, or photos and videos, the essence of what we do on the Internet is about sharing.

Social media communities embrace this and actually take it to the next level. In addition to encouraging members to share via conversations, most social media communities encourage their members to create and share content with other members of the community. Other members are then encouraged to share their thoughts about the content and create their own. This creates an ongoing cycle of creating and sharing.

People in social media communities aren't just sharing their experiences; they're also sharing their knowledge. Forums and message boards are a great place to see this in action. Community leaders, who have been involved with a particular community for a longer period of time and have acquired an incredible amount of knowledge about their particular topic, are generally the people who lead this charge. These community leaders are ready and willing to help out when a community member asks a question or seeks assistance.

The old way of marketing did not allow for a lot of sharing or two-way communications. TV, radio and newspapers were all one-way devices that allowed companies to put a certain message out there. Companies were never really privy to what customers truly thought or even how they used their products or services in their day-to-day lives. Before social media, companies weren't in on the conversations consumers were having about their brands, products or services.

However, social media has changed all of that. Marketers can now listen, understand and even share themselves, which is a concept that can seem very foreign to the classic advertising agency.

Members of a community are sharing both good and bad experiences. If members of a social media community have a bad experience with your company or product, they will probably share it. One community member will warn others, in hopes of helping the rest of the community avoid the same bad experience.

People Want to Belong

We all want to feel that we are a part of something—whether it's a family, neighborhood, group, or community. The sense of belonging is ingrained in all of us. Before the advent of the Internet, we fulfilled that need to belong by joining groups that met in person, such as sewing clubs where members discussed everything from new sewing techniques to their daily lives. Unfortunately, these types of clubs had one major limitation: geography. Before the Internet, it would've been pretty tough for a sewing club in Osaka, Japan, to share ideas with a sewing club in Sarasota, Florida. When the Internet grew in popularity and availability, many clubs and organizations began to form online. Online groups enabled like-minded people from around the world to share the things that were important to them. Now a sewing club in Sarasota can just as easily interact with a similar club in Osaka as they can with a neighbor just down the street. Being a part of that can be quite exciting, especially for members who have barely ventured out of their county or state.

This is important for any business or marketer who is entering the online world. Even the smallest of companies can take full advantage of these kinds of situations. By recognizing that your content and information can be shared globally is important. People like to share content and information that is valuable to others, especially in online communities. This gives people a sense of belonging because they are contributing valuable information. By providing and sharing your company's information you are affording others the opportunity to feel a sense of belonging. That in and of itself can be a greater reward than the satisfaction the person even gets from buying or using your product or service. You've given them the ability to "look good," "belong" and "gain respect." These are things people remember.

Most social media communities foster the spirit of "Come and join us," encouraging people to belong to their community because it's special. You might have a special hobby, skill, or passion that only a small portion of the global population shares. By joining them, you're part of an exclusive club where you can share your experiences with like-minded people who share the same interests.

As an online marketer, my skill set is particularly peculiar. I come from a programming background but also have a degree in public relations. I fit in well with the data analytics professionals because I used to program both Oracle and MS SQL databases. I fit in well with the programmers on IT teams because I used to build web applications for clients. I can move from technical topics to marketing with ease. However, very few of my friends and family members really understand what I do for a living and cannot relate to my "industry" clubs. Their eyes often glaze over when I start rambling on about how you can improve your online marketing strategy. To feel a sense of belonging and not feel so ostracized by my friends outside work, I belong to a few online social media forums and a pretty active Twitter community. This fills my own sense of wanting to belong to something bigger when it comes to one of the passions of my life. I'm not alone. Hundreds of thousands of people every day connect through social media communities. Doing so helps them fulfill some aspect of their lives that friends and family don't.

People Share What They Love

I have a passion for online marketing—particularly social media marketing, as evidenced by this book— and search engine marketing. I love what I do for my clients, and I love to share what I do. I share my passion for online marketing through several different avenues in social media. One avenue is my blog, SearchMarketingGurus.com. On my blog, I speak to topics that fascinate me but that also might get my ire up. I also share my experiences through my photos that I post on Flickr. Another way I share my passion is through videos I create, giving viewers tips on how to improve their online marketing.

You might think I have a lot of spare time on my hands to do all this, but in actuality, I don't. I'm just like every other person working a job. I just put an emphasis on finding a little extra time to share what I love to do with a community who wants to learn from my experiences.

I'm not alone. People will make time to share their experiences if they can do it in a simple and easy way. For example, consider people who collect Legos. People who are passionate about Legos take this interest very seriously—regardless of their age. Forums and fan websites are dedicated to this topic, promoting how they have used their Legos. People are creating SlideShares that show off their Lego creations, and we aren't just talking *Star Wars* or *Indiana Jones* replicas. Fans have created Lego structures that emulate the characters from the *Harry Potter* movies, sports stadiums, and even animals. A church in Stockholm even created a statue of Jesus made of Legos—that's how passionate people are about Legos.

The great thing about all this is that Lego encourages this type of community involvement. The company wants people to share their creations. However, it wasn't easy for Lego to reach that level. At first, the company was a bit skeptical when it entered the social media space. Jake McKee, who was the social media practitioner with Lego, challenged the company and changed its culture to embrace these types of actions in social media. (Blip.TV has the video of McKee's presentation (see Figure 30.1).

In the presentation, McKee speaks to the audience about how Lego's interaction with its adult customers, who make up 5% of the company's consumer base, changed how the company approached all its consumers. Lego realized that these adults were sending powerful messages to other potential Lego buyers. McKee cites the fact that five adults who love building things with Legos could come to a mall and create a 25-square-foot Lego train set that was just awe inspiring. During one weekend, 20,000 people saw this Lego train display. Kids, parents, and grandparents said how awesome it was, and the kids then wanted to buy some Legos. Now that's a powerful conversation that Lego wasn't initially involved with or encouraging.

Figure 30.1   *Former Lego employee Jake McKee talks about how Lego started using social media to its advantage.*

People want to share what they love. If you listen to your audience, you'll learn what they love about you and your products, services, and brands. It's a conversation that you should not only listen to, but also encourage.

When Someone Is Disappointed, They Want to Share Their Pain

Disappointment comes from high expectations. People come to rely on your product or service for certain aspects of their lives. Your product could make their lives more productive in some way, or your service could bring an added bright spot to their hectic lives. If in some way you fail to consistently deliver on your previous expectations, you disappoint your consumers.

When your consumers are disappointed in your company, they tend to share their disappointment with people who can relate. Before the social media boom, those people shared with their families and friends. However, with the rising popularity of social media communities, your consumers can share their disappointment in your company with the online communities they belong to and reach many more people. The opportunity to share their pain and be comforted has widened from the intimate network that people previously took comfort in to a more global community.

On the surface, it can be easy to overreact to negative comments about your company. It can be even easier to decline to participate in social media, for fear of inviting the negative. It's important to know that most members of a community in which your products or services are being discussed probably had some affinity for your company or product before making negative comments. If you take the time to participate in social media, you'll find that it offers you the opportunity to repair damaged relationships and make that previously negative customer happy again.

The restaurant chain Houlihan's experienced something akin to this when it first opened the doors to its Houli-fan community. According to Jen Gulvik, who presented for Houlihan's at the Word of Mouth Marketing Association (WOMMA) WOMM-U in May 2008, Houlihan's had removed the fajitas from its menu. The company made this decision because these fajitas were a nightmare to make operationally and were not a top seller in all the restaurants. In passing, Houlihan's heard that its customers were upset that the fajitas were gone, but the company didn't pay much attention to it.

When the company opened its social media community, it unexpectedly heard a lot more about the topic. The community loudly voiced its disappointment of the fajitas being taken off the menu. Something about the way these fajitas were made had people begging for Houlihan's to bring them back. Although no one in Houlihan's wanted to bring back the fajitas because of the operational nightmares, the company did it anyway because the community voiced its very adamant disappointment.

Houlihan's first told its community that the company was bringing back the fajitas and admitted, "We screwed up." By listening to the customers' disappointment and admitting it had messed up, Houlihan's ingratiated itself with its audience even more and has created a very strong customer loyalty—especially toward the fajitas, which are now top 10 sellers in most of its restaurants.

Sharing Smiles Is Gratifying

Sharing information is always important and valuable. Just as valuable and probably more gratifying is that feeling when you make someone smile or laugh. Sometimes it's just a matter of inspiring someone in the right way, to make all the difference in how they view you and your company in the social media space.

This is also why sites such as I Can Has Cheezburger and Upside Down Dogs are extremely popular social media communities. They make us laugh and smile with their truly funny interpretations of what our pets are doing (see Figure 30.2). Fun videos, photos, and playful but valuable information can do the same thing. The content you share with the community doesn't need to be stone-cold serious all the time.

Figure 30.2 *People love to share "smiles," as evidenced at ICanHasCheezburger.com.*

People want to know that your company has a beating heart and that real people who care work for your company. Sharing a smile, a "laugh out loud" experience, or a touching story doesn't mean that your company loses its edge. On the contrary, it makes your company more appealing to interact with in the social media communities.

It's perfectly fine to share an occasional smile such as these. Each company needs to think about where it draws the line on what kind of content is shared and how often the company shares it. Going overboard can have just as bad of an effect as not sharing. It's a matter of researching the community's limitations. You will also learn "unwritten" rules after you become involved with the community.

You Give a Piece of Yourself by Sharing

People who are in social media communities want to share. By sharing, they are giving a piece of themselves to a greater cause. To most people, that's a very fulfilling feeling. People want to connect with others who are willing to do the same. They really don't want to connect with an "entity," such as a company name. (Entities can be rather cold—and, more important, how does an "entity" share an experience?)

Social media communities want to connect with the people who make up your company. They want to share a piece of themselves with other people. Whether it's their story of how your company's product improved their lives or how your service made them smile, they want to share it with you—you the human being, not the name on the sign of your building.

These online social media communities also want you to share—not just information about how this product is made or what improvements you are slating for the upcoming year, either. They want to know a little bit about you—the people who make up your company. Do some of your employees help out at an animal shelter once a year? Then let the community know—take pictures and videos, and even feature an animal or two that needs to be adopted. Share a piece of what makes your company unique with the audience.

It shows you are human, and that's who people in online communities want to share their experiences with.

31

For It to Work, You Need to Be Social

Many agencies lead their clients to believe that a success-ful social media campaign is a simple matter of building a profile or putting out a social media release. Unfortunately, the companies that buy into that flawed way of thinking become seriously disheartened and even-tually give up on social media marketing because they were led to believe it was that easy and quick. Who wouldn't want to step into the social media pool and swim a few laps if all you need to do is build a profile or send out an email about your social media release?

Contrary to what these agencies lead you to believe, social media isn't the easiest marketing tactic to imple-ment. It actually goes against the grain of traditional mar-keting that has pushed out the message without any interaction or feedback. Social media marketing requires engagement and involvement on both ends for any inkling of success to take root. You need to be social, which means getting out there and actually conversing with your audience.

Social media's heart and soul is its community members sharing experiences. However, that sharing can't happen without conversation. If you represent a company that is considering introducing a new version of its software aimed at a certain niche market, how do you know if it's really needed unless you ask your audience? Lurking in social media circles and listening to what your audience has to say isn't enough. If your audience doesn't know your company is thinking about a new product, you won't know what your audience might think of it. However, if you are actively engaged in the community, you can freely ask, "Hey, we're thinking of adding this version of software to our line. What features do you think would be great to include?"

You Can't Just Lurk

If you are in the early stages of implementing a social media strategy, lurking in the communities that are talking about your industry, brands, products, or services can teach you a lot—it's great for the research phase of your strategy. You can learn how your audience talks about you, what's important to them, and what you can get away with and what you can't. You also learn how comfortable your customers and audience are with you, what lingo they use to refer to you, and what they think of your competition and the industry.

Learning the ins and outs, the winning ways, and the taboos can save you a lot of headaches when you are ready to implement your strategy. The beginning parts of any social media strategy should include a lot of observing—it's the only way to know how to implement your strategy.

Although lurking is great for research, you need to be more active when implementing your strategy. Social media marketing is about being social, which means no hiding in the corner. Being social requires active engagement. Occasionally posting content won't cut it. As we discuss in the next section, you can't just "set it and forget it."

"Set It and Forget It" Doesn't Work in Social Media

Putting up a company profile on Twitter might draw a few friends or fans, but if you don't do anything to support your social media presence, you will likely find that the only fans and friends you acquire are spam accounts looking to get a reciprocal follow back. Marketers who are more concerned with the number of Twitter followers they have than true marketing engagement use automated software to friend new accounts, hoping to get new followers in return. However, these types of accounts are usually spam—they rarely hold any valuable conversations in Twitter.

However, it is a wise move to secure your company's name in the different social media sites, even if you don't plan to immediately enter them. If you decide to give social media marketing a try, you'll be glad that you thought ahead. However, just having the accounts won't do anything for you beyond keeping cyber squatters from benefitting from your brand. Setting it up and forgetting about it won't result in any engagement in these communities, no matter how your agency might claim it's "good for SEO". The search engines are becoming wise require more than just having a Twitter account with your brand name as a ranking factor.

You can personalize some accounts or stylize them around your brand, product, or service. Take a look at the Facebook fan page for the Travel Channel's *Man vs. Food* show (see Figure 31.1). The Travel Channel's strategic thinking prompted this fan page. The company stylized the page to match the show, the company regularly posts relevant content to the page, and, best of all, it converses with its audience.

Figure 31.1 *Stylizing your social media accounts to reflect your company or brand is a smart move.*

If you plan to claim profile names now and possibly begin an earnest social media campaign later, take the time now to fill out the profile with the basics—especially your contact information. If you are more active on some social media platforms than others, add a note to the less active ones indicating where you can more readily be reached.

Just Because You Built It Doesn't Mean They'll Come

Just because you build a social media presence doesn't mean that you are guaranteed fans and participants. Much to the surprise of many companies, social media marketing doesn't just happen because you want it to. Although the magical baseball field in the movie *Field of Dreams* attracted long-dead baseball players, you can't expect your social media presence to magically drag in followers.

It takes much more than just slapping up a MySpace page or sponsoring a community forum to get true engagement. That whole "social" element is a big part of what separates success from failure when launching your social media strategy. Engaging the community is key, so it is imperative that you research the social media communities before launching any type of community or engagement strategy. Doing so will help your social media team know exactly how that engagement needs to happen.

Marketing and promotion also come into play when forming your social media strategy. How do you get the word out about your new community or Facebook group? Natural word of mouth and the viral spread of content helps, but you also must think strategically about how to inform other groups of influencers about your new social media venture. How do you engage them to get them interested enough to participate and possibly spread the word?

Although you will need to do some promotion about what you've built, you don't want to overdo it—your audience could be totally turned off. You need to strike a balance between doing self-promotion and getting your audience to help promote your efforts. Doing your homework and researching the communities before you launch a campaign helps.

If you have done your research, you'll likely find that your audience isn't at just one social media site. Because your audience is at more than one social media site, you need to consider more than just one kind of social media effort. If you have a Twitter account and just launched a forum, tell your followers. If you have a Flickr group, but also have a message board about the same subject, make sure to point your active group members in the direction of the forum.

Conversation Requires At Least Two People

It's tough to have a conversation with yourself. If you aren't listening to your audience, how can you hold an informed conversation? How can your audience view your actions as something other than standing on a soapbox?

Blogs that don't offer the community the opportunity to comment really aren't social media communities. Consider Seth Godin's blog at www.sethgodin.com (see Figure 31.2). Although Godin is a profound marketer and I enjoy reading his books, I don't classify his "blog" as a true blog because he doesn't allow comments. He doesn't interact with his community, which can turn off members of a community. Many people have stopped reading Godin's blog because he doesn't communicate—he just "shouts from the marketing pulpit."

Figure 31.2 *Is this really a blog?*

Godin wants you to socialize his content. He accepts trackbacks and wants you to save his posts on places such as Delicious and Stumbleupon. However, he isn't interested in hearing your thoughts on what he writes. In the spirit of social media and engagement, that's not really social and it's not a conversation.

Marketers who don't have book deals or the biggest names on the "marketing" block find incredible respect and large communities when they engage in conversation. These communities will even come to the defense of such bloggers.

Beth Harte, who writes the blog "The Harte of Marketing," consistently has more than five comments on each of her blog posts. It's not uncommon to see 25 or more comments on a single blog post she writes because she also converses with her community. Harte has built a great following and community because she talks to the people who comment on her posts. When another blogger took issue with

Harte's appearance on a panel at an industry conference, her community came to her defense by pointing to several different references and posts that Harte made. That's what being social is all about in social media.

It Isn't All About Your Content

When it comes to conversation and engaging in social media, it isn't all about you and your content. Conversations can get started around content that you have found and that you want to share with your audience.

Perhaps you are a blogger, or you are thinking about engaging with other bloggers. Sometimes starting a conversation with key influencers in a community won't start with something from your marketing plan. You can start a conversation by sharing a link to another blog entry, a video, a photo, a podcast, or even a list of recipes. Although it might not be your piece of content that gets the conversation started, your act of sharing it with your community can be an icebreaker and gain you the respect you need to build those key foundation relationships in these communities.

The biggest thing to remember when it comes to social media strategies is that it won't work unless you are actively being social.

32

Ask the Audience

An important part of your social media strategy should be to engage your customers, evangelists, and a general audience who might be interested in your products or service. One way to do that is to just ask questions. The key here is that when you are getting started with a social media strategy, your questions shouldn't be all about you, your products, and your brands or services. The questions you ask first should be geared to learning more about what brings your audience to the community and why they feel so compelled to participate, engage, and share.

Everyone has a story, and most people in these communities love to share their experiences, whether they are joys or pains. By asking the members of these communities to share their stories with you, you are taking the time to listen, which many marketers forget to do. Marketing in social media is so much more than just slapping up a Facebook fan page or opening a Twitter account. Realizing this from the beginning of your strategy will help you immensely when you start to engage with community members.

By taking the time to not only ask, but also listen and understand their answers, you glean information that can help you in the implementation of future social media marketing tactics. Also, you are letting the community see that you are giving, too. Most community members will recognize and appreciate the time it takes to ask and listen. In fact, you'll find that most community members will respect you for the effort you are making, as opposed to chiding you because you shove a marketing message in front of them every time you appear in the community.

Established members and the influencers of these social media communities are smart, too. As described before, they can smell a fake a mile away. You can't repeatedly ask the same question of every person in a social media community. Remember, community members talk to one another, and your questions will likely be public, too. Anyone within the community can see what you are up to, and if your actions don't seem genuine, you can bet those members will call you on your actions and most likely ask you to leave. Listen to the community, learn who the key influencers are, and then ask questions.

Personalizing the questions is important, too. Keep in mind that every member of a community came to that community in a unique way. Sure, some of them might have found the community through a web search, but the reasons they chose to join the community and share their thoughts are different for every one of them. The single common denominator is the passion they have for whatever the community is focused upon.

You Always Want to Hear Why They Love You

Asking why your audience loves your brands, products, or services too soon can kill the opportunity to establish a solid relationship with a key influencer and possibly create an evangelist for your company. Don't jump too soon by asking community members why they love your brands, products, or services. Members could interpret this as evidence that you care only about your company, a potential turn-off to the community.

There's time enough to get to these types of questions after you've built the relationships and engaged on a more personal level with the community members. It's always best to ask the members about themselves—establish a relationship with them and *then* ask about your company. Doing so helps establish the fact that your social media efforts aren't solely about professional gain.

Just as important is the way you pose questions about your company to a community. If you ask every member of the community, "Why do you love our Blue Widgets?," you'll quickly become annoying within the community. Asking the question in a different manner every time and tailoring it to each person you ask shows that you have been listening and engaging, and that you aren't just there for market research.

Pay close attention to every member's stories, their pains and their joys, and then work that information into the way you ask the question. For example, let's say you're discussing your key product with someone who joined the community through a referral from another member of the community. You might start your conversation with, "Hey, Bob, I know you got to this community when Jane recommended it to you on Twitter, and I know Jane really loves using the Blue Widgets in her scrapbooking business. What I'd really love to hear about is why you find our Blue Widgets so handy, because I know you aren't into scrapbooking."

By incorporating bits and pieces of what various community members have shared with you into the question of "Why do you love us?," you focus the question on them, not you. You're showing that you aren't just there to continually push a marketing agenda. Instead, you've shown that you are there to listen and engage with members. That's what matters to community members, and that's what will get them to engage with you on a more regular basis.

Don't Avoid the Reasons They Don't Like You

So what if the community doesn't like you? What do you do if a community is upset with your company and is talking negatively about you? Do you avoid asking why? Many companies would rather avoid the situation altogether than ask why a community is so dissatisfied. Doing so means many companies will miss the real opportunity to understand and correct what might be causing them to lose customers. The Kryptonite Bike Lock company that I discussed earlier in this book is an excellent example of what can happen if you ignore a chance to use social media to talk with angry customers. Had the company engaged its social media audience from the beginning, they could have avoided ensuing PR nightmare.

Avoidance gets you nowhere in social media communities. That being said, simply joining a community and saying, "Hey, we're here to fix your opinion of us" most likely won't get your very far, either. Just as you would do when determining what people love about your company, you need to sit back and listen for a while. By doing so, you will learn what has upset the community and you'll likely learn how to approach the situation.

You might find that the community isn't upset about your product. Maybe members are upset about your phone support. Maybe your salespeople haven't delivered on promises of product improvement. Worse still, maybe your customers really are frustrated because your product or service isn't living up to what's advertised. Often the problem boils down to frustration, lack of education, or even lack of good customer support.

I was a fan of GoDaddy.com until March 2010. At one time, I often recommend GoDaddy for domain registration and hosting services. However, I experienced some technical issues with three of my domains not resolving, which concerned me as I could not see any reason as to why this should've happened so suddenly. I contacted the customer service number and was told I would have to use the online chat. What ensued was a nightmare experience. The online chat technician was totally rude and treated me as if I were stupid. The customer service line representative told me the issue was something I had to fix myself. In my frustration, I turned to my Twitter community to find some help. What happened was that many people also started voicing their issues with GoDaddy as well and offered me some great alternatives to my hosting and domain resolution issues.

I wasn't upset with GoDaddy's products. I was upset with their customer service, especially on the chat line and their lack of willingness to help me. I also found the same issues with others in my community. If GoDaddy had been listening, they could have learned some valuable lessons about how their online chat technicians were handling situations with customers and possibly could have turned the situation to their favor.

If you take the time to understand what's causing negative reactions to your company or its products or services, you will gain tremendous insight into things your company might be missing because you are way too close to your own products or services. Listening and then carefully approaching and engaging the members of the community is important. The approach has to be direct yet tactful—and if you haven't spent some time listening, your approach will be that much more difficult.

Consider starting a conversation with something like this:

> I've been listening to your conversations and the others in the commu-
> nity, hoping to understand what my company can do to improve our
> relationship with customers like you. I was wondering if you could share
> with me the experience you had with <company or product name>?

Be taking this approach, you are being transparent and honest while identifying
that you know there's a problem. This approach shows that you are listening and
that you want to know more. By asking your detractors to share, you can learn a lot
more—and possibly even turn them into fans.

Domino's took this approach to heart at the end of 2009 and beginning of 2010.
They asked their community what it thought of Domino's pizzas. What they learned
was many people didn't like it. They received some very negative comments, including "It tastes like cardboard." By listening to their customers, they learned their
products were seriously missing the boat with customers when it came to pleasing
them on taste. Domino's listened, changed their recipes, and launched a new campaign around their efforts. The campaign involved both online and offline efforts
through their "Oh Yes We Did" site at www.pizzaturnaround.com.

Ask the Audience How You Can Improve

Not only can your detractors help you improve, but your most stalwart fans can
help, too. There's always room for improvement, whether big or small. You'll be surprised at how willing your audience is to share thoughts—if you take the right
approach.

You'll also be surprised by how different people use your products in ways you
might not have considered. If you engage both the influencers and followers, build
solid relationships with them, and ask them how you can make your product better,
you can get a lot of insight into areas you might have overlooked otherwise.

For example, Dell started Idea Storm, which allowed people to submit ideas and
vote on products or services Dell could implement (see Figure 32.1). An overwhelming amount of the audience requested Ubuntu Linux options made by Dell
in February 2007. Dell hadn't planned to produce Ubuntu Linux software in the
near future, but because they listened, they ended up partnering with Canonica,
Ltd., in May 2007 to offer their customers laptops and desktops with preinstalled
Ubuntu Linux 7.04 (see Figure 32.2).

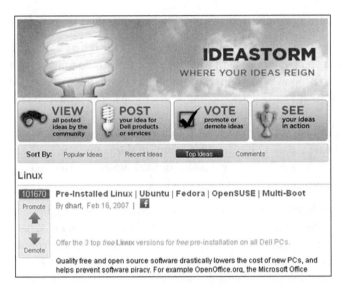

Figure 32.1 *Dell's Idea Storm allows people to submit and vote on product and service ideas.*

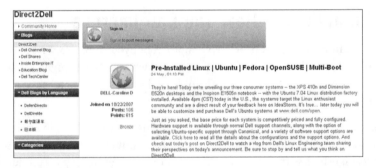

Figure 32.2 *In just a few short months, Dell's open-minded approach led to a partnership with Canonica, Inc., to offer computers with Ubuntu Linux preinstalled.*

Give Credit Where Credit Is Due

Many companies ask for feedback and think that a free coupon, a gift certificate, or a sample of their product is the best way to reward the person giving the feedback. When working with social media communities, these forms of rewards aren't that special. They're the everyday stuff customers can get by calling the number on the bottom of the receipt your store produces when they buy the product.

Community members—especially the key influencers—prefer acknowledgment and special treatment. Remember, they've done a lot more than the person a surveyor stops in a store for a quick five-minute survey. They've shared their time and their experiences with you on a more personal level. They've also lobbied other people to provide their opinions, giving you a compelling reason to implement changes. Consider providing acknowledgment in the form of publicly saying, "It's because of Bob, Jane, and Simon's input through our conversations in this community that we've implemented these changes."

After you've publicly acknowledged the key people, continue to treat them special by making sure they are the first to try a new product or service. Then go one step further and send them a thank-you gift that has nothing to do with your product, but is something you know (through the relationship building you've done) they would really enjoy.

33

You Get What You Give

If you represent a company that has been led to believe that social media marketing is the quick and simple way to overnight marketing success, you are most likely in for a rude awakening. The truth is, the less you put into your social media strategy, the less you will see in return. The more unique, fresh and valuable information or content you give your audience, the more value you will see in the return. The more time and investment of resources (both in research and creation of content) you invest, the more you will surpass the goals you'll set in place.

The "set it and forget it" idea doesn't work in social media marketing because social media requires engaging, conversing, and being social. Communities grow and blossom into engaging, virtual think tanks when key influencers drive conversations and community members actively engage and contribute. You need to invest a lot of time and resources to reach that point.

Success with social media marketing is similar to the Golden Rule—do unto others as you would have them do unto you. If you don't want to invest the time and effort into talking to people in social media communities, then you can't expect them to just start talking to you or about you. If you can't invest the time and resources into keeping a fan page going, then you can't expect your fans to stick around, either. You get what you give in social media.

Community members are smart people. They recognize when a company has made a real effort to be genuine and giving. They also recognize when someone is trying to short-change them for the company's gain. In each situation, the community reacts in kind. If they feel that you don't value their time by simply making token efforts such as posting low value coupons and not actually investing your time, your audience won't take the time to listen to you or engage with you when you make that token effort.

You Need to Invest Your Resources

Everyone's time is valuable. When you are engaging with other people in social media communities, recognizing that their time is just as valuable as yours is important. By giving your time to listening and understanding, you can earn a lot of respect. Community members reward that respect by giving some of their time to share their thoughts, feelings, and experiences. If you think spending 2 minutes answering questions with one or two sentences is engaging with the community, you won't get very far. Taking the time to answer someone's question or sharing your opinion in a one- or two-paragraph reply demonstrates that you are viewing them as valuable, because you've invested the time to reply with a personalized answer or comment.

Creating a Twitter account and letting it run on an RSS feed so that it populates with "conversation" won't get you very far. The same goes for creating a Facebook fan page and letting it sit there waiting for fans to appear. Running your social media strategy this way means you aren't investing what's required to establish real relationships.

You need to make investments to get true value out of any social media strategy:

- Time to research where the conversation is

- Time and resources to develop a strategy

- Time and staff resources to engage community members

- Time to listen to what they are saying in the communities

- Time and resources to measure successes and failures

Recognize the pattern: You must invest time and resources if you expect your social media strategy to succeed.

Giving Valuable Content

To provide valuable content, you must invest both time and resources to discover what your audience will likely find most valuable. Do that and you'll most likely find that your reward is more than you expected.

By taking the time to create content that appeals to your audience and the communities you engage with, you are sending signals to these people that you are listening to them. You won't need to say, "Hey, we are listening to you." That will become very apparent if it's something the community has been asking for.

Providing valuable content can produce many rewards. From forging stronger relationships with influencers who will help your content go viral, to reaching out to new audiences who find your content just as valuable, taking the time to invest in developing content your audience wants is an investment well spent. As you invest more in creating the content that people want and find valuable, your audience will share it with others because they want to be known as members who not only recognize value, but also share it willingly.

It's Similar to a Bank Account

When you start off in social media marketing, you need to make investments to get it off the ground before you see any kind of return. Similar to a bank account where you deposit your money, you don't see an automatic overnight return on your investment. It takes time for that return to accumulate.

Building trust takes a lot of time and investment. But when done in a genuine and transparent manner, over time you will find you've gained a lot of relationships with key influencers and, most of all, you've earned their trust. When people trust you and feel they can rely on you, you have snapped in a very important piece of the success puzzle in social media marketing.

Depositing your time and resources into your social media strategy is important. It's also important to measure your return. You need to make sure you are investing wisely and earning the return you expected. If neither of these is happening, you might need to invest some of your resources elsewhere, to see if you can achieve better gains.

Don't Bribe the Community

You shouldn't pay for someone's friendship. Trying to bribe the communities you want to engage isn't a wise step. The communities are smart—they recognize this kind of action as insincere and begin to doubt your intentions.

By offering to pay someone to be your friend—whether that's by monetary means or by sending them free samples of your product without even knowing if they are a fan—you are missing the entire meaning of social media. Social media is about freely sharing, freely engaging, and freely interacting without reward. Most of the people who make these communities their homes don't do this for money. They do it for the companionship of knowing that they aren't alone and that other people enjoy or feel the same way about something that they do.

Rewards Come in All Fashions

As I discussed in Chapter 30, "Sharing with Others Is Key," Houlihan's restaurants created an exclusive community for its "best fans." Jenn Gulvick also shared another success story Houlihan's had with its Houli-fan community that involved "asking the audience" (see Figure 33.1).Houlihan's first invited its community advisers and then community members from its Houli-fan community, if spots remained, to help them "test-drive" the new seasonal menu that Houlihan's was planning to roll out in the near future. The whole point of this effort was to reward the community advisors and key community members for their participation in a special way.

The community members who accepted the invitation were allowed to bring a guest with them to their local Houlihan's restaurant for a free dinner. All Houlihan's asked in return was for the participants to complete a survey about the menu itself (look and feel) and also about the new items on the menu they were asked to try. Houlihan's went a step better by creating special name placards that indicated the table was reserved for a member of the Houli-fan community.

Figure 33.1 *Houlihan's restaurant is a prime example of social media marketing done right.*

At the time Gulvick delivered her information about Houlihan's efforts at the WOMMA event in May 2007, which was only 2 weeks after it launched, the company already had 600 participants in the effort. A third of those participants had filled out the survey, and 35% of those participants were spreading the word about the new menu. This was a beneficial investment of time and resources for Houlihan's and a great treat for the advisors. They got to try out a new menu before anyone else, and Houlihan's also made them feel extra special about doing it.

Houlihan's HQ community works because it's a network invitation. To become a Houli-fan, either someone from Houlihan's or someone involved in the community must invite you. This definitely gives the community that "special" feel, and it gives Houlihan's the opportunity to engage with an audience that is very focused on a central topic—Houlihan's.

Houlihan's really understood its audience, because the company was paying attention in social media circles while this audience discussed the restaurant. The company used this information to gain more feedback while also providing something of value to each member of the community.

As discussed in Chapter 30, Houlihan's listened to the community about removing fajitas from its menu. The company admitted that it was wrong and the community was right (giving credit where credit is due). Houlihan's rewarded the audience by not only bringing back the fajitas, but also crediting the community for the action. Houlihan's understands that investing in engaging its community, asking them how they feel, and rewarding them in a relevant manner are the keys to the success of the company's social media community.

Here are a few rules learned from the Houlihan's example:

- Research who your audience is
- Give your audience something valuable and/or exclusive
- Don't expect you'll know everything
- Listen to what your audience says
- Admit when your wrong
- Thank your community

V

How Social Media Fits into the Online Marketing Picture

34

People Do Not Want to be Marketed To

Before the Internet arrived, audiences had to endure listening to or seeing advertisements repeatedly. The advertisers were in control of the media that people watched and listed to. Audiences were captive to the messages marketers wanted to push on them as they watched TV, listened to radio, or even drove down the highway.

Then in the mid-1990s, along came VCRs, Tivo, and the consumer Internet, and the entire landscape changed. No longer were audiences forced to sit through commercials to get to the content they wanted. No longer did audiences have to endure seeing or hearing an advertisement seven times within the same hour of programming during their favorite shows. Audiences could search for what they wanted or fast forward through commercials and ignore the "noise" of marketing to get to the information or content they were seeking.

After being marketing to for so long, people are largely weary of advertising. Tired of the claims that each product is the "best," audiences are now turning to communities of likeminded individuals to learn more about the products or services that interest them. In social media communities, people share the "truth" and learn about the real-world experiences others have had with products and services. Social media provides a forum for people to get this information in a natural and more honest way than having marketing messages constantly shoved in front of them.

Now that social media is on the rise and traditional advertising seems to be not quite as effective as it used to be, marketers are looking for new ways to reach their potential customers. Even though social media in concept has been around since the inception of the Internet, marketers have only recently started discovering the possibilities of reaching their target audiences through user-generated content sites and social media communities. The problem is, these users and community members are now in control and don't want to be drilled with marketing messages anymore.

Foisting the same marketing tactics on a social media community that you used successfully five years ago during TV, radio, or print advertising campaigns won't fly in these communities. It's been tried numerous times, and it notoriously fails. As some of the oldest forms of social media, forums and message boards have been able to weed out the "marketers" from the true community members. Many of these social media communities have strict guidelines in place about pushing marketing messages because they've had to deal with the onslaught of marketers thinking their communities are just another place to post marketing messages.

Only There to Push a Marketing Message? Beware!

I recently had the pleasure of speaking with the administrator of the Denver group of the MomsLikeMe.com community. Moms Like Me is a tight-knit group of moms of all ages who get together, mostly based on geography, to discuss subjects that matter most to them. From setting up playdates, to adopting families for Christmas, to ensuring that those less fortunate have a nice Christmas holiday for their kids, the community members of Moms Like Me around the country not only discuss and communicate about topics, but they actually pull together and do things that matter to them as a whole.

When talking to the administrator for the Denver group, I was curious to hear her take about how she and other members felt about marketers coming into the community just trying to "sell" things.

"I personally don't like it, and I know the community doesn't like it, either," Garcia-Gerdes said. "We work really hard to keep those kinds of marketers out. Only the ones who want to really hold a conversation with us do we interact with. The marketers who only want to push their messages of 'buy this' or 'buy that' don't last very long in Moms Like Me."

Warm and Fuzzies Versus the Cold Artic Shoulder

When a new member of a community first attempts to push a marketing message, he or she generally receives a warning to refrain from such activity. If the marketer continues actively marketing, the community usually boots that person out.

Each and every forum has rules—both written and unwritten. The written ones, if violated, could get you banned from the social media community. Violating the unwritten rules will leave you feeling like you're in Antarctica rather than the fun, warm, and sharing community you first discovered. That's why going into a community with marketing guns blazing is a bad idea. Understanding the community and how it functions, as well as how the members interact with one another, is vital.

Some communities tolerate some forms of marketing, but you aren't going to understand how much or how to approach this unless you take the time to research it:

1. Read the rules.

2. Study the community.

3. Most importantly, engage with the community members on a genuine interest level.

Communities dedicated to your brand, product, or service, or even industry type tend to be a bit more tolerant of marketers entering the community. To some degree, it's almost expected that eventually a company representative or even a competitor's representative will show up and start participating in the community.

For example, take the "Flyer Talk" community. There's a representative from Starwood Hotels who has been frequenting this forum for years. The representative has even won awards for his genuine participation and efforts in Flyer Talk. If you have a question about the Starwood Hotels Rewards program, William Sanders, who has gone by Starwood Lurker for years (since 2000), is there to help (see Figure 34.1).

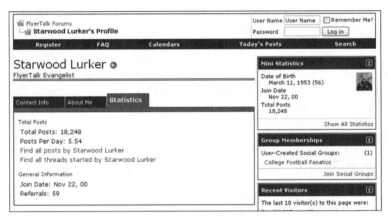

Figure 34.1   *Starwood's Starwood Lurker's profile in the FlyerTalk Forum, is an example of a transparent account set up by an employee engaging in social media.*

Neither Sanders nor Starwood Hotels corporate, which includes the Westin, pushes their rewards program or attempts to sell anything. Instead, they are there to genuinely engage with community members who have questions about the Starwood Hotels Rewards programs and help them resolve issues that have gone unresolved elsewhere (see Figure 34.2).

Sanders has been actively involved with Flyer Talk forums and to date has racked up more than 18,000 posts in the forum. The key to their success is that Sanders genuinely engages with the community beyond just talking hotel rewards points. As you can see from his profile, he lists his interests, which include college football. He even recommends places to eat near the hotel properties, which have nothing to do with Starwood Hotel. It's all genuine interaction and conversation, and that's what endears "Starwood Lurker" to the Flyer Talk community.

Figure 34.2 *Starwood Lurking actively engages—and doesn't market to— the community.*

Let the Rules Help You

Owners and administrators of social media communities establish rules and guidelines for several reasons. First and foremost is to help keep some order in the community they've created. Without them, communities tend to flounder and die out. Another key reason for maintaining order is to avoid allowing spammers and marketers who want to take advantage of the members of the community.

Cre8asite Forums is dedicated to helping search marketers and webmasters understand the world of online marketing (see Figure 34.3). They've been around for more than five years and have a treasure trove of helpful content and valuable advice from which marketers can glean a lot of information. Along with the age of the forum and the wealth of valuable content, they've become one of the heavy hitters that could provide "link juice" to members who have posted links within posts. After being spammed for years by marketers and spammers (who are trying to get a leg up on competitors by placing links in the forum), Cre8asite Forums had to enact a rule preventing links within posts from delivering "link juice" to the referring page.

 Note

Link juice is a term coined by online marketers (not all of them ethical) that refers to the pagerank obtained from collecting backward links).

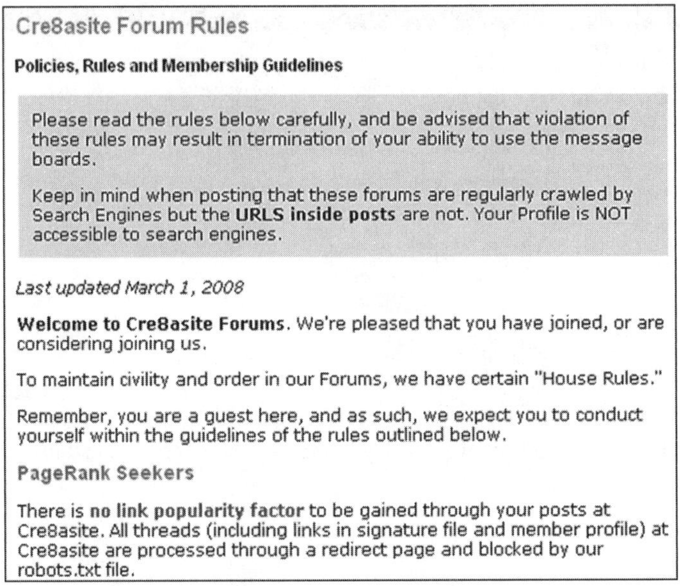

Cre8asite Forum Rules

Policies, Rules and Membership Guidelines

Please read the rules below carefully, and be advised that violation of
these rules may result in termination of your ability to use the message
boards.

Keep in mind when posting that these forums are regularly crawled by
Search Engines but the **URLS inside posts** are not. Your Profile is NOT
accessible to search engines.

Last updated March 1, 2008

Welcome to Cre8asite Forums. We're pleased that you have joined, or are
considering joining us.

To maintain civility and order in our Forums, we have certain "House Rules."

Remember, you are a guest here, and as such, we expect you to conduct
yourself within the guidelines of the rules outlined below.

PageRank Seekers

There is **no link popularity factor** to be gained through your posts at
Cre8asite. All threads (including links in signature file and member profile) at
Cre8asite are processed through a redirect page and blocked by our
robots.txt file.

Figure 34.3   *Forum rules at Cre8asite Forums; you should take the time to read and
understand before actually engaging in a forum or message board.*

By enacting this rule, Crea8site helped to cut down on the link spam it was encountering. Members of the community were tired of being spammed and marketed to
through links in posts that were worthless and not really contributing to active conversations. The administrators of the forum listened to the community and
responded with a solution that worked best for the members. Links are still allowed
because sometimes it's better to post a link to information rather than copying and
pasting entire pages in a reply to a post thread. However, those marketers who were
only out to gain traction by posting links in the forum have now found themselves
out of luck.

35

The Difference Between Buzz Monitoring and Audience Research

If you are an online marketer—particularly if you are charged with setting up a social media marketing campaign—you will hear a lot of talk about buzz monitoring. In fact, an entire subset of the social media marketing industry is dedicated to buzz monitoring that uses tools and services designed to monitor the "buzz" that goes on within the social media sphere.

What do these buzz-monitoring tools do? If you are new to social media marketing, you might also be wondering if the buzz-monitoring tools available are all you need. I hear both of these questions frequently from clients who've heard the hype coming from media outlets, conferences, and online resources. Although they've heard the buzz about the buzz-monitoring tools, many people don't have a handle on exactly what these types of tools are and what they can do. That's the focus of this chapter.

Buzz-monitoring tools are designed to give you insight into what people are saying about your company on social networks, wikis, message boards, and so on. You can also use these tools to learn what people are saying about your competitors, your product category, and more. Some tools can provide you with basic sentiment analysis, while other tools just point you to where the conversation happened. These tools are great for keeping you up-to-date on what's being said and where it's being said.

Buzz monitoring is a vital activity for any company with a social media marketing plan. However, not all buzz-monitoring tools are created equal. In previous chapters, we discussed the paid versions of buzz-monitoring tools, such as Techrigy's SM2 and Radian 6, and the free versions of simple Google Alerts. These tools all tell you the where and the who when it comes to the buzz, but very few of these tools can tell you the why. The why is probably one of the most important and most critical factors for understanding your audience and applying social media marketing strategies.

It's the Difference Between Hearing and Understanding

Buzz-monitoring tools give you only a slice of the information. These tools give you a tidbit to get your social media juices flowing, but they don't tell the whole story. For example, remember the Charlie Brown cartoons in which you could hear Charlie Brown speak to an adult, but when the adult responded, all you heard was gibberish? Many buzz-monitoring tools are similar to this. You know people are talking about your company, but without additional research beyond what your buzz-monitoring tool provides, you won't understand the context for what's being said.

Buzz-monitoring tools are great for giving you a "scent"—that quick glimpse into the community you might never have known about. For example, you might learn about a community that has an acute interest in your industry, product, service, or company. However, you need to create a sound social media strategy before you jump into the conversation. You might find 3 or 2,003 instances of conversation about your company, brands, or products, but you still need more information than what your buzz-monitoring tool tells you.

Buzz Tells You *Where* and *What*—Audience Research Tells You *How* and *Why*

Buzz-monitoring tools can tell you where the buzz is happening. Most of the enterprise-level buzz-monitoring tools can also tell you what that buzz is saying, and some tools even provide a context or sentiment (sentiment analysis) regarding the record they bring back, ranking it as positive, neutral, or negative. However, sentiment analysis is still in its infancy. It's really tough for computers to automatically rank things as positive, negative, or neutral when so many words and phrases can have more than one meaning.

For example, consider the word *spongy*. If your buzz-monitoring software returned a few records using the word *spongy* to describe your product, this could be a bad descriptor if your company specializes in installing brakes. However, if your company is a bakery, the term *spongy* could be a real compliment. In both cases, the buzz-monitoring software likely would have a tough time accurately categorizing the sentiment of the term *spongy* and might classify those records as "neutral." This proves that it's still important to research your audience to understand what they are truly saying.

When your buzz-monitoring tool returns records, you still need to do careful research to determine the *how* and *why* of the conversation so that you can know whether your buzz tools are digging up positive or negative feedback. Sometimes the context of a conversation gets lost when you're viewing individual records that your buzz-monitoring tool returns. You can miss how the conversation started because it might not have started online, or it might have started in a conversation that didn't originally center on you or your brands. Failing to perform due diligence with the records your buzz tools return can mean you don't have any real context for what your buzz tools are telling you.

Relying on the buzz-monitoring data to build your strategy also is a strategic misstep because you can be misled into thinking that all you need to do is start "talking" with the people who are talking about you. Blindly taking the buzz-monitoring data at face value and creating a strategy from it can be a huge waste of time and resources. It is vitally important that you research the communities and the industry to determine how people interact within a certain segment of the market.

Buzz monitoring is similar to using hunting dogs. Dogs can find the scent of what you are trying to eventually find. That's their job; that's what they do best. But the hunter must figure out how to capture its prey, so to speak, after the hunting dogs find it. Although the buzz-monitoring data leads you to where these conversations are happening, only through careful research can you learn why people are talking about your company, why they are in that certain community, what drives them to share and engage, and how you can participate in the conversation in a genuine manner.

Your research can answer a lot of these questions for you. Although some enterprise-level buzz-monitoring tools can give you an inkling into whether the people who are talking about you are influencers, it doesn't give you the full picture. To get the big picture, you actually have to research whether the person has true influence with the people he or she is sharing with. Your buzz-monitoring tools won't show you whether other members of a community actually follow the recommendations of what appears to be a key influencer. Buzz-monitoring data can tell you that a blog mentioned something you are interested in, but it can't tell you how open the blogger is to the strategic tactic you might be considering deploying. Buzz monitoring can tell you that a conversation is occurring about your product, but it doesn't tell you whether the community overall likes you or hates you. You must use human eyes to comprehend that through audience research.

Monitoring Keeps You on Your Toes

If you are contemplating entering the social media sphere, you need to know what's going on before you get there, and that's why buzz monitoring is essential. Even if your buzz monitoring is as simple as setting up Google Alerts on a few key terms, it can keep you ahead of the rising tides and it can help you adjust your online marketing tactics—especially those in social media.

By monitoring what's being said, not only do you have the opportunity to participate in conversations if the research backs that up, but you can also find opportunities to create consumer evangelists and turn upset customers into some of your biggest fans. Buzz monitoring can also lead to interacting with the media, working with other companies, and exposing your product, service, or brand to entirely new audiences that you might not have considered.

In essence, buzz monitoring can open a lot of doors of opportunity for you. Whether you walk through should depend on what your research tells you.

Without buzz monitoring, you are blindly operating your social media strategy in the dark. Doing that is similar to throwing darts at a dartboard while blindfolded. Creating a fan page in Facebook because you saw that someone else had success with it isn't the wisest reason to put resources into that effort. Creating the Facebook fan page doesn't automatically garner you fans unless, of course, you are Oprah. After you have that fan page up and running, how do you engage your fans? How do you get them to interact and share with you?

Buzz monitoring can tell you "Hey, they're talking about you on this fan page," but the buzz monitoring can't tell you how to get those fans from that particular fan page over to your own, and it certainly can't tell you how to get the fans to actually talk to you. That's the tough part of social media—understanding what makes people do what they do. What drives people to want to talk, share, and engage?

Although buzz-monitoring software can keep you on your toes and have you running among communities, it can't tell you what makes people want to share their experiences.

Research Can Pay Off

Buzz monitoring alone can't give you key insights into what exactly your audience is thinking and whether your assumptions and preconceived ideas about what's important to them are truly in line with your audience. Getting that kind of insight involves research. You should also consider using search engines and other tools to dig deeper and get to the root of what these social communities are really thinking, which is something buzz monitoring can only scrape the surface of and something no survey will give you.

A great example of using research in social media to help your marketing efforts is M.D. Anderson, a cancer clinic in Houston, Texas, that provides treatments for different types of cancer. In their book *Groundswell*, Charlene Li and Josh Bernoff describe M.D. Anderson's situation before the clinic started listening to its audience and using that research to help serve its patients better.

Before M.D. Anderson started listening, the clinic assumed that patients were coming because of its prestigious reputation and awards. M.D. Anderson assumed that the new $120 million–plus proton therapy it invested in would bring in more patients. The clinic made a lot of assumptions from a marketing perspective and made decisions from a business point of view. However, its current and prospective patients weren't making *their* decisions this way. When people have cancer, every second going forward from their diagnosis is precious to them—more precious than dollars and coins, more precious than a $120 million proton therapy program. M.D. Anderson didn't realize that although it demanded that patients be prompt for their appointments, the company wasn't respecting the patients' time. Some patients were waiting more than four hours to receive their therapies or treatments.

M.D. Anderson's traditional means of surveying didn't reveal this discrepancy; the clinic learned it through community interaction and actually researching and understanding why a lot of its patients were walking out and never coming back. The company also learned that its awards and accolades from the media didn't mean a thing to the patients, especially when M.D. Anderson wasn't respecting what they valued most—their time.

Another piece of the research revealed that patients don't look at magazines, research, or awards to decide where to go for treatment. Patients mostly rely on physician referrals. It became even more apparent that M.D. Anderson really needed to form relationships with physicians.

Buzz monitoring enabled M.D. Anderson to find conversations, but the research the company did in understanding those conversations became most valuable and paid off.

Although a lot of "experts" might use the terms *buzz monitoring* and *audience research* interchangeably, the difference between them is important to know. Not only can it help you become more successful with your social media strategy implementation, but it can also help your social media strategy complement your other online marketing efforts, such as search engine optimization (SEO), pay-per-click (PPC) marketing, and other online channels.

36

Complementing Both Search Engine Optimization (SEO) and Pay-Per-Click (PPC) Marketing

Social media marketing (SMM) is intricately intertwined with other channels of online marketing. Particularly, SMM works hand-in-hand with search engine optimization (SEO) and pay-per-click (PPC) marketing.

Search engine optimization is the practice of optimizing certain aspects of your website—whether it's content on your web pages, or videos, photos, or podcasts that you create and integrate into your site—for better placement in the search engine results. You can optimize these digital assets to appear higher in the search engine results when searchers type certain keywords.

Depending on what the searcher is looking for and the timeliness of the search, videos or audio can appear before a normal web page listing in the results.

Many other factors across the different search engines enable some content to rank higher in a search engine's ranking of digital content.

Pay-per-click marketing is the practice of bidding a certain amount for your ads to appear on online channels. When someone clicks on those ads, you are charged the amount you bid. Search engines—particularly Google—are most noted for this kind of PPC advertisement. These advertisements appear in the first three positions, are shaded or highlighted, and appear above the natural results that are displayed and the advertisements that appear in a column to the right of the natural search results. Figure 36.1 shows the difference between the paid (PPC) results and the natural (SEO) results.

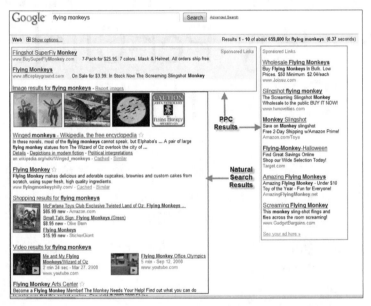

Figure 36.1   *The difference between natural search results and sponsored (PPC) results in Google*

It's advantageous to appear at the top of the search results. As social media becomes more popular and important to the masses, the search engines are starting to include content from these sites in their results. Therefore, you must understand both how utilizing SEO skills can complement your social media strategy and how social media marketing can enhance your SEO and PPC efforts.

People Still Need to Find You

Even in social media, people search for things that they want to learn more about—whether that means they want to know what other people think about a topic or what other people have experienced. As with normal searches, when people are searching in social media, they generally aren't searching for your product or service. Unless your company is a well-known, established brand, brand-type searches are infrequent in the social media arena.

Because you can't rely on people to find your content based on your brand name, it's important to research how people are searching for the type of social media content you are creating and engaging in social media sites. Simply putting "Company XYZ Video" in the title of your video you place in YouTube doesn't guarantee it will be seen by people who are searching for how to use your product. SEO and PPC can help your strategy.

Most search engines are incorporating videos that play directly in the search engine results. The search engines are also starting to incorporate videos into their pay-per-click areas. If you are introducing a new product or service and people are searching for how to use it, your strategy might be more effective if you optimize the videos you produce for the keywords people are searching on. In addition, adding some PPC bids on those keywords and including a video—or a landing page that has the video on it—can help extend your social media strategy to search in a very effective manner.

Social media marketing doesn't happen in a void. One site can't drive your social media strategy, nor should it. Expanding your strategy to include search-marketing components will help you reach beyond one or two sites and increase your chances of reaching those who might not be active in social media.

SEO Is About Links—Social Media Isn't

A huge component of search engine optimization and ranking your digital assets highly in the search engine is based on the number of links your assets receive from other websites. Many people get confused about this linkage between SEO and social media. You can utilize social media tactics to generate links naturally. If your content is valuable to your audience, social media will naturally create links for people who find your content valuable enough that they want to share it with their audiences.

SEO needs links to work properly. Without links, pages will rank for only branded or obscure search terms. Social media doesn't need links—it needs engagement and community. This is the primary difference between these two types of marketing tactics.

SEO and social media complement each other and shouldn't be seen as separate tactics. Your SEO team can help market the content you are creating for your social media audience to additional channels.

Link Baiting Isn't Social Media Marketing

The art of "link baiting" is a particular SEO tactic that sometimes comes under a lot of scrutiny. Link baiting is defined as content or features that entice or "bait" viewers to link to it from other websites. Because social media that is created by users (user-generated content) has a natural propensity to go "viral" and create a lot of links in a shortened amount of time, some companies mistakenly believe that social media marketing is just link baiting on steroids.

Most link baiting isn't social. Infographics, for example, are very popular for link-bait campaigns. Infographics are images that contain a lot of "catchy" information that usually hits home with a particular industry or segment of the population. This type of link bait isn't very "social" but companies can use social channels to promote the infographic and make people aware of it. However, this tactic creates confusion. Companies mistakenly think that because their infographic went to the front page of Digg, it was social media.

If the company created the infographic and just placed it on its website, it's not social. The social aspect is that it's out on a social news site and that site is driving people to come and see the infographic. After people see the infographic, they can vote on it. Occasionally people might comment on the infographic, but that happens on the social media site, not the company's site.

Sometimes link baiting can backfire on a company. Money.co.uk experienced this situation when it employed a person skilled at link-bait creation and propagation to create link bait for the site. The link-bait expert created a story about a teenager who stole his father's credit card to hire prostitutes to play video games with him. Without checking the facts of the story, Money.co.uk ran it. The story hit big on the major news outlets and the piece created many links to Money.co.uk. This process was classic link baiting (not social media). The problem with this link bait came later when it was revealed that the entire story was fabricated.

Money.co.uk was embarrassed as the details about how the story was created and how it was false began circulating on the Web, just as fast and as powerful as the original link-bait piece (see Figure 36.2). It also drew the attention of the search engines, which frown upon such practices to trick both the search engines and users with fake content to generate links.

Figure 36.2 *Money.co.uk apologizing after deploying a fake link-baiting tactic*

Using PPC to Drive Social Media Awareness

PPC isn't limited to search engines, although that is the most recognizable and easiest form of advertising online for most marketers. Different social sites offer different forms of advertising that include hybrid forms of pay-per-click ads. Some blogs offer sponsorships, others work with preestablished content networks that group them within a certain industry niche. Marketers can use this tactic to help raise awareness of certain social media efforts that are launched as part of an overall strategy.

If you've done your research and find that your social media strategy is starting a custom forum aimed at providing support for your customers and a place to share their experience, you might want to add budget for a short PPC campaign. Because the forum will be relatively new, ranking naturally will take time as you get the word out.

A small, very targeted PPC campaign can reach those searchers who are specifically looking for what your community will offer. These types of PPC campaigns can really jump start the awareness factor of your new social media community.

Social networks also offer different types of PPC to marketers. For example, Facebook offers Facebook Ads. Marketers have been successfully using these ads to drive awareness of groups, fan pages, applications, and special promotions, either on Facebook or on their own sites. MySpace also offers marketers different ways to promote their MySpace profiles or other social media activities. These types of advertisement can work hand-in-hand with the natural word-of-mouth propagation that happens when communities learn about valuable content that companies engaging with them in social media spaces have created.

You can't look at social media marketing in a vacuum if you want it to be successful. Planning how to make SEO and PPC complement your strategy is vital to making sure that people are aware of your efforts, especially if your tactic is brand new. Understanding how to incorporate these channels can help your social media efforts reach the goals you've established.

37

Links and Search Engine Results Are Byproducts of Social Media

As I touched upon in Chapter 36, "Complementing Both Search Engine Optimization (SEO) and Pay-Per-Click (PPC) Marketing," social media isn't about getting links to propel your strategy into the stratosphere of success. Links are how search engine optimization experts gain traction in the search engine results for their targeted keywords and phrases. Gaining links to improve your social media tactic or to get to the top of YouTube doesn't work in the same manner.

In social media, links and search engine results are a byproduct of a great social media strategy. A great strategy will

- *Engage your audience through conversations.*

- *Encourage sharing of your information to other members of a community.*

- *Encourage recommending your company and products to others.*

If these results occur, you will gain links. When you gain those links—whether it's to your website or to the social media channels you are actively engaging in—those sites start to rise in the search engine rankings.

Gaining the links naturally as a byproduct of a thorough, well-conceived social media strategy is in line with how search engines view the relevance of the results they provide to searchers. Google, Yahoo!, and Bing want to give their searchers results that are the most relevant. With the advent of social media, searchers can use another piece of information to understand relevancy of content, but social media is not the sole piece to determine relevancy.

My friend, colleague, and mentor, Mike Grehan, who is the vice president of Content at Incisive Media and who oversees the Search Engine Strategies conference series, states it very simply:

> *If a composer writes a review of a symphony by Beethoven on his blog, it's commented on, it's linked to by other composers and music critics, and then a student of music writes a similar review and all of his college friends link to it and comment on the review. Which is more relevant?*

Naturally, when you look at it this way, you see that the composer's review will be more relevant because the search engines will be weighing all factors, including how "socially" active the blog posts are. They will not only look at how many links the site get, but also who's doing the linking. In this case, these two forms of user-generated content could both be relevant, but it takes more than just social media for Google to determine which one tops the other.

Securing Your Social Media Profiles Is Wise, But Don't Count on Them for Rankings

A year or two ago, simply establishing a profile on a social media channel with your company, brand, product, or service name would automatically garner you a ranking in the search engines. That was before the search engines started to weigh more factors in determining the relevancy of a social media profile. Now just establishing your profile on Facebook, MySpace, YouTube, Flickr, or any other of the hundreds of social media sites doesn't mean you will control the top 50 spots in the search engine rankings for your brand names.

However, it's still wise to secure your profile on major social media sites and any lesser-known ones that you might want to become active in. This prevents someone else from "squatting" on your brand name. Similar to domain name squatting, people have been known to acquire social media profiles that are brand names of companies, hoping for big "paydays" from companies willing to pay to acquire the account on the social media site.

Securing your profiles on these social media channels isn't only wise from the cybersquatting aspect, but for two other reasons as well:

1. Similar to cybersquatting, your competitors could actually register an account in your brand name. Although it's not the most ethical marketing strategy, it can occur in today's competitive environment.

2. You should utilize the profiles to your advantage. Inevitably, someone might search for your company on that particular social media channel. Even though you might not be that active on it, you should still fill out your profile with the pertinent contact information or how to find you actively engaging on other channels. It gives the person searching for you an option to engage you where you are actively conversing with others.

You Don't Do Social Media for Search Engine Rankings

A prior boss asked me to build a blog for a client to gain "another foothold in the search engine rankings." Every fiber in my body was against taking such a step; however, I could not appease my boss no matter how I explained that the keywords were too competitive for what the client was attempting to rank this new "blog." In addition, the client had only three pieces of content to put into the blog and, as far as I could see, it wasn't planning to add additional content later. It takes a lot more than just building a blog on WordPress's site to get it to rank for competitive terms.

Unfortunately, many search engine optimization firms think that social media is now a gold mine for search engine rankings. Creating blogs for search engine rankings without adding any real content won't get your company anywhere, no matter how "optimized" it is. If you are writing content to just rank in the search engines, it likely won't be appealing to a real audience that you should be engaging with.

It also takes a lot more than three or four posts in a blog for it to start ranking in a search engine. For a blog to truly be seen as an authority that ranks for keywords, people have to actually be engaging with the content—whether it's by commenting on the posts, linking to them, or socializing them on social channels such as Digg, Mixx, or StumbleUpon. It takes resources to continually create quality content that people find valuable and that will eventually start to rank in the search engines.

Social Media Communities Are Wiser Than an SEO

If content is written specifically to rank in a search engine, it probably won't be popular in the social media environment. That's especially true in sites such as Digg, Mixx, and StumbleUpon. These communities are very wise to the attempts of search engine optimization experts to place content into these channels in the hopes of getting to the popular page.

For example, if Digg gets even a whiff of a notion that you are a marketer—especially if you are foolish enough to submit your own content to the site—they won't be nice to you or your submitted content. The community comes together and actually makes it very clear that marketers are not welcome in Digg. Stories usually get buried within a short time and Digg will sometimes go as far as to mark the site the content came from as spam. If enough reports of spam come through from a site, Digg can ban it as a content source.

Junk Traffic or True Engagement?

People question the tactics some SEO experts employ to socialize content developed especially to either rise fast in the rankings or make it to the front page of the social news sites such as Digg. Making it to the front page of Digg (called "being Dugg") will drive a lot of traffic to your site in a very short amount of time. However, as a marketer, you should be questioning the quality of this traffic.

If your site is a content site with a revenue model based on the number of eyeballs you are getting to the site, Digg will fit your social media strategy. However, if you are selling a product or service, it's likely that the traffic from Digg won't help you much. Typically, Digg (or any other social news site) visitors click the link from the site, take a glance at the pictures or how the site is set up, and decide to vote on it. These visitors don't stay long and usually don't visit other parts of your site, which doesn't provide much opportunity for engaging them.

If your content creation strategy involves a blog and writing content for a very niche audience, you probably shouldn't place your content on Digg, no matter how much your SEO firm claims that "journalists" scour Digg for "new," "interesting," or "unique" content. You have a better chance if you are social within your target audience and give them the content they are craving. Great content will get propagated, including to journalists who would be interested in it.

Your goals for your social media strategy will determine whether your search engine optimization expert's recommendations will be successful in socializing content in social news sites. Leave the optimization of your key content to them, and do your homework on where to socialize your content through your audience research as described in Chapter 35, "The Difference Between Buzz Monitoring and Audience Research."

Link Dropping in Social Media Communities Is Taboo

Another common tactic that search engine optimization practitioners recommend is to "drop your link" inside a forum, message board, or community. Unfortunately, similar to using white text on a white background (a spamming tactic employed years ago that no longer works to gain rankings), dropping links on blogs, forums, or message boards will get you shunned just as quickly as submitting your own content on Digg gets you labeled as an "evil marketer." Dropping links in social media communities is a huge taboo.

Years ago, when blogs first started becoming popular and before Google really started paying attention, search engine optimization experts who skirted around the "ethical" boundaries of marketing tactics deployed scripts that dropped their customers' links in the comments of thousands of blogs and message boards in hopes of raising the ranking of their clients' sites. Often their clients didn't know this was being done on their behalf or they were more concerned about raising their rankings than how these underhanded tactics would affect their reputations down the road.

Now some of these companies are struggling to establish a healthy relationship with social media communities. They are better known as spammers who want to take advantage of a situation than as companies that want to truly engage the community.

Because of the rampant spamming of blogs and communities, webmasters and search engines worked to combat this problem. Google, as well as Yahoo! and Bing, introduced the "nofollow" tag, which says to the search engine "I don't trust this link." When this nofollow tag is deployed on a blog, any comment that dropped a link did not get the value from the link being on the page.

Forums and message boards that were wide open—they didn't hide their content behind a user name and password login—also devised ways to combat the link-dropping problem. Most forums now use a JavaScript redirect that takes the link someone places into the forum and rewrites it so that it's redirected through JavaScripting, which the search engines can't follow to the link's destination.

No matter how coy or superior your search engine optimization expert might think he or she is, remember most of these communities have seen the likes of your so-called "expert" before and are prepared to deal with recommendations that don't benefit their community or their members. Your social media strategy and the tactics you deploy should be governed by your goals for the strategy and how it affects your brand, product, or service—not by how many links you expect to gather or how far up the search engine rankings you can go.

38

Align Offline Marketing Strategies with Social Media

In today's ever-connected world, the online world's effect on our everyday offline lives is growing considerably. It's hard to miss television ads that scream "Join our Facebook fan page" or "Google Pontiac." People go online to search for their favorite commercials, or to find a columnist they've read in a magazine they picked up in the airport.

Companies are making the Web an extension of their brands, and social media is taking a huge role in that extension. The companies that realize their offline marketing strategies need to be fully aligned with their online activities—including email, pay-per-click advertising, search engine optimization, and social media—are the ones most successfully reaching their target consumers.

Companies tend to stumble when they silo their marketing efforts and think that their offline event planning has nothing to do with their social media strategies, or that their traditional marketing (such as TV, radio, and print) has no bearing on search engine optimization, online ad buying, or social media strategy.

Nothing could be further from the truth. Companies venturing into online marketing, especially social media marketing, need to be aware of all aspects of their marketing efforts and how channels can interact. It's no longer "traditional" versus "online" types of marketing. Smart companies realize that it's all integrated marketing.

Social Media Doesn't Happen in a Vacuum

Success in social media marketing doesn't happen merely because you've opted to engage in that channel. Other components—including your offline efforts—affect the success of your social media marketing tactics. This means making sure your TV, Radio, Direct Mail, and even your SEO, PCC, Email, and Affiliate marketing efforts are all working with your social media marketing efforts.

You must connect what you're doing offline with your marketing efforts online because you want people to talk about what you're doing, both in online communities and with their offline connections, and you want people to "join" the conversation and share their experiences with you in that chosen social media channel.

If you simply join social networks and don't encourage people to share, or you don't utilize other channels outside of social media to get your message out, how will people know about you or your services or products?

Encouraging sharing in some social media channels is more difficult because of "walled gardens" (communities that require subscriptions or fees to join). However, social media communities that are free to join offer great potential for spreading the word. But you cannot expect members of a community to just automatically start sharing with you. You have to let your audience know you want to be "social" with them.

Making sure that all your marketing efforts are in sync is critical to any social media effort. You must speak directly to the people in the social media communities about your online efforts and your traditional marketing channels. The marketing people who design your marketing literature for the salespeople to hand out should be incorporating your Facebook fan page address into your marketing pieces. Your ad agency should encourage online participation by mentioning your "branded community" in your print, radio, and televisions ads. Your public relations team needs to work with your social media marketing team to spread the word about offline events and to encourage event participants to come to your social media channel to engage with you.

If you are still siloing your marketing efforts, it will be difficult to get your offline audience to join you online because each silo of marketing is operating independently and won't know of your efforts in your chosen social media channels. You have the resources; why not use them to your advantage and integrate your efforts?

People Consume Media in Many Formats

Regardless of age, gender, job, hobby, or however the statistics you look at are sliced and diced, it's rare that everyone in your audience consumes media in the same way. Some people still trust the old forms of traditional media, such as an article in a trade magazine. Younger generations rarely touch a newspaper or magazine and instead turn to mobile phones or laptops to consume the latest news via an online news website.

Thinking that your marketing slicks will be consumable only by your salespeople handing them to perspective clients can be a tragic misstep in your marketing efforts, especially considering that today's audiences are becoming more environmentally conscious. You also have opportunities to share your printed marketing pieces with members of a social media community.

You must also take a broader view of your radio and TV commercials. If you've produced a catchy commercial that hits home with one particular segment of your audience, it would be a mistake to think that's as far as it can go. The Millennial Generation doesn't have the attention span or the desire to sit in front of a TV to see a funny commercial; instead, they will look it up on YouTube.

You must also consider the reverse—that is, people will share your online digital media in offline formats. Understanding that your digital marketing collateral can have an extended shelf life is important to any marketing effort. Take, for example, having a popular blog. Some of your blog posts could have gone "viral" and are shared across the Internet. Other communities and individuals link to your blog posts. In other words, many of your online audience members find your content valuable.

Thinking that your blog's only "shelf life" is online can be a missed opportunity. What about your offline audience? Wouldn't they find these pieces of digital content valuable, too? You could create a small book of your most valuable blog posts and provide it as an eBook and/or in a printed format. That would allow your offline audience to see your digital content. Just don't forget to include URLs pointing your offline audience to your online content.

Offline Activities Matter Online

Your public relations team might tell you that you don't need to worry about announcing offline activities to your online audience. Or your PR team might tell you that you just need to place an announcement on your company's static web page. If your PR agency has told you this, you should fire them for giving you this bad advice. Then make sure your social media team knows about the offline event.

Trust your social media team to help spread the word about your offline event in a way that appeals to the communities you are currently engaging. If your chosen tactic is a Facebook fan page, they most likely can create an event invite for your fans to participate by either announcing it on the fan page or sending the invite to them individually. You can utilize many ways to let your online social media community members know about what's going on offline, which could make your offline event even more successful.

People Always Search

Hitwise tracks the traffic and the searches for information about the commercials shown during the Super Bowl. These commercials are shown in an offline environment. However, right after the Super Bowl (and even during it), people are looking for those funny or interesting commercials. Hitwise wrote about this in a blog post shortly after the Super Bowl, and charted the most searched-on commercials.

When people are looking for content they see offline, they use Google, YouTube, or the company's website to find it. If the company that produced this information realizes how people look for information online, it can make this process much easier. If finding your offline content is too frustrating for the online user, you've just lost a perfect opportunity to engage a very interested consumer online.

What if you put a small, unobtrusive URL for your commercials at the bottom of the screen? It's not helpful if you upload the commercial to YouTube but don't tell anyone about it. Make sure that you involve your social media team so that they can tell the online world where to find that video clip. Also make sure that your SEO team knows so that they can help people find it when they are searching. Don't miss opportunities to engage your social media audience when you do something interesting or funny offline.

In Chapter 6, "The Conversation Happens With or Without You," I shared an example in which AT&T created a bunch of really catchy commercials that you could not find online by searching for the "Techno Twins" or any of the other catch phrases the people used in the commercials. I talk about these commercials a lot. I reference them to friends, and I wish I could tell them to "Google 'Techno Twins.'"

Unfortunately I can't. Instead, I have to send them a link after I search for it on YouTube because those commercials aren't on AT&T's site.

You might know of the actress Betty White. White has had a resurgence of sorts, but it's nothing that her manager or any fancy PR firm has done. White was in the 2009 movie *The Proposal* starring Sandra Bullock. Bullock presented White with an award from the Screen Actors Guild (SAG). White is probably best known for her role as the airheaded character Rose Nilund on the popular 1980's sitcom *The Golden Girls*, but she's been around a long time. However, nobody expected what happened after the SAG award, not even the Mars company that makes the Snickers candy bar.

Mars featured White in a Super Bowl commercial for Snickers. It was catchy, it was funny, and it got people searching—not just for Snickers, but also for White. Even more amazing was the groundswell of support for this very funny, very talented, and very witty actress who ended up being asked to host *Saturday Night Live*. This support didn't happen in the movie theaters or newspapers—it happened on Facebook (see Figure 38.1). The support even took White by surprise.

Figure 38.1   *"Betty White to Host SNL" fan page—it worked!*

Because of this groundswell effort, Lorne Michaels, the producer of *Saturday Night Live*, announced that White will host an episode in May 2010. Can you imagine if Mars had recognized the fact that the commercial helped create something viral? What if the company had caught onto this "runaway groundswell train" and engaged people on its fan page to support the effort created on Facebook to have White on *SNL?* Talk about a *coup de force.*

If something is valuable offline—whether its value to your audience is educational, economical, comical, or emotional—people will most likely want to share it online as well, especially in social media communities. Recognizing this fact and aligning all your marketing strategies is crucial to your overall success.

39

Create a Social Media-Friendly "Pressroom" and Promote Events

If you're working with classic public relations firms, their idea of social media might be emailing your press release to a bunch of bloggers or journalists with the hopes that someone will care. The reality is most bloggers and journalists don't even read these pitches. Even worse, if it's a "carbon copy" with the same pitch and it's "lame," you might find your press release the highlight of the "Bad Pitch" blog. That's not the kind of "fame" or press you want.

Public relations as we once knew it is changing. The old-style tactics of pushing your carefully worded message to the media with hopes of receiving an email or a phone call doesn't work anymore. You must offer something that will grab their attention. You also need to make the information easy for the media to understand and consume, and for their audiences to understand, consume, value, and share.

Many PR firms miss the boat by not thinking beyond the carefully spun message that's in text.

Attracting the attention and interest of your audience requires more effort. Long gone are the days when a faxed press release to the newsroom of a newspaper or news station would grab the attention of the news desk editor. Now you need something more than a catchy title on a fax or email.

Don't Limit Yourself to Traditional Press Releases

With the dawn of YouTube, iTunes, and Flickr, the days of utilizing only a text press release are quickly fading. In today's world of videos, photos, and podcasts, you need to integrate these types of social media channels into your public relations efforts.

Videos and photos always catch the eye. They make the boring text-style press release come alive. If you are releasing a new product or service, part of your press plan should include creating a video or a photo series of how the product or service works. Including these elements with your pitch to the media or a blogger will definitely catch their attention.

Although the carefully crafted message is still important, you need to think beyond the words on paper to convey your message to the public. The public has become more visual and would rather see an engaging video that conveys a message than to sit and read through a carefully created press release that pimps your product or service. Remember it's not about "your message"—it's about the value that the audience receives from "your message."

Traditional press releases promote what a company feels is important. With the rise of social media and the competition for media attention, companies need to rethink that strategy. Understanding who your audience is and what they are doing in social media should be an important part of your public relations efforts.

In the days before the rise of social media, public relations tried to hit a wide audience, such as offering interviews with the CEO. Hit wide, hope for a certain "open rate," and maybe you'd hear back from a few interested media outlets. With social media, you can now target your public relations efforts more efficiently and effectively. However, you have to understand your audience thoroughly. If you know your audience is more prone to downloading a podcast and listening to it in their cars, writing an e-book about something your company is doing and sending it off to a bunch of industry bloggers won't do you much good.

If you are limited on resources to create a social media–friendly pressroom, external services exist. Services such as PRESSfeed (www.press-feed.com), run by public relations guru Sally Falkow, and MarketWire are designed to make it easier for companies to create "one stop" places for the news media to see the type of news your company is trying to get noticed (see Figure 39.1). Some of these services are free and others have a cost involved. If you don't have the staff to help your create your own newsroom but you want to start integrating different types of media into your releases, this could be the perfect solution.

Figure 39.1   *The PRESSfeed newsroom is a third-party pressroom you can use if you don't have the internal resources to do it.*

Creating the right kind of press release (with easy-to-share and easy-to-consume media) to reach your public is just as important as the way you create your message that you want them to find valuable.

Make It Easy for Bloggers and Journalists

Making these types of consumable media easy to access and share is also key to grabbing the attention of bloggers and journalists. If you make them jump through hoops to locate the media you are creating for them to use in a piece they want to write about you, they might not write the piece. Or worse, it could turn into a piece about "how bad you are" because you made them jump through hoops and they became frustrated with you. Neither is a good situation for your company.

It's vitally important that your media pieces are in one easy-to-reach place. Instead of attaching videos, photos, and portable document formats (PDFs) to an email that you send to your contact, creating a social media–friendly pressroom is the perfect solution for a number of reasons:

- Attaching videos, photos, or audio files can fill up or even max out your contacts' email boxes and annoy them.

- Including this type of media in an email could land your press release in your recipients' spam or junk mail folders.

- Putting this media in one email can overwhelm your contact, and they might move on to the next email without giving yours the attention you want.

Sending a brief email that contains links to a pressroom site enables your contacts to get your primary message without overwhelming them with big attachments. This also enables your contacts to view attachments later. In a subtle way, it shows that you understand their time is valuable and you respect that.

Approaching your public in this manner garners respect and increases the likelihood that your "pitch" won't immediately end up in the deleted folder of your target's email box. The added benefit of making it easier for the blogger or journalist in this manner is that you can actually track the effectiveness of your efforts by analyzing traffic to the landing page. You can see what media is consumed the most, which enables you to continually tweak your approach for the best results.

Integrate and Pollinate

When social media started to become an integral part of public relations, most PR professionals initially viewed it as places where they could push their messages. To some degree, this is true. You can send your press release or other information to a boatload of bloggers. You can also post your press release on PR Newswire. The question is, will anyone notice?

If your press release is just text, it's unlikely that media outlets and bloggers will pick up your information. Copying and pasting the canned press release into an email and sending it off to bloggers doesn't help either. If you are using an automated program to blast an email to hundreds or thousands of bloggers and journalists, stop doing that.

When working with PR online, making a social media–friendly pressroom is likely your best shot at making sure your message gets noticed and stays on track. It's also helpful to approach each media contact you research (meaning indentify, read, and make a relationship with) on an individual basis. Although it's more time consuming, it provides a better payoff in the long run. Integrating your approach is even better.

Sending personal emails to the bloggers or journalists that point them to the integrated information (text press release, video, photo, audio, and so on) enables your targeted individuals to create a story from their own perspective but still include the message you want to disseminate. But don't stop there.

Make sure your social media team is aware that you've created a social media–friendly pressroom and they know about everything you are putting out there. Your team can then leverage this media you've put together and pollinate it across other channels for you. Doing so increases the likelihood of someone you hadn't even known about picking up your story and running with it.

Your social media team understands how to best present your video, photos, or other digital assets to the communities who would most likely consume it and share it with others. What good does it do if your press release is sitting in one spot and only one area of your company knows about it? The key is to make sure all areas of your marketing team (SEO, PPC, social, and traditional) know about your PR efforts and they work together to pollinate your efforts to the online channels that would be most effective.

Make Sure Your Teams Work Together

You can hinder your online marketing strategy by thinking that your PR team's efforts are limited to offline promotion and writing press releases. PR and social media go hand in hand, so you need to change your approach. The old style of "write it and release it" doesn't work very well in social media because these communities want to engage, share, and actually talk to a human being who is involved with the company.

This illustrates why integrating your PR team's plans with your online efforts is so important to your overall marketing efforts—not just PR or social media. When you integrate your efforts, it's a win–win for both areas of your company.

Although your PR team's expertise is carefully crafting your message, your social media team's expertise is engaging communities with that message. If your PR team doesn't know about your efforts in social media, they can't make a special effort to tailor and reach that audience. If your social media team doesn't know about your PR team's efforts, they can't disseminate the message.

The other part of the equation is that if each of these teams is operating in a vacuum, it can actually look bad for you. Imagine a reporter picking up your press release and learning that the message presented there is different than the message your social media team is tweeting about. What happens then? Who does the reporter believe? Most likely not the PR person, as the reporter has been well trained to understand that PR people are masters of "spin."

40

YouTube is the Second-Largest Search Engine

Although YouTube isn't technically a search engine, it is the second most popular site used to conduct searches on the Web. Since late spring 2009, YouTube has consistently outranked Bing and even Yahoo! for searches conducted on a site. According to a 2010 comScore report, YouTube cemented itself as the second-ranked site for conducting searches (see Figure 40.1).

Consumers and members of your audience probably don't know that YouTube isn't technically a search engine. To them, it's a place where they search for videos. As a marketer, knowing that YouTube is such a well-used site to search on should spur you to use this knowledge to your advantage when implementing your strategy.

When people find videos valuable, they do more than just post them to their Facebook pages or Twitter accounts. They play them on their phones, email the link to their friends, and tell their neighbors to "Come over here and see this."

People search for everything on YouTube that they do on Google—from how to tie a tie, to "Granny DJ" (search for "Granny DJ" on YouTube and you'll meet viral sensation Ruth Flowers).

comScore Expanded Search Query Report December 2009 vs. November 2009 Total U.S. – Home/Work/University Locations Source: comScore qSearch			
Expanded Search Entity	Search Queries (MM)		
	Nov-09	Dec-09	Percent Change Dec-09 vs. Nov-09
Total Internet	22,280	22,741	2%
Google Sites	13,751	14,019	2%
Google	9,878	10,101	2%
YouTube/All Other	3,873	3,918	1%
Yahoo! Sites	2,622	2,629	0%
Yahoo!	2,599	2,605	0%
All Other	23	24	4%
Microsoft Sites	1,521	1,620	7%
Bing	1,324	1,399	6%
Microsoft/All Other	197	221	12%
Ask Network	715	696	-3%
ASK.COM	348	332	-5%
MyWebSearch.com/ All Other	367	364	-1%
eBay	635	680	7%
AOL LLC	611	588	-4%
AOL Search Network	349	325	-7%
MapQuest/All Other	262	263	0%
craigslist, inc.	568	583	3%
Fox Interactive Media	447	424	-5%
MySpace Sites	439	416	-5%
All Other	8	8	0%
Facebook.com	354	351	-1%
Amazon Sites	250	302	21%

Figure 40.1 *ComScore ranks YouTube as the second most searched on website.*

Unfortunately, we aren't privy to the same search data on YouTube that we can access with the keyword tool that Google provides to the public. You can only imagine the type of data we'd see if YouTube provided this functionality, and how incredibly valuable that would be to marketers. So we have to be content for the moment knowing that YouTube is the second-largest search engine that really isn't a search engine.

It Isn't Just About "Going Viral"

Companies are mistakenly led to believe that if their video doesn't go viral on YouTube, it's not a success. If you are judging your success and failure based on what happened to the BlendTech videos or the Diet Coke and Mentos videos, then you might not ever attain a successful implementation of a social media tactic using YouTube. If you are trying to measure the success of your social media tactics against media that was created by others who had no inkling it'd go viral, you are setting the bar a lot higher than you can realistically attain.

You can do more with YouTube than utilizing it in hopes of going viral. By adding videos showing how to use your product, or perhaps demonstrating what your product really looks like, you can enhance your return on investment in other ways. For example, you can increase conversion rates, generate more interest in your products, or increase ending-sales figures. All these examples are measurable results that you can see if you use YouTube or other video shares.

GovernmentLiquidation.com uses videos for this purpose. The online auction company deals strictly with auctioning lots of surplus items. You wouldn't believe the "stuff" that our government buys in excess and never uses. Government Liquidation started slowly. First, it offered videos showing what would be available at upcoming auctions. Before using video, potential bidders had to rely on simple pictures or written descriptions.

As a test, Government Liquidation took several identical lots and created a video of just one of those lots. The other lots were left with picture and text descriptions. The company expected perhaps a small lift in participation on the bidding, but it was amazed by the results. Not only did bidding increase on the lot with video, but the ending bid amounts increased exponentially. Because the bidders could actually see from multiple angles what they were bidding on, they considered the items more valuable and therefore bid higher. Government Liquidation also found that it could drive traffic to its auctions by placing auction videos on social media sites.

Although the videos did not go viral, they were still a huge success for Government Liquidation. In the future, Government Liquidation hopes that conversation on social media sites will help drive more sales of surplus items.

Video Is More Engaging Than Text

The Government Liquidation example in the previous section illustrates that video is more engaging than just text. Conversion rates go up when people can see what they are buying, whether it's products or services. Whether you're looking to drive purchases, newsletter subscriptions, support for a cause, or any number of potential calls to action, video is more likely to get the results you want.

I run a blog called SearchMarketingGurus.com. On that blog, I have several videos that discuss online marketing tips—everything from integrating email, using Twitter, optimizing your web pages for better search engine results, to reasons why you want to apply analytics to your website. When my video posts go up, they get a lot more buzz, comments, and interaction than when the posts on the site just include text and pictures. My audience enjoys hearing me talk to the points that I've explained in past blog posts. Even if the video features just me talking and using a whiteboard, people enjoy these posts more than if I used simple text and pictures.

The videos that I create are simple and easily done. They are made for a very specific niche audience, and by no means do I ever expect them to go viral. They aren't meant for that purpose. Instead, the videos are meant to educate my audience and get them to start incorporating the topics into their online marketing strategies.

Video Results Appear in Search Engine Results

Before mid-2008, when people searched for a particular subject, they were presented with a list of 10 blue links—the websites that the search engines deemed most relevant to the search. But in 2008, Google decided to "change the game" by incorporating different forms of digital media into the results it was returning to the searchers. This change included thumbnails of videos that were relevant to what its spiders had found. Video results were included from YouTube (owned by Google) and other sites such as Yahoo! Video, Vimeo, MetaCafe, and a few others. Eventually, Google added the capability to play some of the video results in a small viewer on the results page.

By not relying on text-only results, Google was realizing that searchers would be more engaged with the search results if those results contained more than just textual links. As I explained in Chapter 29, "Your Content Must Have Value," soon after Google changed how it delivered results to its searchers, Marissa Mayer, vice president of search products and user experience at Google, explained that Google understood that text web pages aren't always the best nor the most relevant results for a person's search.

Google further expanded this idea by enabling businesses to include links to their videos on YouTube in local search results. Businesses appearing in local results also can include up to five photos that appear on the search results page.

By allowing these other forms of media into the business profile, Google can deliver better and more engaging results that are narrowed to specific geographic locations. Videos will often appear at the top of the search results when a user searches for a specific company.

If you searched for information on Lady Gaga or Beyonce, would you find a list of 10 blue links very helpful? When you are searching for "Beyonce," you probably want to know about her latest music or see her latest video (see Figure 40.2). This explains why all the search engines are incorporating video into their search results. If you are looking for the latest results from an episode of *American Idol* or *Dancing with the Stars,* you'll likely want to see video clips of the latest performances. If you're searching on "how to unclog a sink," a text web page won't help you that much, but a video certainly would.

Figure 40.2   *Search results for "beyonce" on Google returns videos that can be played directly in the search results.*

This illustrates why it's important to understand your audience and know how they consume their media online. Would a text web page, a set of photos, a podcast, or a video be the best form of serving up your valuable content to your audience? Videos are extremely engaging and can often be more effective in explaining what you are trying to get across to an audience because they are so visual.

When incorporating video into your social media strategy, remember it's not about you. Instead, it's about the value the end user who's viewing the video content will receive. Regardless of whether the video goes "viral," your audience will let you know in many other ways whether the video is valuable. It might take a few tries to determine how to best present your video content, so be prepared to modify your approach. You might even change things up so your audience keeps finding the value in your content.

41

Social Search Is All About the Now

Although it's helpful for consumers to learn about an ongoing problem with your product or service, they want to know more. They want to know what's happening right now with that product. Has the company addressed the problem? Is the company taking steps to fix it? Have other consumers who've encountered the same problem found a workaround or a solution? What kind of experience have other customers had with the company?

People are increasingly looking to social media outlets to find this kind of information. People use social media not only to learn about a company's products and services, but to get opinions on music, games, books, and just about anything else you can possibly think of. If you are a concert promoter, perhaps it would be good to know where people are going online to learn about experiences they had at other concerts your company promoted. If your company runs vacation resorts, it would be good to know what people are saying about their experiences in your resorts. If you own a restaurant in a popular tourist location, it would be good to know what experiences people are having at other nearby restaurants and even take the opportunity to build some goodwill for your restaurant.

People are searching social media sites for this kind of information, whether it's from several years ago or from yesterday. Although older information won't be very relevant to the searcher, what happened last month or yesterday is relevant. People want to know the latest experiences because nothing in life ever stays the same. A review from a year ago about a hotel that has been recently renovated isn't as strong as a review from last week praising the new renovations. Search engines are always looking for the freshest, most relevant information to serve, so in this case, understanding that the newest reviews are likely the most relevant is important.

The search engines are taking notice of these types of searches and are increasingly serving up results from social media sites that have the newest information. Google would much rather you come to Google and do your search on "the best time of year to go to Key West" than go to Travelocity. So Google now includes Travelocity reviews and other travel review sites as part of its search results. By giving you all the most relevant information in their search results, Google is keeping the visitor engaged on their site longer and not sending them off to another site to do another search.

Instant Gratification

The evolution of search has led people to expect instant gratification when they conduct a web search. Think about it: You probably tap your feet, huff and puff, and generally get annoyed when a website takes a long time to load, or you have to wait more than five minutes from the time you place your order in a drive-through until the time you pull away with your food. We have all become accustomed to instant gratification.

This is part of the reason why social media sites, tools, and platforms have become increasingly popular. If something happens that upsets me, I want to know if others are experiencing the same thing so that I can commiserate with them. Better yet, I hope that the company might be listening and offer to help me correct the situation that I'm finding so distressing.

Companies that know their audiences and customers and that are communicating in real time on social sites have the opportunity to rectify situations before they get out of hand. They might even have the opportunity to turn an angry customer into a fan.

I've written about Southwest Airlines several times throughout the book. Southwest is a company that knows people are communicating about their experiences with the company on Twitter and Facebook. Recently, I was at the Fort Lauderdale airport checking into my Southwest flight home after speaking at a conference and enjoying a day or two at the beach. Before arriving at the airport, I had checked in online, but I still needed to check in my luggage. I arrived more than two hours ahead of the advised check-in time. Thank goodness I was there early because I had to wait for more than an hour just to check in my luggage.

Apparently, outbound flights from Fort Lauderdale on Saturday mornings create a mad house at the airport. I snapped photos from my cellphone, uploaded them through Twitpic, and tweeted about it from Twitter. I wasn't angry, just frustrated. Obviously Southwest knows this situation happens every Saturday, so why wasn't it working on the situation?

What happened next really surprised me. Southwest, who searches for what's happening "now" with its brand on social media channels, tweeted to me. They apologized for the frustration I was encountering, recognized it was an ongoing problem for them, and confirmed they were actually looking into ways to alleviate the situation from happening every Saturday morning. I actually had a nice private direct message conversation with the person who was manning the account at that time, and it impressed me to see that Southwest Airlines really did care about what I thought.

By not being afraid to address my frustration that was happening "now," Southwest kept a customer and really helped cement the fact that I'm a true fan of Southwest. My frustration was "instantly gratified" by being acknowledged and receiving an apology. Anyone searching on Twitter for Southwest or for the Fort Lauderdale airport could see our conversation and see how it was resolved. It was a win–win situation for Southwest—all because it engaged in social media and was paying attention to what was "happening now."

Social Media Site Users Share Their Most Recent Experiences

When people use social media sites, they are sharing what's happening in their lives in real time. Whether it's by posting status updates to their Facebook account, uploading photos to Twitpic via Twitter, or uploading videos to YouTube via their iPhone, people love to share their current life experiences with their friends in social media communities.

Through questions and answers, reviews, and blog posts, members of social media communities are looking for answers to their current questions, expressing their recent experiences, and looking for feedback from other members.

Although people search to find similar experiences, you'll often find the same questions posted repeatedly on Yahoo! Answers, forums, and message boards. If your company is joining the conversation, you shouldn't think that you need to answer a question only once. You'll likely answer the same question again soon. You cannot expect all members of a community to know that you already answered this question three months ago.

However, some people will dig through old conversations and posts. They might find prior photos, blog posts, videos, and other digital assets after the initial buzz of the content has died. This could mean the same content might enjoy a second (or third) round of buzz.

Social Media Sites Often Are Faster Than Major News Sites

About a year ago, the major news outlets learned that they can no longer claim to be the fastest source for up-to-the-minute news. When China was hit with a devastating earthquake, it wasn't CNN, MSNBC, or FoxNews that first reported what had happened. Instead, it was Twitter users reporting it to the world. In fact, blogger Robert Scoble was using tweets as a primary source of what he was reporting to his audience.

The same thing began to happen with other major news events. News about the uprisings in Iran and the earthquakes in both Haiti and Chili hit Twitter before major news sites could report it. Recognizing that fact, CNN started paying attention and incorporating Twitter to help it be the first major news outlet to share the news even before it could send a news crew to cover the breaking story. The time of the citizen journalist has come to the forefront, and CNN puts it front and center with its "iReport" section of its website (see Figure 41.1).

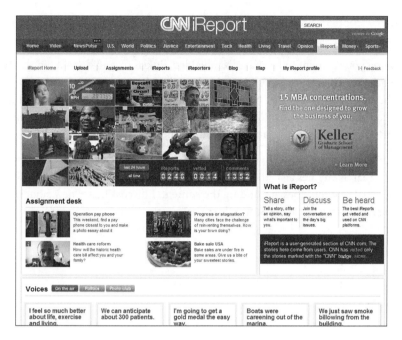

Figure 41.1   *CNN's iReport section of its website*

By recognizing that it can't be everywhere all the time, CNN turned to using social media to let its community help the company break the stories it might not be able to get to as fast. CNN receives more traffic to its site, a growing and very dedicated community, and word-of-mouth publicity that no traditional advertising could ever garner.

Search Engines Want the Freshest and Most Relevant Content

As I stated several times throughout this book, search engines want the most relevant and freshest content in their databases so they can deliver that to their searchers. This is why social media communities are so appealing to the search engines. Active social media sites always have a constant source of new, fresh, user-generated content being added to their sites. Members are always adding new posts, photos, videos, or audio content that can be extraordinarily valuable to not only the social media communities audiences, but to searchers looking for it as well.

The old ways of thinking about your content—that it's yours and that its value will be realized only on your own website—is an outdated way of thinking if you are planning to be successful with your social media strategy. If you don't enable your content to be shared, how will anyone find value from it? Housing the media in your newsroom or pressroom on your website without any way to share it is a lost opportunity for your company.

Enabling your content to be shared, embedded, linked to, and distributed through-out social media communities has a side benefit—discovery by the search engines. Just because the content isn't housed on your site doesn't mean it's not valuable to you. You should view it as another avenue to engage with a wider audience and an opportunity for others to learn about you via these social media communities.

Search engines are starting to incorporate social media content into their search results. Search engines also are incorporating ways of understanding how valuable these social communities are finding the content. I discuss these "new signals" in Chapter 43, "New Signals to Search Engines."

42

It's Not Just a Web Browser Anymore

In 1989, Sir Tim Berners-Lee invented a way to join hypertext with the Internet. He never imagined that his Hypertext Transfer Protocol (HTTP) for linking a series of pages would evolve into what it has today. He couldn't have envisioned HTTP being able to handle much of the media served up on web pages today.

First, a little clarification: The Internet is not the same as a web browser. The Internet is a "place" in which different forms of content and media are connected and served to users via a web browser. A web browser is a tool used to view and interact with content in various forms located on the Internet. The web browser isn't the only means of viewing and interacting with Internet data, but it is the most popular way today.

HTTP today is merely a combination of hacks to the original HTTP. These hacks take the original text-based web pages that first appeared in the late-1980s and add the capability to view videos and photos, listen to audio files, *and much more. However, ask yourself this: Just because a web browser can do all these things, does that mean it's the best tool for the job? Today the answer to that question might be "No."*

As more companies and content producers realize that a web page might not be the best way to serve up content on the Internet, they are beginning to develop new and improved ways to consume and share content. Social media–site developers have also begun to realize that a web browser isn't the only way that their users are accessing social media, and they are developing new ways for their members to participate in their communities that aren't tied to a web browser.

Your Audience Consumes Media in Many Different Ways

The best way to understand how your audience is accessing your data is to look at your own analytics. Your log files provide insight into how many people are accessing your site via mobile phones or social media channels. Some web analytics applications (if they can decipher the data) tell you the type of smart phone being used to access your site (such as iPhone or BlackBerry).

Other tools also show that people don't always access data via a traditional web page. One look at an active Twitter user can show you that he or she accesses content via many different applications. Twitter developers have been quick to create applications for users to access the microblogging platform in easier ways.

Today you can access Twitter from dozens of mobile applications and many desktop applications. Personally, I can't remember the last time I "tweeted" from the Twitter.com web page. I consume my content from Twitter via a desktop application called Tweetdeck, which enables me to not only see what my friends are saying on Twitter but also to see the photos and videos that people put in their tweets—all without bringing up a web browser.

Tweetdeck is self-sufficient and independent of a web browser. I can even conduct searches on Twitter without going to Twitter's search page. The desktop application provides it in the platform I'm using to communicate on Twitter.

The same functionality is possible for videos. Apple's iTunes platform enables you to stream videos straight to your TV. Some cable providers are offering the same style access to YouTube—you can search for the videos you want to watch on YouTube and view them right on your TV. Apple isn't alone in trying to keep the viewer on a different platform to connect with social media channels. Roku, for example, which is well-known for streaming Netflix to televisions, is now offering access to various social media channels straight from its receiver to your television. Access to Flickr, Pandora, BlipTV, Facebook Photos, and even the MLB.com (Major League Baseball) can all be accessed on your TV via your Roku receive and your remote control, keyboard, and monitor not needed.

The content you add to social media communities won't always be consumed via Internet Explorer or Firefox. Realizing this and understanding how your audience likes to consume the content you are creating for them could eventually determine the success or failure of your chosen social media tactic.

The Rise of the Smart Phone

Web-enabled cellular phones—otherwise known as smart phones—have changed the face of how content is being delivered to consumers. When the iPhone debuted with its "Apps" store, it was as if a flood gate opened. Developers took notice and began making applications that made it easy for smart phone users to access information.

Social media communities especially took notice. Today you can download apps for any number of smart phones—iPhone, BlackBerry, and Google's Android platform—that enable you to easily connect to many social communities. Interacting with social media via your smart phone provides instant gratification and is extremely easy to do.

If I'm on the street in downtown Philadelphia with my friends and we're looking for a certain type of food but aren't sure of which restaurant is best, which is easier: Whipping out my netbook, hooking up my air card, waiting for it to connect, booting up my web browser, and heading to Yelp's website to look up recommendations? Or using my Yelp application for BlackBerry, which geolocates me and serves up recommendations based upon my current location? These applications have become popular because they make finding information easier (see Figure 42.1).

Figure 42.1   *Yelp recognizes that its community members aren't just using a web browser to access its site, so the company built mobile apps for a variety of smart phones.*

Even news sites, financial institutions, and other businesses are becoming increasingly aware that making their content accessible via smart phone applications will be vital to their future success. It's not just about how their website looks in a web browser for the phone, it's about making an application to best present their content to the mobile phone users. Enabling users to easily access data helps ensure that their content gets distributed, propagated, and shared.

Mobile phones and the opportunities for marketing and advertising through them is a fast-growing area. Cindy Krum, author of *Mobile Marketing: Finding Your Customers No Matter Where They Are,* has a great book that delves into the ins and outs of mobile marketing (see Figure 42.2). If you are considering putting together a mobile online marketing strategy, I highly suggest adding this book to your library. Krum is an expert on the topic and speaks at several conferences about it. Her book is a wealth of knowledge in this area.

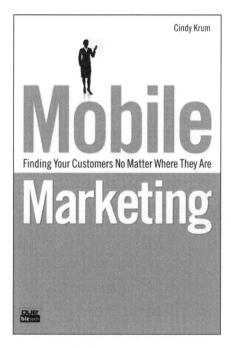

Figure 42.2 *Learn more about mobile marketing in* Mobile Marketing: Finding Your Customers No Matter Where They Are, *published by Que.*

Identify how your users consume their content online. Doing so is important for your immediate and long-term success. You should also watch how people share and distribute your content, and recognize that it might not always be done via a web page.

By offering applications that access your digital content for the desktop, smart phone, or even a TV, you increase the opportunity to reach more audiences who are likely very social. The future certainly points to the fact that audiences are becoming less attached to a computer desktop and are more mobile. Adapting to your consumers' needs makes you more valuable to them in the long run.

43

New Signals to Search Engines

Before I start this chapter, I need to give credit and applause to the foremost thinker on this subject, Mike Grehan. Without his constant influence on not just myself but an entire industry of search marketers, a lot of this information wouldn't be tied together as it is. Grehan is likely one of the most forward-thinking people in both search and social media about how social networks are affecting search marketing. In his paper "The New Signals of Search," available on Search Engine Watch (www.searchenginewatch.com), he goes into greater depth on this subject.

Vannevar Bush, one of the world's first hypertext thinkers, sparked the idea of the World Wide Web more than 60 years ago. Bush is the author of "As We May Think" (www.theatlantic.com/magazine/archive/1969/12/as-we-may-think/3881/) and is also known as "the man behind the atomic bomb."

When World War II ended, Bush started to question whether the work fellow scientists were doing could benefit humanity instead of destroying it. In his "As We May Think" essay written after World War II, he argued that scientific efforts should turn to making all collective human knowledge more easily acceptable.

Guess what Google wants to do? (See Figure 43.1.)

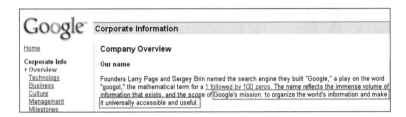

Figure 43.1   *Google's mission is "to organize the world's information and make it universally accessible and useful."*

Bush is better known for developing a system he called "memex" that probably made him the earliest of hypertext thinkers and also light-years ahead of other scientists and inventors of the time (see Figure 43.2).

> Consider a future device for individual use, which is a sort of mechanized private file and library. It needs a name, and, to coin one at random, "memex" will do. A memex is a device in which an individual stores all his books, records, and communications, and which is mechanized so that it may be consulted with exceeding speed and flexibility. It is an enlarged intimate supplement to his memory.

Figure 43.2   *A quote from "As We May Think" by Vannevar Bush, first published in 1945 by The Atlantic Monthly*

Why am I telling you all this? Because it's an important concept for all marketers to understand in learning how search and social media work.

As you can see, Google and Bush are on the same track. Regardless of whether Google's founders intended to follow Bush's logic, it's clear that the company's efforts were predicted long before hypertext was created. To a great degree, Google has already realized Bush's ideas. However, with today's technologies increasing the ease that any human can put information on the Internet and can share information via social media channels, it's becoming very difficult for Google to access all that information via links to web pages.

Google Relies on Social Media

A few years ago, Google announced that its link-processing system had hit the one trillion URL mark. That means Google knew of at least one trillion links. Google also estimates that billions of links are now being added each day with the rise of social media. That's pretty hard to get your head around. Billions of links in a single day? How can any search engine crawler scour that many links? This truth is the search engines can't.

Although Google knows of at least a trillion links doesn't mean that it crawled all those links. Too many impediments prevent that from happening—bandwidth issues, coding issues, time issues, refresh issues, and so on. Because many web pages live in databases or password-protected sites, it's understandable that Google can't crawl the entire web.

If search engines rely on the links to gauge relevancy and they can't get to every link, what can they use to help them? You guessed it: social media.

Matt Cutts, Google's head of web spam, said in 2008:

> Marketers need to embrace universal search by integrating video, images, books, etc. As far as Google trends for 2009, they will affect SEOs (search engine optimizers) as well.

If you haven't already been heeding his advice, you should start now. Take a look at how Google is integrating images, video, audio, and "tweets" into its search results. Even more relevant is that tweets returned in search results update live within the search results (see Figure 43.3). How's that for "real-time search" and relevancy?

Figure 43.3 *A search for "Sandra Bullock" displays videos and real-time results from Twitter and blogs. The results update in real time in the search results as Google finds them. Note the "Pause" link.*

Real-Time Search

Every search engine is trying to fill the needs of searchers. Google, Yahoo!, and Bing are leading the way. They've made deals to incorporate live Twitter streams into their searches. They've also made deals with Facebook to deliver similar "public" information. Videos and images from their social media properties and ones they don't own are now appearing in the results. For example, as photos are added to Google's Panaramio social media photo-sharing site, they are appearing on Google maps (see Figure 43.4).

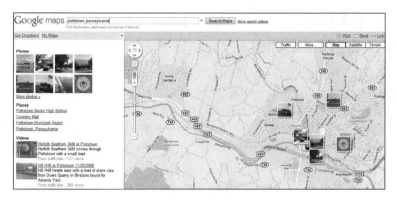

Figure 43.4   *Photos loaded into Google's Panaramio photo-sharing site now display in Google Maps when community users geotag their photos.*

Search engines seek to deliver the freshest, most relevant content that they believe their users will find valuable. Before the launch of Google's "Universal Search," links were the chief component in determining relevancy for search engine results. The more links a page acquired, the higher that page ranked in searches. This method of gauging relevancy became ripe for manipulation and spamming. Unscrupulous marketers would buy up links to point to their web pages in an attempt to control their spot in the search rankings, even if their page really wasn't relevant for the search term. For example, think about those search results that used to rank for "Britney Spears" or "Paris Hilton," but when you clicked on the link, you were taken to a page that really sold lawn chairs. Much of that type of manipulation (essentially baiting and switching) was done by buying links.

This is part of the reason why search engines are now investing in integrating real-time search results with the universal search. It's harder to manipulate real-time results because you would need to continually broadcast the same tweet. Not even spammers have that kind of time on their hands.

Real-time search also fills that just-in-time marketing need. Marketers need to be keenly aware of how the search engines' results are changing to incorporate social media results if they want to be able to fill their own just-in-time marketing issues. Of the following two options, which is more relevant and impressive to a searcher?

1.   A search result that has all your company's digital assets from different social sites appearing in the search results, including tweets from your Twitter stream

2.   A search result that has your static website URL listing at the top

If you chose the first option, you're on the right track.

Links Still Matter, But They Aren't the Only Heavyweight Anymore

Links will still matter to Google, Yahoo!, and Bing. Links do affect your ranking in search results and that will continue to be true. Links will always play a heavy role in weighing what's relevant to a search engine and what it displays for results. However, the search engines aren't using the number of links as the only factor for determining search-result relevance.

In addition to including real-time tweets in search results, the search engines are weighing other kinds of digital content. The search engines look at how videos are shared on other sites (such as Facebook and MySpace), how they are rated, and so on. The search engines use these signals to determine whether people think a video is relevant. The same goes for other forms of digital content, such as photos, podcasts, e-books, presentations, and even PDFs.

Bottom line: It's vital for marketers to understand that it's not just about how many links you acquire anymore. Search engine ranking is about how valuable your content is to the end user.

44

Choosing a Social Media Consultant

As you're nearing the end of this book, you might be think-ing that you will need some help creating a social media strategy if you don't have your own in-house social media team already assembled. Who do you turn to? Your PR agency? Your ad agency? Maybe your local SEO expert? Many people are claiming to be social media experts who are ready and willing to take your money because they think it's a quick and easy way to make a buck.

Social media is definitely "hot" right now. Everyone wants a piece of the pie and the success stories that go along with it. The biggest thing to keep in mind when entering social media is that not every company is the same. Don't choose a social media company (or marketing, PR, or SEO company) that hands you a marketing slick indicating that you should "pick one of our packages" and you'll be up and running in a few hours.

By now you know it's not that simple. If a company claims that it is that simple, you shouldn't invest your hard-earned dollars with it. That's why I've included this chapter in the book. I've come across a lot of people who claim to be social media experts. When I look at what they've done with clients, I find that they don't use much strategy. Instead, I see mostly gimmicks or things they've done for themselves.

Another tip is that you should avoid social media experts who claim they can help you because they've "done it for themselves." If they can't prove that what they did for themselves also works for other clients with the same rate of success, how can they say it will work for you? Every business is different. Repeatedly applying the same tactics in the same style won't work in the real world of social media. If your consultant is trying to apply the same techniques to your company's social media strategy without any research into what your company does, the techniques might not be successful if your company doesn't work the same way or has a different type of audience.

Finding the Right Social Media Consultant

Someone might claim to be a social media "rock star," but the proof is in the pudding. Experts should be able to show you how they will tailor a strategy that works for you instead of just rehashing what worked for them.

Look at the Consultant's Website

Before hiring a social media consultant, look at his or her website for clues that the consultant really understands the social media world. Does the consultant also understand search marketing, usability, and online marketing?

If the company's website is designed entirely in Flash, my advice is to think twice about hiring this company. The company obviously doesn't realize that sites created entirely in Flash aren't search engine friendly (a common mistake). If the company isn't aware of this simple fact, how can you rely on it to make sure your digital content will be fully optimized to be found in both search and social media sites?

Take a look at the title tags and the content on the consultant's sites. Is the consultant "sharing" knowledge and ranking for more than just the company's name? Does the company seem to be social? Does its website integrate the company's Facebook, Twitter, MySpace, Flickr, YouTube, SlideShare, or Scrib'd accounts?

If the company's salespeople are talking the talk, the website should be walking the walk. It should be clear that the company understands how to incorporate social media into a sound online strategy.

Who's on the Consultant's Social Media Team?

If the consultant's social media team isn't varied in knowledge, you might be banking your social media strategy on one type of technology. I know companies that have built their entire reputations on being a company of "power" Digg users. If you are going to bank your strategy on just Digg, you better be prepared to be with that company for a long time. Digg traffic numbers can be very addicting, especially if a company of power users is getting your content to the front page consistently.

Think about this for a moment: What happens if Digg bans the company's power users? Or even if just one or two of them get banned? What happens if you have a disagreement with your consulting firm about the direction of content and you want to end the relationship? Where does your strategy go? What happens to your traffic numbers? If you are relying on companies promising you huge traffic numbers from social news, social bookmarking, and hybrid sites such as StumbleUpon—and that's their only strategy—you might want to think twice about hiring them.

If the social media team has a varied mix of people—including experts in research, strategy, and analytics—then you've got a good team of people. Each team member can help your strategy become a better success because he or she won't rely on just one social media strategy.

Is the Consultant Social?

Another aspect to look at is whether the consultant's team is actually social? Are members of the team blogging and sharing their thoughts? Are team members on Twitter engaging in conversation and following people? Or are they using Twitter as a broadcast channel? What about the company's blog, Facebook fan page, or Twitter account? Are they being social by propagating their own blog posts and posts made by others? Do they practice what they preach? Figure 44.1 shows how I use social media to share with my company's audience.

Figure 44.1   *How I share with my audience and clients through blogging and other social media communities such as SlideShare.*

Remember that it's not about "rock stars" either. Although rock stars might be big names in the social media communities, your customers won't know who they are, nor will they care. Your customers care that you are there to engage with them. If you have a good, sound team advising you where to have those conversations and how to gauge your success, and providing advice on trying new tactics, you don't need the "social media rock star." Often the real rock stars are the quiet ones who do this day in and day out successfully for their clients and who find complete satisfaction in that. People who would rather tweet their own names, gain thousands of followers, or comment on their own blogs about their own greatness probably won't make your social media strategy a winner. Look for the social media pros who share their knowledge but who aren't chest thumping to show how important they are. Don't be fooled by the glitter.

Who Are the Consultant's Clients?

Many social media marketing companies are under nondisclosure agreements (NDAs) with their clients, and they can't talk about the work they do for them because of the competitive nature of their industries. However, it's unlikely that all their clients place them under an NDA. A good social media consultancy will offer clients for you to speak with about how the company approaches social media. Generally, if a social media marketing company is doing a great job, its clients are willing to privately recommend them if asked.

If the consultant can publicly name its clients, look at the social media efforts of those clients. Simply search on the client company and undoubtedly the consultant's work will pop up—if the consultant knows what it's doing. You'll see profiles on social sites and videos, photos, or other digital media assets. All this is pretty easy to find—you just need to know what to look for.

I've highlighted numerous examples throughout this book of things you shouldn't be doing with your social media strategy. If you are employing a consulting firm to help you firm up that strategy, make sure to look at what the company has done with other clients. Make sure that you do your due diligence in researching the company and don't fall for the dog and pony show of slide decks and pretty pictures. See for yourself. Are the consulting company's current clients being social? Are the clients engaging in an upfront and transparent manner? Are there skeletons in the closet that the company hasn't resolved? If so, are the company's clients dealing with the negative situations in ways that would be respectful, and actually turn negatives into positives?

You should determine whether the consulting company is just guiding its clients or if it is doing the implementation. Is the company tweeting, blogging, and so on for its clients? You'll be able to tell that right away. Companies have a distinct way of speaking and customers know it. If what's being done for one client looks the same as another client of the consultant, definitely take a second look at how the consultant operates. The last thing you want is a consultant who offers to tweet and blog for you and is doing the same for 10 other clients. At the end of the day, your customers will call you out for not being "real" and any trust you had built up is lost. Why take the chance on investing money, time, and resources in this type of tactic?

It should be your company implementing the tactics of the social media strategy. The consulting company is the guide. If the consulting company is guiding its clients successfully, it will be easy to see and you can feel more at ease hiring the consultant to help guide you.

What Successes Is the Consultant Talking About?

Success isn't just "We got to the front of Digg" if you are a retailer selling merchandise that someone on Digg would never buy. Success isn't "Our game went viral" if you are selling services and you hope to also get a subscription. Success isn't "We got hundreds of links to our top 10 list of vacation spots in Europe" if your hotel is in Pottstown, Pennsylvania, and you want people to book rooms there.

If the consultant you are looking at is touting these types of things as success, the company might not really understand you, your audience, or the social media environments it's "pimping." Take a close look at what the company is touting as a success.

If a company is new, it most likely has no brand recognition in the marketplace—either offline or online. Success with social media marketing would be the lift in brand exposure and the brand lift the company receives by engaging with an audience of potential consumers. If a company has a poor reputation, success would be turning those negatives into positives, not the number of Facebook fans it has.

Although increasing those numbers is important, having thousands of fans, subscribers, or followers doesn't necessarily mean success. An engagement factor must come into play with those fans, subscribers, and followers for it to be successful. If the company you are looking at to be your consultant is only stating "We generated X number of fans to a fan page" as a success, I suggest that you move on to the next candidate.

Is the Consultant Giving You a Laundry List or a Strategy?

The last piece of advice I want to give you when looking for a social media consultant is to listen carefully to the consultant's "pitch." If the consultant is saying "Oh yeah, we can make you a Facebook fan page, a Twitter account, a viral game or application, an ambassador community, a forum or message board, and we can get those all launched within three months," I suggest you ask the company this question: "How do you know my audience is active in those places?"

If this is your first or second meeting and the company is suggesting these tactics without saying "We've done some high-level research and we think these are some possible pieces of your strategy," the consulting company might believe that social media is a laundry list of tactics that every company should implement.

Remember every company is different. Even if you are in the same industry or you are looking at your competition, your audience is still a bit different than theirs. Just because your competition is using certain tactics doesn't necessarily mean you should also be implementing those tactics. If the social media consulting companies you are interviewing to be your guide are just arbitrarily listing things you can do, move on to the next candidate.

When it comes to picking a social media marketing consultant, you will need to do a lot of research yourself, almost as much research as the company should be doing about you and your audience. You will be with this consultant for a long time. Social media marketing success doesn't happen overnight and you need to trust the company to guide you in not only where to engage, but also how to properly engage your audience. Don't spend money, time, and resources with a vendor who really doesn't understand you, your audience, or the social media communities you should be targeting.

45

Putting It All Together

You've made it to the end. You're likely ready to start your own social media strategy or improve an existing one, aren't you? This book has a lot of information, so I hope you can take it along with you when you start putting your strategies together. I intended this book to be for readers to highlight and mark up with your own notes and thoughts, just as I do with the books I read and find valuable.

I decided to end this book by helping you piece together the 44 chapters that came before this one into a clear cohesive action plan. Social media marketing boils down to having the information you need to put together a strategy, defining your goals, implementing your strategy, measuring the tactics you implement, and then honing it all until you attain success. If you're not successful, then it's time to stop doing what you are doing and craft a new plan.

Remember these important points as you create your action plan:

- *Not all companies are the same—even if you are competitors, your audience will be different.*
- *You need to truly understand your audience before you engage them.*
- *Cookie cutter solutions don't exist.*
- *Don't be afraid of the negative; embrace it as an opportunity.*
- *Measure what you are doing; if it isn't working, stop doing it.*

Understand Your Market

Many companies make the mistake of inaccurate assumptions when they step into social media marketing. The biggest advantage for implementing a social media strategy is knowing your audience—both your online audience and offline audience because they can differ. Understanding that marketing offline is targeted to people older than age 60 and marketing online is targeted to people between the ages of 30 and 40 will help you define strategies for social media that could actually reach both markets.

By understanding your market, it gives your research a leg up. You'll know where to start looking and who to start listening to. By listening, you might even discover more opportunities than you thought possible if you assumed that your initial marketing plan encompassed every possible demographic.

If anything is certain in social media, it's change. Every day new communities are created, new relationships are formed, and new ideas are given wings. All this has the potential to create a new opportunity to reach or possibly scatter your target market. That's why understanding how your target market consumes data is so vitally important.

Research Where Your Audience Is

You can't assume you know your audience is on Facebook or on Twitter just because Oprah and Ashton are there. If something has gone mainstream, it's likely that your audience knows about it; but knowing if your audience is really engaging there is an entirely different ball of wax.

Understanding that people converse on multiple channels—Facebook, Twitter, blogs, Wikipedia, event-sharing sites, and so on—is an important concept to embrace when you are planning your social media strategy and looking at communities to research. Your audience could be concentrated in two main areas but also have a slight presence in a number of smaller communities. Sometimes those smaller communities might be where your most intimate and best relationships form.

By understanding where your audience is, you will understand how they communicate and share with one another. You'll understand the norms and the taboos—what you can and cannot talk about. People can be very passionate about things that they love, so knowing how to converse with that type of passion is important, especially if that passion can help your company meet its goals in social media.

Define Your Goals

Before you define any tactics that set up your social media marketing strategy, you need to define what you want to accomplish. Your goals will define how you gauge whether your social media strategy is successful. Remember goals are different than just measurement.

Measurement is counting things such as the number of fans, subscribers, or followers. An example goal is "We want X percentage of brand lift in the next year by engaging in social media." The measurements are a means to an end—if you can meet these measurements overall, you'll hit your goals of brand lift.

Your goals shouldn't be decided by one team either. Social media can affect many aspects of marketing, both online and offline, both new and traditional—from branding and public relations to website traffic and search optimizations. Understanding that integration is a key part of social media will help you better define and meet your goals.

Decide Who Owns What

Remember that anyone in your company can have an impact on your social media strategy. Before you launch into a huge strategy of implementing several different tactics, make sure you do a few things first:

- Define the message you want shared in social media communities.

- Make sure everyone in your company is aware of what you want to implement.

- Involve every department:
  - HR to help you define policies
  - IT to make sure you have the technologies to implement the plan properly
  - Legal to make sure you can say what you want to say without getting in trouble
  - Marketing, PR, direct, email, SEO, and PPC to stop siloing your efforts and instead integrate them
  - Customer service to provide insight into stories and help you relate better with people in social media communities
  - Senior and executive staff who are already looked to as leaders, so use them to your advantage
  - Everyone else because if they don't know what's going on, they could potentially harm your efforts in the most unwitting ways
- Integrate your efforts. Make sure all your departments are sharing information. Different communities in social media appreciate and value different types of information coming from a company.
- Define who's responsible for what:
  - PR should provide the social media team with a list of events being planned.
  - Marketing should provide the social media team with a list of marketing efforts (slicks, commercials, and so on).
  - SEO and PPC should share with the social media team the keywords they are targeting and their efforts in creating content.
  - Analytics should help you report what is happening in the different social media channels in relation to both your efforts and your existing website.

Understanding who owns the conversations is just as important as making sure everyone is involved. By deciding who owns the conversation, you must decide if your employees are tweeting, and are they doing it from work or home? Are they blogging on a company blog or are they maintaining a personal blog? If they are in a forum, what's the handle they need to go by? Be careful not to have many of your social media resources assigned to one employee. If that employee quits, your audience might go, too.

Define who owns the conversation before you start conversing.

Create Your Strategy

When you've got the basics down of who your audience is, where they are, how they engage, what you want to get out of building a relationship with them, and who does the talking, you can get to work on planning a strategy. A strategy is more involved than a laundry list of tactics to be implemented.

A strategy includes things such as determining the why, how, when, and with what. It's about defining stopgap measures in case whatever you do doesn't take off, or putting technology in place to handle the mass influx of interest in case you are very successful.

The other piece of your strategy is measuring. I'm not just talking about the tools you use; your strategy must define what you will measure. Will you measure buzz in volume, in sentiment, or both? How about the traffic that comes into your website? Does the traffic coming from your blog count toward your overall goals with social media? Is your content being shared and how is that affecting things such as your Google page rank?

I discussed these points in earlier chapters, so now it's time to put them to good use and create a strategy that you can successfully measure.

Implement and Measure

When your strategy is in place and everyone's on board, it's time to implement and then measure what that implementation is doing. Very few social media tactics are overnight successes. It often takes time for the tactics that you implement to grow roots and become successful. You need to be prepared to measure whatever impact occurs.

Those tactics that do take time will likely become more valuable during the course of your strategy. If you are properly building solid relationships—meaning the audience is finding value—those relationships can eventually garner more word-of-mouth referrals and customer acquisition than any wildfire viral piece. Remember, a social media tactic that's part of a sound strategy doesn't have to go viral to be successful.

Tweak, Retweak, and Stop If It's Not Working

Taking the time to measure your success helps you understand how to adjust your methods. Technologies will change, disappear, or improve, so tweaking your strategy to adapt for that will be just as important as making sure you maintain the same levels of engagement that you have from the start.

Don't be like the United States government either. If something isn't working for you, don't be afraid to pull the cord on it and stop. The U.S. government is known for its wasteful spending on programs and policies that make no sense or do not work, often because of political interests.

No one on your staff should have that much personal or political involvement in one social media tactic of your strategy that he or she refuses to give it up if it's not working. Remember the term "Stop beating a dead horse?" Let that be your mantra if you find a tactic you implemented isn't working in social media.

The opposite is also true. If you find some of your tactics are extremely successful, you might want to tweak your implementation of that tactic to include more resources (money, time, or people) to make it even more of a success. No one says that you have to maintain what you start with, especially in the world of online marketing in which technologies are changing at such a rapid pace.

You will find there's always room for growth and learning. Those lessons can help you and your team turn your company's marketing strategies into full-blown success stories if you keep an open mind and learn to adapt.

Index